T0305201

Public Procurement and Innovation

Public Procurement and Innovation

The Role of Institutions

Max Rolfstam

Department of Business and Management, Aalborg University, Denmark

Edward Elgar

Cheltenham, UK • Northampton, MA, USA

Published by
Edward Elgar Publishing Limited
The Lypiatts
15 Lansdown Road
Cheltenham
Glos GL50 2JA
UK

Edward Elgar Publishing, Inc.
William Pratt House
9 Dewey Court
Northampton
Massachusetts 01060
USA

A catalogue record for this book
is available from the British Library

Library of Congress Control Number: 2013933490

This book is available electronically in the ElgarOnline.com Social and Political Science Collections, E-ISBN 978 0 85793 052 1

ISBN 978 1 84980 287 1

Typeset by Columns Design XML Ltd, Reading
Printed and bound in Great Britain by T.J. International Ltd, Padstow

Contents

Figure and tables

FIGURE

TABLES

Acknowledgements

This book relies on research carried out through financial support from the Ruben Rausing Foundation, the European Commission, VINNOVA (the Swedish Governmental Agency for Innovation Systems); Sigfrid och Walborg Nordkvist Foundation; Kungl. Fysiografiska Sällskapet and Trygghetsstiftelsen (the Job Security Foundation); the Danish Council for Strategic Research; and the BHJ Foundation.

The author wishes to thank the following people: Bo Göransson, Gerd Johansson, Erik Andersson and the floorball team of the Department of Design Sciences in Lund for the good spirit; the Sønderborg Fire and Rescue Department for support; Sven-Eric Harjeskog for sharing his vast experience as a public procurer; Nina Widmark for the always sound reflections and the inspiration; Sue Arrowsmith for the legal aspects of public procurement and the encouraging attitude toward legal novices; Susana Borrás for encouragement; John Warrington for some nice discussions; the late Leif Hommen for supervision; Thomas Kaiserfeld for helping me finish my PhD thesis; Wendy Phillips and Elmer Bakker for being great people; Ben Matthews and Trine Heinemann for being role-model researchers; Luke Georghiou for starting the field of public procurement of innovation this time (and being the opponent for my PhD defence); Jacob Edler and Elvira Uyarra for many interesting discussions (when should we finish our common paper?); John Rigby for the reflections; Lena Tsipouri for being one of the good people; Patrick McCutcheon, Agnieszka Skonieczna, Bertrand Wert and Lieve Bos for the European perspective; Bo Balstrup, Jeppe Kristensen, Marie Louise Thomsen and Ole Helby Petersen for the Danish procurement perspective; Hans Hansen for outlining a work strategy; and Christian Clausen for helping me to understand Danish culture. Acknowledged is also the kind support (and patience) from Edward Elgar staff helping to finalise this book. There is also an array of people I have not mentioned, including all the people with expertise relevant to the public procurement of innovation whom I have met over the years: thank you.

This book is dedicated to Gösta Persson, who made it his trademark consistently to accept like a gentleman whatever joys and hardships his life brought about.

1. Introduction

A BOOK ON THE TOPIC THAT IS ON EVERYONE'S MIND

This book concerns the role of public procurement as a means to stimulate innovation. It manifests an attempt to summarize some thoughts regarding the utilization of 'intelligent' public demand that ultimately prompts private sector innovation. Over the last decade the topic has evolved from initially being a matter attracting only scattered attention (mainly in academic circles) to the current state where few would question the idea of using public procurement as a demand-side innovation policy instrument. The Organisation for Economic Co-operation and Development (OECD), for instance, has established that '[p]ublic procurement is at centre of recent demand-side innovation policy initiatives. Because of their large purchasing power governments can pull demand for innovation and can also create a signalling effect as lead user and influencing the diffusion of innovation broadly' (OECD, 2011, p. 11).

Although the role of public procurement of innovations has attracted attention in many parts of the world, such as Canada (Currie, 2005), China (US–China Business Council, 2010; Li, 2011), New Zealand (Ministry of Economic Development, 2005), India (Mani, 2003) and Japan (Myoken, 2010), the main concern of this book is the developments in the European Union (EU) in the last ten years or so. For the EU, public procurement was identified as an important tool for reaching the innovation targets drawn up in the wake of the Lisbon Agenda goals, set to increase competitive advantage in a global economy (European Council, 2000; European Commission, 2003b, 2005; Edler et al., 2005). An array of reports has since then been published in order to promote a discussion and utilization of public procurement as a means to stimulate innovation. In the last few years, public agencies both at the EU level and at other levels in the member states have initiated concrete projects where public procurement is used to stimulate innovation. The fact that 'public procurement' occurs 14 times in the EC communication from 2010, *Europe 2020 Flagship Initiative: Innovation Union*, indicates that public procurement of innovation as a policy instrument will continue to move towards the centre of innovation policy making for many years to come (European Commission, 2010).

It is this developing interest in public procurement as an innovation policy instrument that is the basic justification for this book. Although public procurement of innovation has gained increasing attention, a more profound and updated analysis that could help to inform policy and methods development and implementation is lacking. The purpose of this book is therefore to try to ameliorate this situation by drawing on relevant recent research. The underlying concern here is the impact of public procurement on innovation, that is, the extent to which public procurement generates innovations (other than process innovations within the procurement processes themselves). In other words, the concern here is primarily public procurement of innovations, rather than innovations in public procurement. In some places, however, innovation in public procurement might be required in order to accomplish public procurement of innovation. This book relies on the assumption that public procurement is a useful innovation policy instrument. Such a position does not automatically assume an ideal world free from any problems that might occur in activities aiming at applying these ideas. On the contrary, any agent engaging in public procurement of innovation will face problems and challenges, as would anyone engaging in any activities aiming at delivering innovation. Any sound analysis should acknowledge these potential problems, but perhaps foremost try to gather some insights useful for making public procurement of innovation successful. The ambition here is to contribute to such a sound analysis.

Some theoretical considerations reflect the character of this book. As would be typical of any work carried out with scientific aspirations, this book consists of statements and analysis of facts, what Chalmers calls 'observation statements' (Chalmers, 1999). The formulation of observation statements does not happen solely by facts entering the brain through the senses. Instead, 'the formulation of observation statements presupposes significant knowledge' and also 'that the search for relevant observable facts ... is guided by that knowledge' (Chalmers, 1999, p. 13). This means that scientific knowledge cannot be derived from *any* fact but is the result of a knowledge-dependent (ibid., p. 14) selection mechanism: in the words of Kuhn, a paradigm (Kuhn, 1996). Although, it might be somewhat of an exaggeration to talk about a paradigm in this context, this book has nevertheless followed some paradigmatic rules that have affected what facts have been collected and observed and how they have been analysed. The particular topic itself would also probably never have been 'conceived and none would have [carried out further research on it] without a paradigm theory to define the problem and to guarantee the existence of a stable solution' (Kuhn, 1996, p. 28).

One paradigmatic nominator for this book, especially in the initial stages of the work, was the volume edited by Edquist, Hommen and Tsipouri (2000). Their volume provides a thorough introduction to the field, at least in the way that what was then called public technology procurement was perceived at the time. Although things have evolved since then, the book suggests a 'sensitizing' direction on what knowledge to look for and collect that is highly relevant for a book like the current one. For example, what follows naturally from Edquist, Hommen and Tsipouri (2000) is the interest in the procurement legislation and how it might affect possibilities for the public procurement of innovation. Although the current book will also demonstrate some of its weaknesses, the perhaps most important contribution is the theoretical link established between innovation theory and public procurement. Very briefly, this link can be summarized as follows: viewed as an act of innovation, public procurement becomes a special case of user–producer interaction (von Hippel, 1988) where interactive learning takes place (Lundvall, 1988, 1992). Rather than being the result of anonymous market processes based on price information, public procurement of innovation (as distinct from procurement of regular goods or services) becomes a process where the social and collaborative aspects need to be stressed. What comes naturally from such perception is the interest for what governs these social and collaborative aspects, namely institutions.

There prevails what appears to be an expanding research stream concerned with public procurement of innovation. The topic has been brought up in contexts such as the International Purchasing and Supply Education and Research Association (IPSERA) Conference, the International Public Procurement Conference (IPPC) and the Procurement Law Academic Network (PLAN). The Danish Research Unit for Industrial Dynamics (DRUID) has also over the years facilitated a discussion on the topic. There are also publishing venues stemming from these contexts or elsewhere facilitating the development of new knowledge on different aspects of public procurement. One example is the Participatory Innovation Conference organized by University of Southern Denmark in 2011, which had a special track dedicated to 'public procurement of participatory innovation'. In 2012, Manchester Institute of Innovation Research organized a conference where public procurement was a central theme. An important part of the debate is also evolving in the policy realm, manifested in reports issued by public agencies and/or consultants working on behalf of them. Although about to emerge, there is not yet an

institutionalized research context, with reoccurring conferences and jour-
nals, for public procurement of innovation per se. The approaches and
perspectives applied are also scattered. The current book attempts to add
to existing perspectives a particular emphasis on innovation, useful for
academic as well as non-academic development of new knowledge and
practice on this topic. The assertion is that public procurement viewed as
a special case of innovation, that is, essentially as a social process
governed by institutions, calls for understanding of the 'rules of the
game' of public procurement and how these rules may affect the
possibilities for public agencies to procure innovation. This book sets out
to make such an analysis. The generic research question derived from
such a perspective can be formulated as follows: how do various kinds of
institutions affect the possibilities for public procurement of innovations?

This book builds on research carried out between 2004 and the present
time (for example, Edler *et al.*, 2005; Rolfstam, 2005, 2007a, 2007b,
2009a, 2010, 2012a, 2012b, 2012c; Gavras *et al.*, 2006; Hommen and
Rolfstam, 2009; Rolfstam *et al.*, 2011). The empirical material drawn on
consists of a set of case studies (Eisenhardt, 1989; Yin, 1994). The book
also relies on innumerable discussions with people from academia, the
public sector and private industry, and reflections made after attending an
array of meetings, workshops and conferences dedicated to developing
more knowledge on the public procurement of innovation.

The subsequent sections of this chapter provide an introduction to the
topic, by initially discussing some definitions of public procurement of
innovation and what types of innovation can be delivered. Then follows a
brief discussion on innovation policy in general and in particular the
rationale behind utilizing public procurement as an innovation policy
instrument. The chapter concludes with a brief account of the recent
historical developments in this field, which is a story about a topic that
has moved from an almost unknown existence to become something on
everyone's mind, a development that in itself is a justification for a book
like this one.

WHAT IS PUBLIC PROCUREMENT OF INNOVATION?

Some ambiguity prevails among available definitions of public procurement of innovation. There is also a variation in what terms are actually
defined. 'Public procurement of innovation', 'innovation procurement',
'public technology procurement', 'innovative procurement' and 'pre-
commercial procurement' are some of the terms used in the literature and

in discussions. Although it is possible to pinpoint discernible differences among these concepts, they all share some characteristics that make them relevant here. There is typically a public agency engaged, together with one or several private firms or other organizations, in activities that may lead to or promote innovation of some kind. Sometimes the difference in wording and meaning is merely a matter of taste. In some cases, however, there are assumptions hidden in the terms that may create confusion if precautions are not taken, especially in cross-national settings.

Some countries have developed concepts describing relationships between a public agency and a private firm that primarily are used and understood the same way among actors in that particular local context. One such example is 'public private innovation' (Weihe *et al.*, 2011). This is a well-established term in Denmark used to describe learning activities taking place in collaboration between a public agency and research organizations and/or private firms that may lead to innovation, at least in the sense that these arrangements tend to function as test-beds for innovative products and services that have not yet been introduced to the market. The term however does not necessarily include procurement of a tangible item. 'Public technology procurement' is another concept well known in Sweden, and is even legally defined in Spain, but is perhaps less known and applied in other countries. One concept developed and used extensively in Australia and the UK, typically used for large infrastructure projects, is the private finance initiative (PFI). Another notion closely related to PFIs is public–private partnerships (PPPs) (Tvarnø *et al.*, 2010). Although the use of PFIs has diffused elsewhere, it has been adopted only sparsely in some other EU member states (see Petersen, 2011 for a comparison between Ireland, a country with extensive experience of PPP, and Denmark, a country with rather modest adoption of PPP). Yet another term, 'developing pair', is used to describe long-term collaboration between a public agency and a private firm as seen in some Scandinavian countries in the twentieth century, for instance in telecom (Fridlund, 1999).

From an institutional perspective, where nations can be understood to manifest national contexts developed according to system-specific and path-dependent trajectories, it would not be a far-fetched expectation to encounter context-specific concepts and procurement traditions (for example, Hollingsworth, 2000, p. 621). Allowing internalizing and locali-zation to fit local contexts is, according to the same logic, central both for the promotion of public procurement of innovation policies and for successful practice. To fully give an account of the different develop-ments of local concepts in the EU or elsewhere is however outside the scope of the current book. Public procurement of innovation, as for any kind of innovation, is also very versatile in terms of how outcomes should be understood and defined. This complexity, which holds for any kind of innovation, is yet another factor that adds to the challenges for anyone seeking to clarify the meaning of the concepts used by people engaged in discussions on public procurement of innovation. In the light of that reality, what follows is an elementary discussion on definitions.

Understandings of Public Procurement of Innovation

Procurement 'refers to the function of purchasing goods or services from an outside body' (Arrowsmith, 2005, p. 1). Public procurement occurs when this function is performed by a public agency. From a legal perspective, procurement carried out by private firms acting on behalf of a public agency also in principle comes under the definition, as such procurement needs to comply with public procurement laws as well. Although procurement is synonymous with, for example, purchasing, buying, sourcing and so on, and although technically speaking it could be referring to any actor, the assumed agent, if the term is used without a qualifier (for example, 'private', 'public'), is usually a public agency. Public procurement can take place at any level in society – in a department in a local council of a municipality, or on the regional, national or even supranational level. In fact, essentially all public functions are supported by public procurement (Thai and Grimm, 2000, p. 231). Following these definitions, for public agencies goods (and services) of any kind are acquired through public procurement.

What is needed for the purposes here, however, is a definition that reflects not only the activity of procuring but also the delivered outcome, innovation. One way to meet this requirement is to draw on the classical writings in innovation studies, for example those of Joseph Schumpeter. One way of defining innovation is to distinguish between production and innovation, as Schumpeter did. According to him, production concerns the utilization of 'materials and forces within our reach' (Schumpeter, 1934 [1969], p. 65). Innovations (although Schumpeter used the word 'development') are new combinations manifested as the introduction of a new good, a new method of production, the opening up of a new market, or the use of a new source of supply of raw materials or new ways of organizing industries (ibid., p. 65). Essentially echoing the words of Schumpeter, Edquist (1997, p. 1) states that '[i]nnovations are new creations of economic significance', distinguishing, at least implicitly, between innovation and invention. An invention, unlike an innovation, has not yet proven its success on a market, as discussed by Fagerberg (2005, pp. 4–5). With reference to Schumpeter (1934 [1969]), public procurement of innovation could then be understood as a purchasing activity that delivers any of the development aspects mentioned above.

One concept that emphasizes Schumpeterian understanding of innovation as the creation of something new is technology procurement. This is a concept that ontologically belongs to technology policy, not innovation policy. Several authors also make this connection explicit, for instance Lundvall and Borrás (2005). Technology procurement is understood to occur 'when a public agency acts to purchase, or place an order for, a product – service, good, or system – that does not yet exist, but which could (probably) be developed within a reasonable period of time, based on additional or new innovative work by the organisation(s) undertaking to produce, supply, and sell the product being purchased' (Edquist and Hommen, 2000, p. 5). Westling (1991, p. 43), writing about the Swedish construction sector, maintains that '"[t]echnology procurement" is a form of purchasing aimed at directly stimulating innovation'. The Swedish Energy Agency uses a definition essentially similar to the one suggested by Edquist and Hommen (2000) cited above. It does, however, provide a more elaborate interpretation of what that means in practice: 'Technology procurement is a complete tender process with the purpose of promoting and speeding up the development of new technology. The purpose of technology procurement is to develop new products, systems or processes that meet the procurer's demand' (A. Persson, 2004, p. 5, author's translation). Persson's broader understanding comes close to another concept available in the literature, market transformation. The purpose of market transformation is 'to introduce new products and services and to increase adoption of new products and services as well as existing but underutilised products and services' (Neij, 2001, p. 68). This concept concurs to some extent with a general understanding of public procurement of innovation. One ontological difference is the aims, which are typically energy efficiency and sustainability, that is, qualitative change. The perspective places a focus primarily on the effects of procurement activities on the market, not necessarily on strategic concerns for increased competitive advantage. It can be seen as complementary to public procurement understood as an innovation policy tool. The concept is also broader in the sense that it sometimes also includes private procurement.

The definition of technology procurement implies that there is also a type of procurement which does not deliver innovation. This is consistent with the life cycle dynamics most products go through. An innovative product does not remain an innovation forever but becomes eventually a mature product that at some point vanishes completely from the market (cf. Utterback, 1994). The distinction thus offers a demarcation line between procurement activities that are plain sourcing activities of well-known products and procurement activities that lead to innovation. This in turn offers a way of operationalization. It is relatively easy to determine whether or not innovation has been delivered in a particular case by asking questions about what aspects of the procured item were novel, if the supplier performed any research and development (R&D) in order to deliver the product, if there were any changes in the organizations after the procurement was completed, and so on (see Edler *et al.*, 2005 or Rolfstam, 2008 for examples of case study questions applying that understanding). Procurement of items such as fuel, stationery or any off-the-shelf product would then belong to the non-innovative category of 'materials and forces within our reach' (Schumpeter, 1934 [1969], p. 65), that is, what is sometimes referred to as 'regular procurement' (Edquist and Hommen, 2000). As will be discussed below, the public procurement of innovation versus public procurement of regular goods dichotomy is not always adequate, and might blur the analysis if applied too persistently.

To discuss further the differences between public procurement of innovation and public procurement of regular goods it might be useful to reflect on what innovation is and to what extent something 'does not exist'. Such an exercise relates to the discussions in the first few years of the 2000s that sometimes evolved in the early workshops organized to diffuse information on public procurement of innovation. When introduced to this at the time new topic, people sometimes assumed innovation to mean exclusively the creation of something radically new, and the discussions developed around that idea and to what extent it would be possible for public agencies to stimulate radical innovation. Although innovations can be radical and ground-breaking, they can also consist of incremental improvements (Utterback, 1994), perhaps based on new combinations of already existing knowledge. So, when a public agency procures something which 'does not exist', what did not exist before the procurement might in reality vary in magnitude of radicality. One definition that partly takes these other forms of innovation into account stipulates that public procurement of innovation is 'the purchase of goods and services that do not exist, or need to be improved and hence require research and innovation to meet specified user needs' (European Commission, 2005, p. 5).

Apart from stressing the understanding of innovation as combinations, Schumpeter also makes distinct the difference between product and process innovation, where the former is the 'introduction of a new good' and the latter 'the introduction of a new method of production' (Schumpeter, 1934 [1969], p. 66). Therefore, it might be argued that the definitions on technology procurement discussed above 'do not account for innovation through the recombination of existing goods or services, innovation in the delivery of existing services, and exclude most process innovations' (Uyarra and Flanagan, 2010, p. 124), which is of course a severe limitation. At least for products, it is well established that the 'innovative focus' initially set on product innovation is later in the life cycle of the product replaced by process innovation (Utterback, 1994). It could then be argued that even public procurement of mature products could include innovation. For a public procurer it would be a matter of shifting focus from product innovation to process innovation. Examples of public procurement of process innovation are for instance when a public procurer decides to buy computer time, rather than physical machines, or when certain environmental criteria are specified for the delivery of procured services. Such specification strategies may stimulate supplier process innovation without necessarily affecting the tangible features of the product.

Two other concepts related to innovation are diffusion and adoption. Diffusion, adoption and innovation are to some extent overlapping concepts. Sometimes, however, it is necessary to keep them distinct. An innovation may be seen as an invention that becomes commercially successful on a market, that is, it is adopted by users, or diffused (Rogers, 1995). An innovation may also be incrementally altered over its diffusion time, that is, exposed to post-innovation improvements (Coombs *et al.*, 1987, p. 130), which might affect the diffusion curve. In that sense, diffusion and innovation are interlinked. As will be discussed below, public procurement can indeed be used to diffuse innovation. One relatively neglected type of public procurement of innovation related to diffusion is unsolicited bids, that is, when a supplier approaches a public agency with an offer of an innovative product without being prompted by a specific tender call. Such a situation can clearly lead to public procurement of innovation if the public agency exposed to the offer is able to act. It is also a situation that falls out of the definition of technology procurement, owing to the lack of an initially given specification of something which does not exist.

Understanding public procurement of innovation as a way of acquiring knowledge needed to innovate has also been brought forward in policy discussions. The National IST Research Directors Forum Working Group (2006, p. 19) uses the notion of R&D procurement

> because it refers to acquisition of knowledge – collected by the supplier by carrying out intellectual investigation services – (R&D services) consisting of

critical solution analysis, prototyping, field testing and small scale pre-product/service development – with the objective to prove the feasibility or unfeasibility to transform a technologically innovative idea into a first working batch of pre-commercial volume and quality pre-products/services according to the requirements in the tender specifications.

This is also consistent with innovation research, where a generally accepted claim is that 'the most fundamental resource in the modern economy is knowledge' and that 'the most important process is learning' (Lundvall, 1992, p. 1). In a similar way Dosi thinks of innovation as '*the search for, and the discovery, experimentation, development, imitation, and adoption* of new products, new production processes and new organizational set-ups' (Dosi, 1988, p. 222, italics added). Viewing public procurement of innovation in such terms brings focus onto the process of innovation, that is, the cognitive activities that lead to innovation, rather than the Schumpeterian perspective which mainly deals with innovation as an *ex post* outcome. It also highlights the role of public procurement of innovation as a device for knowledge accumulation beyond a single procurement project. Eliasson, for example, in his study of the procurement and development of the Swedish military aircraft JAS talks about procurement as a 'technological university' enabling knowledge spillover to other projects (Eliasson, 2010). Kaiserfeld (2000) has also shown that even projects failing to deliver the intended product innovation may still be useful as instruments accumulating knowledge facilitating innovation elsewhere. (For a discussion on public procurement of innovation as public procurement of knowledge see Cabral *et al.*, 2006.)

The knowledge aspect of public procurement of innovation is central to 'pre-commercial procurement', a term that has been increasingly promoted by policy makers on the EU level as an 'approach to procuring R&D services' (European Commission, 2007a, p. 2). The emphasis here is on generating new knowledge that can be commercialized at a later stage. In essence, pre-commercial procurement can be seen as a pedagogical 'package' drawing attention to the exception in the European procurement directives that allow direct procurement of R&D services, that is, procurement which does not deliver commercial applications. The model gives an opportunity to develop different ideas in parallel where one or a few of the initial ideas will eventually be selected for commercial public procurement in accordance with the procurement directives. At the same time, competition must be maintained in order to avoid transactions that constitute state aid. In that sense the pre-commercial procurement model is the outcome of a balancing act defined by the two legal frameworks regulating public procurement and competition. Public agencies applying this package may assume that they will violate neither the EU treaty nor the procurement directives. Pre-commercial procurement is described in detail elsewhere (for example, National IST Research Directors Forum Working Group, 2006; European Commission, 2007a). One of the benefits of the model is that it offers a way of handling risk and uncertainty. The first phase in pre-commercial procurement may involve a pre-study or 'solution exploration' where several different solutions are explored. A second phase may include prototype development of the solutions that are judged most promising. This can be followed by the development of a small test-batch of some of the remaining solutions. Eventually, when the procurer has reached sufficient knowledge, one or more of the remaining solutions are selected for commercial roll-out.

Although pre-commercial procurement is an interesting attempt to highlight possibilities for public agencies to procure innovation within existing legal frameworks, it is still relatively untried in practice in the EU context. One potential problem with the pre-commercial procurement model is that it does not require the execution of commercial full-scale procurement. Although certainly leading to the Dosi kind of learning, applying the pre-commercial procurement model per se does not necessarily lead to a finalized product diffused on a market. Critics have also claimed that the model is unnecessarily expensive, especially for smaller or local procurers. These remarks do not however mean that the pre-commercial model is not an interesting tool, but only that its success will probably depend on complementary activities in the specific contexts in which it is applied. What is probably the most important factor is that pre-commercial procurement processes should be driven by a genuine interest to actually procure the outcome. Otherwise there prevails a risk that pre-commercial procurement will become a tool for producing 'yet another pilot' that never reaches the commercial stage.

Finally, it is interesting in this context to note that the central legislative package for public procurement within the EU, the EC directives on public procurement, do not include any definitions of *the act* of procuring that relates to the *real outcomes* of the procurement activity. The concern of the legal texts is the *contracts*, that is, the formal agreements of 'pecuniary interest' made in writing (European Parliament and Council 2004a, 2004b). Legally, a procurer may be the state, regional or local authorities, bodies governed by public law, or associations formed by such authorities. The directives also define a set of procedures to be invoked by public procurers. These are: the open procedure; the restricted procedure; the competitive dialogue; the negotiated procedure;

and design contests. There is also an array of definitions on different types of contracts that can be awarded. These are: public works contracts; public supply contracts; public service contracts; different concession contracts; and framework agreements. The legislative package does not however regulate in any sense the content of procurement activities, that is, what is procured. Neither does it discriminate between public procurement that delivers innovation and public procurement of off-the-shelf goods. This makes any assertion that the EC rules inhibit innovation somewhat off-target on formal grounds, as innovation per se is not an element regulated by the rules.

Here, public procurement of innovation is understood as *purchasing activities carried out by public agencies that lead to innovation*. This relatively broad understanding means for example that activities carried out both before (what is sometimes called the 'pre-procurement phase') and after the formal tender process should be taken into account or, to follow the terminology suggested by Murray (2009), activities that belong to the commissioning cycle and the procurement cycle respectively. Examples of activities in the pre-procurement phase would be the scanning of markets and emerging technologies, market consultations, facilitating the communication of public need, or match-making events where solutions can be connected to existing problems. Examples of activities after completion of the formal tender process would be the evaluation of project outcomes and collection of lessons learned to improve procurement projects in the future. The definition incorporates not only products or systems, but any kind of innovation that might be delivered. The relatively broad understanding would also include procurement activities carried out on behalf of a public agency, which also fall into public procurement from a legal perspective.

What at least implicitly follows from this definition is that one instance of public procurement of innovation might not be the same as one call for tender. A large project might consist of several tender calls, all with a different purpose (see for example Gavras *et al.*, 2006). There might be tender calls aiming at awarding contracts where suppliers will perform pre-studies, prototype development, consultancy services and so on. Although not all of the individual tender procedures themselves technically speaking deliver innovation, they should be considered as part of purchasing activities that lead to innovation, if conducted to acquire support or resources to be used in a context leading to innovation. In this light, the attempt to make a distinction between regular procurement, understood as the procurement of already existing goods, and public procurement of innovation, as Edquist and Hommen (2000) do, is somewhat misleading. Implied in the definition is also the position that any sound tender call should be set up in an innovation-friendly way, where the initial requirements from the procurer are met, without excluding the possibility for suppliers to suggest innovative solutions not initially known by the procurer. This means that public procurement of supplier-driven innovation is also included in the definition.

PUBLIC PROCUREMENT AS INNOVATION POLICY

The understanding that innovation is beneficial from a long-term perspective is well established, as is also the underlying rationale for developing innovation policy. It is therefore not particularly controversial to claim that innovation is the most important determiner for sustaining competitive advantage and growth. By innovating, a firm can present a better product on the market, or produce it more efficiently than its competitors, and thus achieve competitive advantages. With the understanding of a firm as an actor in an economic environment with actual or potential innovating rivals, innovation is far from a one-off event. A firm that wishes to stay competitive in the long run must continuously evaluate its activities to seek out opportunities for innovation. In other words, firms must handle the underlying mechanisms on which capitalist economies develop, what Joseph Schumpeter poetically described as 'the perennial gales of creative destruction' (Schumpeter, 1976, p. 84). Indeed, innovation does not become any less important in an economy characterized by global competition.

Appreciating firms as central loci for innovation does not mean, however, that relying solely on innovation generated from within the market will be the most beneficial option for economies (for example, regions, nations or supranational entities such as the European Union). Public agencies on different levels can and may want to develop 'knowledge policies' to promote for example scientific progress or development within a specific sector in order ultimately to stimulate innovation (Lundvall and Borrás, 2005). By using this term, these authors want to stress that innovation and competence building involve 'many different sources of knowledge and that innovation itself is a learning process' (ibid., p. 625).

There exists an array of different means to stimulate innovation, and public procurement has not been one of those much emphasized in the last few decades. In general, innovation policy instruments can be ordered under three different headings: environmental, supply-side and demand-side measures (Rothwell, 1981). Examples of environmental measures are tax allowances for firms which engage in R&D. Another measure that falls into this category is intellectual property laws that give monopolistic rights to commercialize a product developed by a firm. This temporary exclusion of competition makes it possible for firms to secure a return on investment in development. Supply-side measures are typically research infrastructure provided by public agencies. Examples of this category are public provision of scientific training, public laboratories and R&D grants. One measure listed on the demand side is public procurement (E. Braun, 1981). In a similar way, Geroski (1990) put public procurement and regulations on the demand side and subsidies and infrastructure investments on the supply side. A recent taxonomy of innovation policy tools also includes public procurement as a demand-side measure alongside systemic policies (cluster policies), regulation and standardization in order to target technical development and support for, or articulation of, private demand (Edler and Georghiou, 2007). Although the potential of public procurement as an innovation policy instrument is fairly well established, policy making in the last few decades has emphasized supply-side measures such as providing technical infrastructure, R&D grants or subsidies in order to stimulate innovation. Demand-side innovation policy instruments such as public procurement have been relatively neglected (Rothwell, 1981; Edler and Georghiou, 2007). For the European Union it has been emphasized that 'the main area of neglect in recent years in R&D and innovation policy spheres has been demand-side policies. Certainly many countries have attempted to stimulate aggregate demand via the use of a variety of macroeconomic instruments, but few have actively sought to link supply and demand directly via the use of instruments such as Public Technology Procurement' (European Commission, 2003a, p. 64). Accordingly, it has been argued that EU policy makers should take into account both blades of the scissors of demand and supply (Georghiou, 2007, p. 4).

The common underlying idea is that public agencies could help to stimulate private sector innovation by putting out for tender public contracts on products, services or systems which, in order to be delivered, require some kind of innovative effort by the supplier, such as R&D. Such contracts may provide efficient incentives for the private sector to carry out R&D, especially in situations characterized by uncertain market conditions where firms would otherwise hesitate to carry out R&D. In short, public demand for innovation may stimulate R&D among suppliers. The knowledge and capabilities gained by firms responding to public demand for innovation will render competitive advantages that contribute to firm growth. Potentially, the process also has a reciprocal effect, in the sense that firm growth increases tax income for economies, both through increased intake of company taxes and through increased intake of individual income taxes. In principle, then, a successful chain of events initiated by public demand for innovation would in the end increase public purchasing power to be exercised in further public demand for innovation. Another aspect of public procurement of innovation concerns the effects on the procuring agency. An innovation satisfying intrinsic needs may lead to the same service provided by a public agency being delivered at less cost. The other possibility is that a better public service can be delivered at the same cost. A sometimes neglected effect is the potential market transformations associated with public procurement of innovation. Even firms not directly involved as suppliers may have to respond to innovations delivered in public procurement of innovation projects, in order to stay competitive on a specific market.

One basic justification for making public agencies more prone to innovation generation lies in the fact that public procurement represents 16 per cent of EU GDP, a purchasing power which if directed wisely could significantly boost supplier-side innovation. The importance of public procurement of research and development and the fact that countries such as the US and Japan which have adopted more strategically focused procurement policies have run ahead of the EU in terms of creating demand for R&D further justify this policy focus (National IST Research Directors Forum Working Group, 2006). In a comparison between EU and US expenditure on 'R&D procurement', it was found that 'EU spending here is four times less (approximately $3.4 bn) than the US – after the elimination of expenditures on military procurement, with the addition of which the US lead over the EU increases to a factor of 20' (ibid., p. 10).

A BRIEF HISTORICAL OUTLOOK

It should be noted that the idea of using public procurement as a policy tool is not new. Over the years, public procurement has been used to accomplish a variety of policy objectives: to increase overall demand, stimulate economic activity and create employment; to protect domestic firms from foreign competition; to improve competitiveness among domestic firms by enticing 'national champions' to perform R&D activities; to remedy regional disparities; and to create jobs for marginal sections of the labour force (J. Martin, 1996). McCrudden (2004) discusses procurement initiatives addressing social goals that took place in the nineteenth century. For example, in 1840, US president Martin Van Buren issued an executive order that established the ten-hour workday for those working under certain government contracts. Similar initiatives were also made in Europe, in particular France and the UK. The same author even states that '[i]t is not too much of an exaggeration to say that modern procurement systems evolved alongside the development of the welfare State, and it is hardly surprising that the former was used in part to underpin the goals of the latter' (ibid., p. 258).

In the 1980s, studies were carried out to explore the phenomenon of technology procurement and to assess its potential as an industrial policy instrument in the telecom sector in four countries (Denmark, Finland, Norway and Sweden). On a general level it was concluded that, 'although there are several indications that private and public technology procurement is an efficient means of generating economically viable innovations, it does not follow that government policies to stimulate public and/or private technology procurement are easily implemented' (Granstrand and Sigurdsson, 1985, p. 202). Ove Granstrand (1984) also produced a paper providing a general framework for describing and analysing patterns of buyer–seller interaction with special reference to technology procurement. Cases collected from the areas of telecommunications and power transmission were provided. One attempt to think of public agencies as technology users important for a national innovation system was made by Gregersen (1992). One of her points was that public agencies can stimulate innovation *either* through establishing stable long-term incentives for private sector innovation *or* by being forced to act innovatively in unstable situations. Her second point was that public procurement is one tool that could be used in concert with others, in order to simulate innovation in a global economy.

If one makes the jump from history to recent history, studies have shown that public procurement can be used to stimulate technical development in the building sector (Westling, 1991); for creating environmentally friendly technology (IEA, 2000; Erdmenger, 2003); and as a way to coordinate demand and bring new technology more quickly to the market (Phillips *et al.*, 2007) or induce market transformation (Neij, 2001). Older European examples are available in Edquist *et al.* (2000); examples of projects carried out by the Swedish National Board for Industrial and Technical Development (NUTEK) are given in Suvilehto and Öfverholm (1998, cited in Neij, 2001). It has also been shown how public procurement public agencies can stimulate innovation and help in maintaining or even increasing competitive advantage for a country. Scandinavian cases supporting this point include the formation of a development pair with the Royal Board of Waterfalls (Vattenfall, the Swedish Power Corporation) and ASEA (later ABB) in the twentieth century. The public agency provided the necessary willingness to take risks associated with the development of innovative technology as well as pressure to do so in situations when the private supplier hesitated (Fridlund, 1999). The important role played by public telecom operators in the 1980s to stimulate innovation in telecom in a similar way, in both Sweden and Finland, has also been brought up in the literature (Palmberg, 2002; Berggren and Laestadius, 2003). Taking into account also work by Dalpé, DeBresson and Xiaoping (1992), Geroski (1990) and Rothwell (1984), we are left with the conclusion that rather profound insights existed on the topic even then.

In the last decades of the twentieth century, however, the prevailing perception of the relation between the market and the public sector was not conducive to promoting public procurement as a demand-side innovation policy tool. This was the time of the free market approach that stressed market mechanisms rather than public sector management as the way forward, as promoted by world leaders such as US President Ronald Reagan and UK Prime Minister Margaret Thatcher. In many countries this trend typically led to the contracting out of non-core activities in the public sector or to sales of government business enterprises (Callender and Mathews, 2002). In Sweden, for instance, the policy discourse in the 1990s was 'characterized by more generally oriented policies than before, at least within the area of industrial policy. Instruments of a more selective character, implying stronger intervention in the market economy [e.g. public technology procurement], were not in fashion' (B. Persson, 2008, p. 22). These neoliberal policies were also visible in the way public procurement legislation was designed: to prevent nationalistic, protected and (therefore) inefficient procurement and instead promote the creation of a common European market (Cox and Furlong, 1996). Other references elaborating on this development are the European Commission (1998) and S. Martin *et al.* (1997). Similarly, Gavras *et al.* (2006, pp. 70–71) argue that the EC directives were stressing regulation rather than strategy, the free market rather than interventionist orientation, European rather than national competitiveness, competition rather than protectionism, equal opportunity rather than collaboration and learning, and competitive markets rather than public sector monopolies.

PUBLIC PROCUREMENT OF INNOVATION IN THE EU

What can be seen as a demarcation line between the neoliberal policies of the past and what was about to come was the Lisbon European Council meeting in 2000. At the meeting a process was initiated in which public procurement as a means to stimulate innovation would become increasingly emphasized. The meeting established that the European Union, although in a fairly good state in terms of inflation levels, interest rates, public sector deficits and education level of the workforce, still had to address the challenges imposed by global competition and the shift towards a knowledge-driven economy. As a response to the perceived situation, the goal was set for the European Union 'to become the most competitive and dynamic knowledge-based economy in the world' by 2010 (European Council, 2000). One of the ways forward to achieve this goal was to form 'better policies for the information society and R&D, as well as stepping up the process of structural reform for competitiveness and innovation' (ibid.).

Two years later, the European Commission (2002a, p. 23) concluded that 'a stronger European impulse is needed' to achieve the Lisbon goal. At the Barcelona European Council that year it was also agreed that R&D investments needed to increase from the level of 1.9 per cent of GDP in 2000 to 3 per cent of GDP in 2010. A second issue concerned the level of business funding of R&D. The goal was set that the current levels of 56 per cent should be increased to two-thirds of total R&D investment (European Commission, 2002b). In the general effort to develop research and innovation-friendly regulations, public procurement started to gain attention as a potentially useful funding source for public infrastructure. The tendency of governments to buy established rather than new technologies was acknowledged, however, and also that '[c]hanges in these areas could have a substantial impact on increasing private R&D' (ibid., p. 14). In 2003, research carried out for the European Commission based on the perception that the targets initiated at the Lisbon Council would not be met without support from governments and the European Commission, emphasized (among other things) the importance of the right mix of different policies adapted to a given context. Among the measures listed was public technology procurement. It was also concluded that:

> Policy instruments which attempt to link supply with demand have been relatively neglected ... despite the fact that public technology procurement entailing a measure of R&D is the largest potential source of the financial resources needed to meet the Barcelona target. Public authorities should be encouraged to be less risk-averse and take steps to increase the amounts of R&D associated with procurement decisions. (European Commission, 2003a)

The same year, the European Commission concluded that public procurement 'is a leading or major component of demand in a number of sectors ... where the public sector can act as a launching customer' (European Commission, 2003b, p. 20) and noted that '[a]n important objective is to raise public buyers' awareness of the possibilities offered to them by the legislative framework, and to support the development and diffusion of information enabling them to make full and correct use of these possibilities' (ibid., p. 20). In 2005, public authorities were described as 'big market players' which 'have powerful means to stimulate private investment in research and innovation' (European Commission, 2005, p. 8) for the purpose of assuring economic growth in the face of global competition. In the same year, the Council of the European Union recommended that member states should (among other things) focus on 'encouraging public procurement of innovative products and services' (European Council, 2005, p. 6). The Aho report from the European Commission published in 2006 outlined the role of public procurement as a way of creating lead markets. This idea draws on the notion of lead users developed by von Hippel (1988) and a belief that public procurement could be used to build on lead users creating lead markets, by driving demand for innovative goods, while at the same time improving the level of public services (European Commission, 2006, p. 6). The lead market initiative seems not to have managed to live up to the great expectations with which it was born, mainly, it has been claimed, because of budget constraints (CSES and OR, 2011). One could also argue that the idea was built on unrealistic expectations of the lead user notion. The fact that this phenomenon occurs and may create lead markets does not in itself allow for the conclusion that lead users can be generated by top-down intervention. Although 'knowing where innovation occurs would seem to be a minimum prerequisite for exerting effective control' (von Hippel, 1976, p. 238), it appears unlikely that such 'knowing' would become anything but probabilistic in character.

In 2007, the European Council published a guide for innovative solutions in public procurement. In addition to providing a list of ten 'elements for decision makers who want to develop and implement a public procurement policy that promotes innovation' (European Commission, 2007b, p. 5), the guide explicitly emphasized the role of public procurement as a tool for innovation: 'To have the greatest impact, then, public procurement for innovation needs to be a part of a general innovation policy. What is needed is a system providing for education, for research, for finance, for knowledge transfer and support for small business, for intellectual property management and for a high quality regularity environment' (ibid., p. 4). Another example of a project with a clear focus on promoting innovation was the Open Method of Coordination – Public Technology Procurement (OMC–PTP) project set up to bring together policy makers, practitioners and suppliers (Bodewes *et al.*, 2009) to establish a platform for learning concerning various forms of procurement leading to innovation. Yet another project, the STEPPIN Project, dedicated attention to the role of standards in the procurement of innovation (Europe Innova, 2008). In 2008, the European Commission also set up an expert group on public procurement and risk management (Tsipouri *et al.*, 2010). The European Commission has also launched coordination actions, essentially aiming at diffusing or promoting, for instance, the use of pre-commercial procurement (Turkama *et al.*, 2012).

The increasing emphasis on public procurement of innovation on the EU level has also started to become apparent in rather concrete activities on the national and sub-national levels. This is evident not only in the UK and the Netherlands, the countries with the most developed policies and practices (see Edler *et al.*, 2005 for a survey of the initial state of public procurement of innovation policy development). Other member states have also initiated fairly concrete activities. For instance, innovation-promoting agencies such as the Finnish Funding Agency for Technology and Innovation (TEKES), the Danish Enterprise and Construction Authority, and the Swedish Governmental Agency for Innovation Systems (VINNOVA) have in the last few years intensified their efforts to develop and launch concrete programmes aiming at promoting different forms of public procurement of innovation. Initiatives are also visible on the sub-national level, where the region of Southern Denmark is a perfect case in point, having launched a €6.5 million project devoted to developing demonstration projects and new knowledge that may inform public procurement of innovation practice in the future (OPI-Lab, 2011).

In sum, it would not be an exaggeration to say that the pendulum has swung in the other direction, and the emphasis on 'free' market forces has lost ground in favour of the public sector as a pacer of innovation (Gregersen, 1992). 'Government is suddenly seen as a fundamental provider rather than an adjunct to the business of running the economy' (Callender and Mathews, 2002, p. 230). The beginning of this chapter also cited an array of documents signalling the particular emphasis on public procurement as a tool to remedy the innovation emergency. In other words, getting involved in research in this field, with an attempt to support, inform, analyse and maybe sometimes criticize the policy development, is easily justified.

AN INSTITUTIONAL APPROACH TO PUBLIC PROCUREMENT OF INNOVATION

Two observations from the development outlined above emerge. The first one follows from the policy development per se, meaning that public agencies in EU member states are exposed to innovation policies emphasizing and encouraging the implementation of public procurement as a means to stimulate innovation. For some public agencies this means very little deviation from what is currently business as usual. To many others, however, this discourse is a rather profound shift in perspective from prevailing practices derived from the neoliberal policies in vogue in the last decades of the previous millennium. The second observation, which is connected to the first one, is that there is at present support and persuasion on the EU level for the implementation of these policies among EU member states. This means that public agencies may increasingly try to adapt to these policies and start to develop new procurement practices where innovation is given more attention. This creates a situation rather different from what would have been the case if no such support existed. Any public agency striving towards increasing its role as a 'market player' and a demanding customer may find useful support in terms of concrete funding possibilities as well as opportunities on the national level. The focus here is not so much on the external incentives, however, as on the endogenous institutional change required in many places.

One of the virtues with an institutional analysis of society in general is that it opens up an understanding of human behaviour as taking place in relation to already established 'rules of the game'. From an institutional perspective it follows for instance that any single action can never be understood as a stand-alone and disconnected phenomenon. In order to make sense, it can only be studied in relation to its context, which in turn is evolutionarily determined. An emerging complementary policy development emphasizing innovation, in a context affected over many years by policies emphasizing 'efficiency', may bring about different types of institutional clashes. Although this book does not take a position regarding the pace of EU policy implementation, it is at least noteworthy that, a decade after the first concrete reflections about utilizing public procurement as an innovation policy instrument emerged, the opinion is still that 'Europe has an enormous and *overlooked* opportunity to spur innovation using procurement' (European Commission, 2010, p. 16, italics added). The aim for the institutional analysis attempted in the current book is to provide some understanding that could inform the policy development further towards a situation where public procurement of innovation is not overlooked but utilized to a greater extent than it is today.

STRUCTURE OF THE BOOK

After this introductory chapter, there follows in Chapter 2 a discussion of what institutions are and how an institutional analysis can be applied in order to understand public procurement of innovation better. Chapters 3 to 6 each highlight different takes on endogenous institutional analysis, essentially by drawing on case studies. Chapter 3 deals with a case of public procurement of innovation that was a success story and can thus be seen as a falsification of the general claim that the EC directives on public procurement prevent innovation. By drawing on additional cases, Chapters 4, 5 and 6 scrutinize other reasons on endogenous levels why problems sometimes occur in public procurement of innovation. Based on a cross-case analysis of an array of cases, including the cases discussed in these chapters, Chapter 7 discusses some factors shown to be important determinants for success in public procurement of innovation projects. Chapter 8 provides some concluding remarks.

2. Public procurement of innovation theory

Any attempt to discuss theory in social sciences may run the risk of at least implicitly assuming the existence of a dichotomy between 'academic' or 'theoretical' knowledge on one side and 'practice' on the other. Although such framing may sometimes be justifiable it would be a misleading assumption for a theoretical discussion on public procurement of innovation. New knowledge on this topic has evolved in such a way that 'theory', 'policy' and 'practice' are intertwined. Public procurement of innovation is a knowledge domain that, at least in the last decade, has been propelled by three main drivers: academic research, innovative policy making, and practice. For instance, in the early years of the 2000s, the development of the field was highly influenced by academic innovation researchers.

Academics such as Georghiou and Tsipouri played a pivotal role in formulating the initial ideas concerning using public procurement to stimulate demand for innovation (Guy *et al.*, 2003). Policy makers have acted by establishing innovative instruments. Examples at the European level are the lead market initiative, or the development of pre-commercial procurement as a model for procuring innovation. In the wake of these concrete initiatives, expert groups and coordination actions of researchers, policy makers and practitioners have been set up to evaluate and promote the initiatives. On the national levels public agencies have made available different types of support and funding. Practice, in particular cases of 'best practice', has played an important role as examples offered as inspiration to others. Academics and policy makers have in that sense tried to capture and diffuse knowledge attained from skilled procurers with practical experience of public procurement of innovation projects. One early example is the case discussed in Chapter 3, of Telenor procuring a new digital radio system. The case, collected in the context of a study initiated by the European Commission (Edler *et al.*, 2005), helped to clarify the role of the EU procurement directives in relation to innovation. The case also brought about new knowledge for the academic community (Rolfstam, 2007b). One example of policy-driven knowledge production is the Nordic Lighthouse initiative by Nordic Innovation promoting public procurement of health. Although this initiative was not technically speaking a funding programme for research, the expected outcome included both new knowledge and innovation in practice in the field of public procurement of innovation. There are also examples of events where the contribution from academia is relatively modest. One such example was the Ecoprocura conference organized in Malmö, 2012 on sustainable procurement and innovation. This was an event dominated by contributors from the non-academic or practitioner realm, almost making the few academic participants present a peculiar element. The publication patterns of researchers corroborate the point. Publication lists for researchers within this field typically include not exclusively conventional academic publishing venues. Research results are externalized also through project reports and/or policy documents that are often produced in collaboration with non-academics and non-academic organizations. Citations of academic work within this field may appear not only in other academic works but also in policy reports and government enquiries.

Academic research undertaken on public procurement of innovation must therefore be conducted with a certain degree of 'humbleness'. While being confident of its own value, it must take into account that not all relevant knowledge useful for public procurement of innovation prevails and develops within academia. Being able to engage in interaction with other stakeholders of public procurement of innovation, both as a learner and as an informer, is a central feature as well as a success factor of the paradigm it represents. An epistemological landscape accentuating the importance of 'staying connected' does not however disqualify a theoretical analysis. On the contrary, especially when public procurement of innovation diffuses into national or regional innovation systems, the importance of monitoring, scrutinizing and informing, based on a more rigorous analysis, will be even greater. This chapter sets out to summarize some theoretical considerations on public procurement of innovation developed over the years that are useful for such analysis. The chapter addresses two aspects of public procurement of innovation. First, it discusses what kind of innovation public procurement *can* achieve. Second, it outlines a way of analysing public procurement of innovation drawing on institutional theory. The claim here is that such analysis may shed light useful for understanding *how* public procurement of innovation can be achieved.

THE HOMMEN MATRIX EXTENDED

One attempt to summarize different types of public procurement of innovation led to the development of the Hommen matrix (Hommen and Rolfstam, 2005), named after the late innovation researcher. This is a typology that has been used as an analytical tool in research (e.g. Edler *et al.*, 2005), and also in practice, for instance by the Flemish government (Bodewes *et al.*, 2009). The typology displays a matrix built on two dimensions that define public procurement of innovation activities. The first dimension captures the mode of interaction from which the social need that motivates the procurement process has evolved. The other dimension concerns the impact of the procurement in relation to the market. The Hommen matrix can be seen as an improvement of a preliminary typology distinguishing between 'direct' and 'catalytic' procurement (Edquist and Hommen, 2000, pp. 22–3). The version presented here is extended by one new element on each dimension. The social need dimension has been extended with 'distributed' public procurement of innovation. On the market dimension the element of 'destruction' is added. These concepts draw on Schumpeter and recently developed ideas concerning new open and/or distributed forms of innovation (Schumpeter, 1976, p. 84; Pénin *et al.*, 2011).

As was mentioned above, the first dimension of the Hommen matrix refers to the origin of the social need that will be satisfied by the procurement. The assumption is that public procurement of innovation can take place with different degrees of bundling of demand. The reasons for a public agency to execute public procurement of innovation can be intrinsic, that is, take place in order to satisfy its own need. In the typology this is called 'direct' procurement. The procurement of a new type of police car provides an example of this type of procurement. Here a public agency, in this case the police, procures an item for its own use. The societal need that has motivated the procurement can in this respect be said to have been intrinsic to the public sector buyer. It is an item procured by the public agency to deliver the services it is set up to deliver. Another situation occurs when the public procurer is not the only potential user but seeks to promote market acceptance of the procured item by other potential users. In such a situation the procurement is based on needs that are shared or 'congeneric'. This is referred to as 'collaborative' procurement. One example, as will be discussed further below, is what happened in Norway some years ago, when several emergency response agencies collaborated to procure a new digital radio system (Gavras *et al.*, 2006). The third element on the axis of social needs is extrinsic or catalytic procurement. This refers to a situation where the primary effect obtained is of less intrinsic use for the public procurer itself. Instead, the public procurer acts on behalf of other end users, for instance private consumers. Examples of catalytic procurements can be found in the market transformation programmes in the energy sector that were carried out in Sweden and elsewhere during the 1990s. These programmes were similar to what has been applied by the International Energy Agency. Such programmes involved, for instance, the procurement of energy-efficient home appliances, where the main end users would not be public sector organizations but rather private individuals and households. Although the monetary rewards for these procurement projects were often very modest, firms participated for strategic reasons. Catalytic procurement may take place as a conscious process but may also occur as an unintended effect. The fourth element of the dimension is distributed public procurement of innovation. This is also an extrinsic form of public procurement of innovation, but taken one step further. Here the public agency publishes some kind of opportunity without either specifying a problem or making a commitment to procure anything. It is the task of the supplier to explore and exploit the opportunity. One example of such distributed public procurement would be if a public agency publishes different types of data and information that could be used for development of mobile services, for instance targeting local tourism.

The other dimension in the Hommen matrix refers to the market effects rendered by the procurement and relies on the assertion that public procurement of innovation takes place at different stages of technological development, or phases in the technology life cycle (Dosi, 1982; Utterback, 1994). It is relatively well established that public procurement of innovation can play a vital role in the emergence of new or 'young' technologies. What is usually not taken into account is that public demand can also play an important role with respect to the diffusion of new or alternative technologies, once they have been developed, since public demand for innovative products also sends strong signals to private users. The four elements in the market dimension hence take into account that innovation may occur in any stage of the technological life cycle. Sometimes public procurement of innovation can lead to market creation. The role of the procurement would then be market *initiation*. In situations where a market already exists, the effects of public procurement of innovation may be characterized as 'boosting' or *escalating* an already existing market. A third type occurs when the role of a public procurement process leads to *consolidation of markets*. This refers to a situation where the market is fragmented by different products and solutions and where there is a perceived need for harmonization or standardization of all or some selected aspects of a product or solution. The fourth element incorporates the role of public procurement of innovation in relation to the end of a product's or technology's life cycle, that is, *destruction*. Destruction is one neglected aspect of public procurement of innovation, which is a bit odd, as destruction is central to the Schumpeterian understanding of innovation (Schumpeter, 1976, p. 84). A combination of the two dimensions creates a matrix consisting of 16 possible types of outcomes for public procurement of innovation. This typology, which addresses variation in the social and economic contexts of public technology procurement, can be used by analysts as a framework for characterizing and comparing different instances of public technology procurement, and by policy makers as a tool for identifying and assessing different contexts of possible intervention. This typology is outlined in Table 2.1.

Table 2.1   The Hommen matrix extended

Role in Relation to Market / Type of Social Need	Initiation / Development	Escalation / Adaptation	Consolidation / Standardization	Destruction / Removal
Direct Needs intrinsic to public agencies	Direct Initiation	Direct Escalation	Direct Consolidation	Direct Destruction
Co-operative Congeneric, or shared needs	Co-operative Initiation	Co-operative Escalation	Co-operative Consolidation	Co-operative Destruction
Catalytic Extrinsic needs to public agencies	Catalytic Initiation	Catalytic Escalation	Catalytic Consolidation	Catalytic Destruction
Distributed Need identified and satisfied externally through exposed public opportunity	Distributed Initiation	Distributed Escalation	Distributed Consolidation	Distributed Destruction

Many examples of direct/initiation type of public procurement of innovation involve what were originally defence technologies such as computer, radar and sonar technologies. These technologies did not exist previously, but were primarily developed to meet needs intrinsic to the military, and they eventually created new civil markets. One interesting state-owned company in the Swedish context is Vattenfall. The procurement of offshore windmills carried out by Vattenfall over a number of years is one example of the direct/escalation type of public procurement. The procurements were for commercial purposes, with the effect of reinforcing the market for windpower technology, that is, a product that initially was relatively modestly diffused in Sweden. Direct/consolidation public procurement takes place when a public agency decides to procure only technology meeting certain environmental criteria, excluding products that do not meet these standards. This typically creates pressure on suppliers failing to meet the standards to innovate to remain a supplier. Sometimes such consolidation procurements are carried out by a central procurement agency on behalf of several other public agencies. This would then be an example of catalytic/consolidation public procurement. One example of an agency conducting such procurements on behalf of other public agencies in Denmark is National Procurement Ltd.

Cooperative/initiation occurred for instance when Norwegian emergency response authorities (including for example the police, fire departments and ambulance services) procured a new digital radio communication system to replace the old analogue system (Gavras *et al.*, 2006). The cooperative/initiation type of procurement is also illustrated by the procurement of alternative fuel vehicles (AFVs) in the US initiated some years ago (Cave and Frinking, 2003). For this kind of initiative it is likely that organizations and individuals other than the initial public procurer would also become users of the innovation. In Denmark, as in many other countries, public agencies are forced to consider environmental issues and energy efficiency in all their procurement activities. Ultimately, such an initiative leads to products that are used by others apart from the public procurer. In this way such initiatives stimulate broader markets, that is, a cooperative/escalation type of innovation.

The listing of 'best practice' products, for instance by the Federal Procurement Challenge in the US, corresponds to a cooperative/consolidation type of procurement. In this case, it is possible that there are other potential users apart from the procurer, and the list would also potentially create incentives for innovation in those competing products that are currently underperforming according to the requirements. In Sweden, the Commission on Environmental Technology has for many years stimulated and facilitated the procurement of sustainable technologies. It has in collaboration with users formulated functional specifications for environmentally friendly products with the aim of creating new products, processes and technologies. This initiative represents an example of a catalytic/initiation type of procurement, where the procurer does not obtain anything, but potentially contributes to the creation of new markets. Some of the activities carried out by the International Energy Agency (IEA) would be examples of the catalytic/escalation type of public procurement. One such example would be the IEA DSM Awards of Excellence, where companies are challenged to develop technology meeting certain environmentally friendly and/or energy-saving criteria (IEA, 2000). An energy-efficient lightbulb developed in a public procurement project will most likely also become useful for buyers other than the public procurer once the technology is generally available. Another example of this kind of development would be if a public authority procures energy-efficient refrigerators with minimal Freon levels, to stimulate the market for example for a particular environmentally friendly technology. Another type of public procurement initiative that is fairly widespread internationally is labelling. One example is the 'Energy Star' assigned to products that meet recommended efficiency levels (Cave and Frinking, 2003). Typically, labelling is carried out by an agency to satisfy extrinsic needs leading to consolidation. Thus, labelling can be seen as an example of catalytic/consolidation procurement.

The destruction element takes into account that innovation is often associated with some kind of destruction or replacement of what currently exists. When innovation involves the replacement of whole architectures, this might make complete systems of skills and components obsolete (Henderson and Clark, 1990). When public agencies set up procurement standards regarding for example energy efficiency, this not only triggers innovation among suppliers currently not meeting the standards but at the same time has a destructive effect on existing technology. To some extent, then, destruction is coupled with consolidation procurement. However, initiation and escalation public procurement of innovation can also be destructive. One example is the introduction of a TETRA-based radio system for the Danish fire brigades. Immediately, the existing analogue radio system became obsolete, and public demand for everything related to the 'old' technology in principle reduced to zero. It also destroyed the market for analogue listening devices used for instance by journalists, as these devices were incompatible with the new system.

Destruction works however not only as an effect but also sometimes as a precondition for success. The removal of existing contracts may be necessary to free resources to allow for procurement of innovations not previously utilized by an organization (Rolfstam *et al.*, 2011). Including this de-spending issue is important, because it tends to be neglected. It is much more interesting to pay attention to the new, rather than things that need to be abandoned. Rather than being a problem, destruction can sometimes be the point of the whole procurement, as it may help to remove from the market undesired components or products. One example of such 'constructive' destructive procurement is the activities carried out by the Jegrelius Institute for Applied Green Chemistry (Jegrelius, 2010). This is an institute, connected to the Jämtland County Council in Sweden, that works to remove hazardous chemicals in healthcare products through public procurement of innovation. One project that drew attention was devoted to developing a PVC-free blood bag. The project essentially attempted to replace a hazardous chemical component of an already existing product. Destruction could also be an element already considered at the initiation stage of a product's life cycle, as emphasized by cradle-to-cradle thinking (McDonough and Braungart, 2002). Public procurement of innovation could facilitate demand not only for innovation in general but also for destruction. Tender call specifications could also prompt responses to how the innovation should eventually be removed at the end of its life cycle.

Working with boxes that form a matrix is associated with certain risks. The outcome of such an exercise might invite interpretations that are unintended and/or too literal. In innovation studies in particular, where concepts almost always suffer from overloading problems owing to the nature of the topic itself, these risks are apparent. Anyone attempting to fill the boxes in the matrix with empirical material would soon discover these problems in this context. One category of problems is temporal. The effects on the market can be established only *ex post* and are in principle out of the procurer's control. Apart from the catalytic technology projects conducted with an explicit aim of market transition, the market effects of public procurement of innovation are probably mostly unintended. It is also possible that the demand for innovation alters between the private and the public sector over the life cycle of a product or technology. Public procurement may initiate an innovation followed by a phase where private demand becomes more qualified as an innovation driver, eventually leading to a state dominated by consolidating and/or destructive public procurement of innovation. Matching problems occur because of naturally occurring irregularities. Cases might qualify in several of the cells in the Hommen matrix.

The claim here is that valid points generated with the Hommen matrix as an analytical point of departure should not be ignored just because the world cannot be 'neatly divided into ... quadrants' (Henderson and Clark, 1990, p. 13). One point is for instance that public procurement of innovation is not limited to new technology as is sometimes implied. Public procurement of innovation can lead to radical innovation, but also probably more often to other less radical forms of innovation. It can occur as a classical principal–agent relation, but also in collaboration with others, and even with relatively modest involvement of the public procurer. Another point is that there might be different requirements when it comes to what skills and capabilities are needed depending on where in the matrix a particular procurement project belongs. The general pattern is that the closer one gets to the upper left corner of the matrix the more important in-house technological procurement competence becomes. Correspondingly, the importance of coordination skills increases with the increased degree of cooperation. What could be inferred is also an expectation of an increased share of process innovation with increased maturity (Utterback, 1994). A third point is that the effects may take place among firms which did not participate in any particular procurement projects. One example is public procurement leading to market transformation where one or a few suppliers' direct involvement in a particular project might prompt innovative responses from other non-participating firms in the same sector.

In sum, it appears as if the indigenous public procurer will always have the opportunity to deliver innovation. The rest of the chapter could be seen as an attempt to outline a theoretical foundation useful for explaining why these opportunities are not always realized.

INSTITUTIONAL ANALYSIS OF PUBLIC PROCUREMENT OF INNOVATION

Analysis based on mainstream economics tends to treat public procurement, including public procurement of innovation, in the light of auction theory (Edquist and Hommen, 2000). Public procurement is considered a game in which the buyer and the supplier each try to take advantage of the other's weaknesses. The supplier's supposedly superior knowledge of the solution stands against the buyer's advantage in being in control of the actual design of the auction rules. Applying this perspective to a procurement process would, regardless of procurer (public or private), yield a quite straightforward analysis: the lowest bid to meet the specifications should automatically be awarded the contract. This efficiency-based thinking has had a great impact on procurement behaviour, as evolved in neoliberal times, leading to a tendency to prioritize the lowest price over value for money in contract award decisions. The position maintained here is that considering public procurement of innovation as an auction works less well, as such analysis fails to capture relevant aspects when *innovation* is studied. One central point, for instance, is that the buyer probably holds crucially important knowledge about the need or problem for which a solution is to be developed. This knowledge needs to be shared with the supplier. In contrast to mainstream economics, innovation theory treats public procurement of innovation as a special case of user–producer interaction. This means that the process is regarded not as the result of an anonymous market process, as a mainstream economics perspective tends to suggest, but as an instance of learning that takes place between actors governed by a set of 'rules', in other words, institutions. The assertion here is that such institutional understanding would be useful to inform innovation policy making and thus subsequently help to promote the utilization of public procurement as a means to stimulate innovation. Such an institutional understanding, which is useful for understanding public procurement of innovation, is developed in this chapter.

Apart from what is essentially a critique of earlier research alluded to in the previous paragraph the pursuit endeavoured here can also be justified on practical grounds. There is a clear perception that this complementary policy discourse emphasizing innovation rather than efficiency policy has not managed to materialize in concrete and successful projects to the extent envisaged by policy makers. This perception has in turn led to different debates aiming to explain this perceived failure, where the EC directives regulating public procurement have been a central issue. Innovation researchers have for instance claimed that the EC directives on public procurement are not innovation friendly (Edquist *et al.*, 2000; Nyholm *et al.*, 2001). Others have asked for clarifications concerning the law (IEA, 2000). In mass media and in other contexts views are raised on what public agencies should do, or not do, in order to become more innovative. Another theme brought up for scrutiny has been public procurers' averseness to risk taking (Tsipouri *et al.*, 2010). The current process aimed at revising the procurement directives can be seen as one element in a general interest in making the procurement system 'better suited to deal with the evolving political, social and economic context' (European Commission, 2011, p. 4). For the contemporary research community the situation is an implicit call for help to ameliorate the shortcomings of earlier research. The claim made here is that innovation research drawing on institutional theory, as outlined in this chapter and applied in this book, would provide useful insights that could contribute to this amelioration.

However, making a claim that innovation research based on institutional theory is useful is far from original. Of somewhat higher news value is the attempt to make a connection between innovation theory and public procurement of innovation. This was initially done in a volume edited by Edquist *et al.*, (2000). The argument maintained here is that the approach would provide a useful framework for research conducted to inform the current public procurement of innovation policy discourse after some improvements and clarifications have been made. A brief summary and critique follow.

With institutions as a central analytical pillar, Edquist *et al.*, (2000) summed up what was then the state of the art in research on public procurement and innovation. The volume analysed public procurement in the light of innovation theory and also included a number of case studies of public technology procurement in Sweden, as well as case studies of public technology procurement projects in the telecom sector in several European countries, conducted by a team of researchers. The findings of a comparative analysis of these cases stressed the importance of user competence and user–producer interaction for successful technology procurement projects. These were also central points of argument in the analysis of the EC directives on public procurement. Edquist *et al.*, (2000, p. 308) concluded that there is 'a considerable degree of tension between the EU procurement rules and the need to accommodate informal co-operation in the form of user/producer interaction related to technical change'. They also argued that the EU policy development related to the EC directives on public procurement was 'almost exclusively concerned with the regulatory aspects' of policy, while the authors, in contrast, emphasized another policy dimension, 'the strategic aspect – i.e. the use of public technology procurement as an instrument of innovation policy by the EU or by national government agencies' (ibid., p. 7). However, research aimed at testing this proposition found that following the EU procurement rules could actually facilitate successful innovation on the part of public sector organizations, depending on their adoption of appropriate organizational practices (Rolfstam, 2007b, 2009a). Edquist *et al.*, (2000) did not manage to analyse the institutional set-up for public procurement of innovation in a fully integrated manner, and their discussion therefore fell far short of being fully comprehensive. Further, the empirical aspects of their work – and also of the other chapters collected in the same volume – pre-date the introduction of the former public procurement directives put in force in 1997. Their analysis also relied heavily on studying the legal text about to be implemented. Consequently, the findings and conclusions of these authors cannot be directly applied to the current empirical and policy context. What should be stressed then is not that the problems encountered in earlier studies of public procurement of innovation should be taken as discouragement for an institutional approach. Instead, what is important is to take into account the part–whole aspect of institutions. As will be argued below and by Amable (2000, p. 647), analyses that focus on single institutions 'may altogether miss the genuine importance of institutions in the economy, which is of a combinative nature'. Making claims based on one institutional level, in this case the EC directives, on a reality affected by multiple levels of institutions is associated with obvious risks. As will be discussed further below, this tendency to ignore (typically) lower institutional levels is a problem noted by many scholars, including Edquist himself (Edquist and Johnson, 1997). If Edquist had taken into account his own advice on that point, maybe the claims concerning the EC directives would have been less bold in the 2000 volume.

To develop this discussion further, the remaining sections of this chapter outline an innovation research perspective drawing on institutional theory that offers also some critical insights regarding earlier work, as well as suggestions for further research. This commences with defining what institutions are, followed by making the connection between public procurement of innovation and institutional analysis. As a response to some of the problems in the institutional analysis seen up to this point, the chapter develops three institutional 'modes' for institutional analysis of public procurement of innovation: multilevel institutional analysis; endogenous versus exogenous institutions; and institutions as rationalities. The chapter closes by briefly discussing the implications for research and some concluding remarks.

WHAT ARE INSTITUTIONS?

The fundamental assertion underlying the institutional analysis attempted here departs from a view of human collaboration as governed, supported, affected and/or regulated by institutions understood as at least effectually collectively agreed on *ex ante* structures. A word of caution is necessary here. Although the term 'institution' is widespread, there prevails no consensus on what the term actually means. This is a situation which can sometimes cause confusion. The term 'institution' may refer to a formal public organization, or maybe a unit within a public organization, such as a library, a prison or a hospital. In the Swedish language, for example, the word 'institution' can be used in the same way as the English word for (university) department. In that way of using it, 'institution' becomes almost the same as a (formal) organization. This is not the way the term is used here. The assertion here is that, although institutions certainly can prevail within an 'organization' understood freely as any social coherence (such as a country, a region, a firm, a street gang, etc.), institutions may also transgress organizational borders and exist only in parts of an organization. This does not however exclude the possibility of considering a particular organization as a 'container' of a specific set of institutions. One could perhaps say that the analysis such a perspective renders makes the importance of the formal organization secondary. In that sense, institutions are 'the rules of the game in a society... that shape interaction' (North, 1990, p. 3) or the 'sets of habits, routines, rules, norms and laws, which regulate the relations between people and shape human interaction' (Johnson, 1992, p. 26). Institutions can also be regarded as 'systems of established and prevalent social rules that structure social interactions' (Hodgson, 2006, p. 2) or as 'the prescriptions that humans use to organize all forms of repetitive and structured interactions including those within families, neighborhoods, markets, firms, sports leagues, churches, private associations, and governments at all scales' (Ostrom, 2005, p. 3). One way of distinguishing institutions from what are not institutions is to consider to what extent a certain phenomenon would exist without any relation to human attitudes. In this sense, Searle (2005) distinguishes between observer-dependent and observer-independent entities. Observer-independent entities are physical entities such as force, mass and gravitational attraction. These would exist even if there were no people on earth. Examples of observer-dependent entities are money, government and marriage, that is, entities that 'exist' only because a certain group of people subscribe to a common interpretation of what they are. It should be noted, however, that an entity might have both observer-independent and observer-dependent features (ibid.).

The virtue of institutions is that they typically function as assets or resources. Without institutions, any human-performed activity would require problem solving and decision making about what to do and what to do next that would hinder any more advanced action from being performed. Institutions such as language, technical standards, and rules regarding what side of the road one should drive on work as informational devices that 'make it unnecessary to start life from scratch every day' (Johnson, 1992, p. 25). Without institutions a social system would not be able to accumulate knowledge or enable communication and would therefore be unable to sustain innovation. The argument is related to, but not the same as, the basic one used by transaction cost economics to explain the existence of firms, as was suggested by Coase (1937). Following that line of thought a firm exists as long as transaction costs for economic exchange are lower for the firm than other ways of conducting the exchange. This condition would also explain the existence of any institution, as implied by Johnson (1992). One should note, however, that apart from 'static' transaction costs 'there still remain some interactions that ought to be internalized' (Dahlman, 1979, p. 141), which refers to transaction costs associated with changing ways of economic exchange. This means that, although alternatives offering lower trans-action costs exist, an institution might still not change if the cost of the change itself is too high. Although differences in transaction costs of the exchange between actors are part of the explanation, the cost of changing per se is not an explicit part of the transaction cost model proposed by Coase (1937).

Thus, one complicating factor for the cost of institutional change is externality (Buchanan and Stubblebine, 1962). Externality is usually understood to mean other costs or benefits not captured in the price of a certain item. You could for instance consider as a positive externality the friends you meet when buying a drink in a crowded bar. You will be charged for the drink, but not for the value of meeting your friends. The corresponding institutional argument is that most institutions don't exist exclusively under their own control in isolation from any other institution. This explains why you might continue to visit the bar even after an increase in bar prices. You might accept paying a higher price for a drink as long as your friends keep coming there. Also, if a violation of a current institution is attempted, this might typically cause some kind of problem or punishment. The reason for this is that the violation or attempted change might threaten to impose additional transaction costs on any other institutions in control of the violated institution. Although expressed in another way, what is described here is the same principles that lead to institutional isomorphism (DiMaggio and Powell, 1983). In order to avoid institutional punishment, organizations and embedded institutions will tend to converge with organizations and embedded institutions where there is connectedness (ibid., p. 148). This means that institutions sometimes function as constraints. What in this regard adds to the problem side is that institutions also tend to evolve slowly and reactively. This may lead to mismatch problems 'which prevent the full realization of the productivity potentials of technical innovations, which forestall the reallocation of resources and efforts from mature to emer-ging technologies, and which generally favour established technological trajectories to new ones' (Edquist and Johnson, 1997, p. 55). A principal argument is that institutional change, and its influence on economic activity, is much more difficult to direct and control than technological change, and hence prevailing institutions often are drags on economic productivity and progressiveness (Nelson, 2008, p. 2).

INSTITUTIONS FOR PUBLIC PROCUREMENT OF INNOVATION

Having outlined an institutional understanding of human collaboration above, this section discusses how an institutional approach relates to public procurement of innovation. In a way this is a rather straightforward thing to do, as an institutional approach to innovation studies in general is well established (Lundvall, 1992; Nelson, 1993). Indeed, the fundamental starting point for innovation studies is the assumption of 'a set of institutions whose interactions determine the innovative performance' and 'a set of institutional actors that, together, plays the major role in influencing innovative performance' (Nelson and Rosenberg, 1993, pp. 4–5). It is assumed here that these general assertions also hold for innovation involving the public sector (Gregersen, 1992). The claim made here is that public procurement of innovation should be regarded as a special empirical phenomenon in the field of innovation studies. The most basic form of public procurement of innovation consists of a public agency that needs to procure a solution to a problem or satisfy a particular need. The procurer may be an expert of its problem, but not typically on the exact details of the solution. The supplier may have in possession knowledge, skills and resources to come up with a solution, but lack specific knowledge about the need the public agency wants to satisfy. The ultimate goal of the procurement process is in that sense to find a supplier that, compensated with a certain amount of money, will satisfy that need by applying its tools and skills to solve a particular problem. This process requires interaction between procurer and supplier and maybe other stakeholders where the supplier eventually learns how to apply its tools and skills. The solution, that is, the procured service or goods, is at least partly created after the formal agreement between procurer and supplier has been made. This implies also that at least parts or aspects of the procured item are initially unknown. This in turn creates certain characteristics that distinguish public procurement of innovation from procurement of regular off-the-shelf goods studied in the light of auction theory. Public procurement of innovation becomes in this light a complex and interactive process where the central activity is learning 'which involves interaction between people' (Lundvall, 1992, p. 2). Viewed as an act of innovation, public procurement becomes a special case of user–producer interaction (von Hippel, 1988). As 'almost all learning processes are interactive, influenced, regarding their content, rate and direction, by the institutional set-up of the economy' (Johnson, 1992, p. 23), an interest in institutions becomes natural in order to understand further determinants of public procurement of innovation. From this follows also the justification for pursuing further an institutional approach; if public procurement of innovation can be considered as a special case of innovation, innovation research based on institutional theory would make sense and also have some potential in delivering results that could inform current public procurement of innovation policy development.

To further scrutinize the relevance, Searle's (2005) understanding of observer-dependent facts, that is, 'facts' agreed as such within a community, as different from physical facts is useful. It is not hard to identify institutional facts or observer-dependent entities within the realm of public procurement in general or in public procurement of innovation in particular. Public procurement takes place within a public agency, institutionalized to provide a specific public service, for instance health, education or safety. A public procurer deals with money, specifications, and legally binding contracts that may include clauses that will punish a supplier failing to meet agreed deadlines. A public procurer is also assumed to comply with formal rules, and also other kinds of instructions, guidelines and policies. For procurement of most standard items, use might be made of standardized routines and standard contracts, or even framework agreements where most aspects, apart from the number of units to be procured, are settled in advance. A supplier unhappy with a decision to award a competitor a contract might complain and ultimately bring a case to court in the hope of a changed decision or compensation. For public procurement of innovation, there might also be issues related to intellectual property rights and how these should be distributed between the public procurer and the supplier. The formal institutions that provide the 'rules' for public procurement within the EU are the EC directives on public procurement. According to these rules, public procurers need: to advertise new contracts Europe-wide; to hold a competition between interested firms to determine the winner of the contract; to exclude firms lacking the necessary financial or technical capacity; to respect minimum time limits to ensure that all interested firms have time to participate; to award the contract on the basis of criteria stated in advance; and to provide information on the decisions made (Arrowsmith, 2005). The formal legal system set up for public procurement in the EU illustrates also how the EU is organized, drawing on the EC Treaty and the forms of legal actions defined therein. Examples of these actions are regulations, directives, decisions, recommendations and opinions. All of these have different applications. Regulations, for instance, are binding in their entirety, that is, they must be complied with fully by those concerned, whereas recommendations and opinions have no binding force at all. Directives are binding, too, but only in terms of the result to be achieved. National procurement laws among EU member states are thus transposed versions of the directives. The consequences for public procurement is that, although EU member states are supposed to implement the same directives in national law, the way this is achieved may vary. Some countries have also made certain amendments not seen elsewhere, for instance special rules for public procurement under the threshold values, not regulated by the directives.

INSTITUTIONAL PROBLEMS AND WAYS FORWARD

Establishing the virtues of an institutional approach, as attempted above, does not mean that it is a problem-free approach. For instance, most scholars working with institutions would agree that '[t]he notion of institutions itself is not yet a coherent concept, at least not across the various users of the term' (Nelson and Sampat, 2001, p. 32). For innovation studies, attempts have also been made to suggest structures for institutional analysis that would help scholars to comprehend how their work interrelates (Hollingsworth, 2000). Another problem in innovation research is for example the tendency to assume an exogenous view (Jacoby, 1990, p. 139) of institutions, where institutions are viewed mainly as constraints on human behaviour (Nelson and Nelson, 2002, p. 269) or as incentives or obstacles to innovation (Edquist and Johnson, 1997). Actions in firms and other organizations are seen as essentially reactive responses triggered by the institutional set-up. The analyses typically remain on the level of formal institutions – the legal and regulatory framework associated with a given innovation process – even though the concept is much broader in scope (Edquist and Johnson, 1997; Hollingsworth, 2000). Another limitation of this approach is its tendency to neglect the variety of organizational models and strategies among individual firms and other organizations (Coriat and Weinstein, 2002, p. 274). The literature also discusses the difference between formal and informal institutions (Borrás, 2004). This is a dichotomy that may or may not converge with the exogenous–endogenous dichotomy. Although exogenous institutions such as laws are formal, not all exogenous institutions are. Certain cultural traditions might be exogenous but still informal. Similarly, endogenous institutions may be formal or informal. An example of a formal endogenous institution would be a written work instruction used by an organization. What is perhaps the most significant difference is that the exogenous–endogenous dichotomy takes into account that institutions are relative and may have a different 'range'

(Jepperson, 1991, p. 146). They may manifest themselves as formal national law only when applied in a particular country and not in other countries; a manager may have authority over his or her employees but not over other managers' employees; and so on. This is an aspect that is not captured well by the informal–formal dichotomy.

Edquist *et al.*, (2000) provide a starting point for a more contemporary institutional analysis of public procurement of innovation. Their volume analyses 'public technology procurement' in the light of innovation theory based on a number of case studies of public technology procurement in several European countries. These authors concluded that there is 'a considerable degree of tension between the EU procurement rules and the need to accommodate informal co-operation in the form of user/ producer interaction related to technical change' (Edquist *et al.*, 2000, p. 308). This conclusion suffered however from an exogenous bias and failed to take variation into account, as discussed above. The claimed negative effects on innovation inherent in the rules were based on analysis of the legal text only, a problem already identified in the literature (Edquist and Johnson, 1997; Hollingsworth, 2000). The shortcomings of this approach have been demonstrated elsewhere (Rolfstam, 2007b, 2009a). Although formal rules are indeed a central component in an institutional analysis of public procurement of innovation, the findings and conclusions based on analysis of the legal text only cannot be directly applied to the current empirical and policy context.

The following sections develop this holistic argument by discussing three modes or perspectives helpful for an institution-based innovation research approach that may also help to avoid some of the shortcomings discussed above. These modes are multilevel institutional analysis, endogenous and exogenous institutions, and institutions as rationalities.

MULTILEVEL INSTITUTIONAL ANALYSIS

For research on public procurement in the EU, what follows from an institutional approach is the need to understand how compliancy with the EC directives on public procurement may affect the possibilities for public agencies to procure innovation. As pointed out above, the analysis of these directives alone does not complete an institutional analysis of public procurement of innovation. What should be emphasized, following Hollingsworth, is that, '[w]hen we do institutional analysis, we must engage in configurative analysis, recognizing that actors are not coordinated or governed by a single type of institutional arrangement'

(Hollingsworth, 2000, p. 605). Furthermore, institutional analysis should consider the 'part–wholeness' of institutions, that is, that what at first glance might be counted as an institution also consists of institutions, as well as potentially being part of another institution. 'Consequently, the institutional analyst faces a major challenge in identifying the appropriate level of analysis relevant to addressing a particular puzzle and learning an appropriate language for understanding at least that focal level and one or two levels above and below that focal level' (Ostrom, 2005, p. 12).

For public procurement within the EU several institutional levels are discernible that each may be considered in an institutional analysis of public procurement of innovation. One could distinguish between the global level, the EU level, the national level, the level of the public agency, and the level within a public agency assigned to carry out public procurement, referred to here as the level of the procurement division. To the global level belongs the Agreement on Government Procurement (GPA) of the World Trade Organization (WTO) and the United Nations Commission on International Trade Law (UNCITRAL) model law. The GPA agreement is essentially set up to safeguard transparency and non-discrimination in public procurement. The UNCITRAL model law has been set up to be used as a legal template for countries wanting to regulate public procurement, and has been used by many transition economies (Arrowsmith, 2004a).

On the EU level are the EC directives on public procurement. There prevails some consistency between the EC directives and the GPA, as the former should comply with the latter. There is also consistency with the UNCITRAL model law on the general principles on transparency and non-discrimination, although the UNCITRAL model law also includes some special aspects not included in the EC directives (ibid.). European countries other than EU member states also comply with the EC directives on public procurement. Iceland, Liechtenstein and Norway, being members of the European Free Trade Association (EFTA), have signed the Agreement on the European Economic Area (EEA). This makes these countries 'full participants in the EU's Internal Market' (Bryn, 2010, p. 5), which also includes the requirement to conform to procurement rules applied in the EU. On the national level, public procurement is regulated in national public procurement law. As was mentioned above, the EC directives are transposed among EU member states into national law according to the subsidiarity principle, which means that all EU member states implement the same directives. Within a country, public agencies on different levels can carry out public procure-ment. Here one can distinguish between public agencies on the national, regional and local (municipal) levels. The lowest level in this hierarchy is the department within the public agency that executes the actual procurement process. These levels are summarized in Figure 2.1.

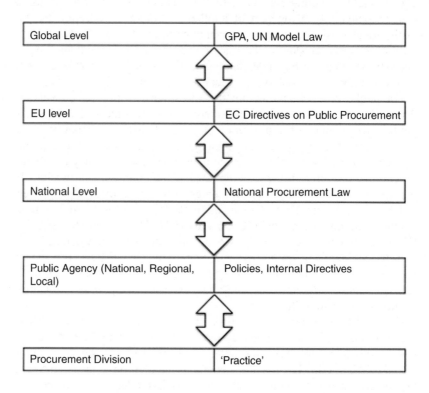

Figure 2.1   Example of institutional levels relevant for analysis of public procurement of innovation

Viewing public procurement as an activity determined by several institutional levels opens up analytical possibilities not offered by a single-level analysis. A multilevel analysis would regard public procurement carried out by a procurement division as determined by endogenous practices and routines, affected by policies and directives established for the specific public agency, and by national law, which for EU member states is determined by the EC directives, which in turn have been developed in interaction with global institutions. Such an analytical assumption would help the analyst to avoid seeking single-level institutional solutions to what are actually often multilevel problems. One example is research from the UK that has reported on the evolution of the informal practice of public procurement 'that may be compatible with the principles of non-discrimination and, to a large extent, competition, but not with a strict interpretation of the law' (P. Braun, 2003, p. 597). Such informal practice is, although technically speaking violating institutions on the national level, still in compliance with institutions on the EU and the global level. The chances are that an institutional analysis conducted exclusively on the national level could lead to the conclusion that some procurers should be punished. If, on the other hand, a multilevel institutional analysis is conducted, the conclusion reached might be that the national procurement law should be rewritten in such a way as to make currently 'illegal' procedures legal, in order to give procurers legal freedom of action to comply with institutions on the EU and global levels.

The multilevel institutional mode becomes interesting if one considers the current policy development with the EU as institutional change. As was discussed above, institutional change takes place as the result of contextual factors such as transaction costs and externality. In other words, the effects of a certain change, for instance a new revised version of the procurement directives, will depend on the particular context. Although literally the same legal text will be transposed, practices in different public agencies, policies, and general attitudes in particular member states will help to interpret the text and make choices about its implementation that reflect the particular institutional set-up. Although implementation will happen in compliance with the directives, the implementation might therefore still not be the same. One challenge for rule makers on the EU level (or in principle any higher level) is to construct the rules to allow such institutional negotiation between the institutional levels. Another advantage with a multilevel institutional mode is that it draws attention to questions regarding the importance of determining the institutional origin of a certain behaviour. One could argue that the remedy of innovation 'unfriendliness' in a procurement division (the lowest institutional level elaborated here) might not necessarily be realized by a revision of the EC directives. If a local municipality is constrained by lack of resources, with a political leadership not emphasizing innovation, making procurers risk averse, surrounded by a local business community failing to see the public sector as a source for innovation, one could question to what extent an increase in emphasis on public procurement of innovation would occur only because the EC directives are revised.

A final comment at this stage is that it should be noted that the model on institutional levels relevant for public procurement of innovation discussed above is a simplification very far from an 'all-component' analysis as outlined by Hollingsworth (2000). What is lacking, for instance, is any other law not specific to public procurement that may be applicable. An analysis also including, for example, relevant institutional arrangements and institutional sectors on all institutional levels would however only lead to further support of the crude point made here: like many other elements in a society, public procurement of innovation is best understood as a multilevel institutional phenomenon. Although simplifications and practical limitations will always be associated with research on this topic, the awareness of the fundamental principles of multilevel institutions and the interconnectedness between the levels may still help researchers to avoid too hasty conclusions.

ENDOGENOUS AND EXOGENOUS INSTITUTIONS

Coriat and Weinstein (2002) argue that innovation research has followed two separate trajectories, capturing either an organizational or an institutional dimension. The organizational approach has attempted to grasp how firms develop competitive advantages through innovation by taking organization-specific decisions into account. This would correspond to endogenous and informal institutions. The problem with this approach is that it 'largely ignores the contributions of [exogenous] institutional approaches' (ibid., p. 274). Conversely, the institutional approach, while successfully disparaging standard economics' view of innovation as an exogenous process, and incorporating societal (often national) institutions into the analysis, has failed to grasp fully the role of individual organizations. This approach 'implies the major risk of forgetting the key role of diversity within a system, and of the ways actors' behaviours remain largely autonomous and non-determined, and thus to underestimate the flexibility of a system and its possible transformations' (ibid., p. 280).

The solution proposed by Coriat and Weinstein is to bring these two trajectories together through the development of a typology that distinguishes between universal and organization-specific institutions, and between institutions concerned with long-run societal reproduction and those designed to operate on a fixed-term basis (ibid., pp. 281–4). Here we will use the notions 'exogenous' and 'endogenous', respectively (drawing on Jacoby, 1990). Exogenous institutions are 'based on the criteria of authority and enforcement and posed on all the agents' (Coriat and Weinstein, 2002, p. 283). These are typically formal law that applies to everyone. There is also often an enforcement system that punishes any violation of this type of institution. Endogenous institutions are the rules that individual agents decide to give themselves; they are '"private" collective agreements between groups of agents' (ibid., p. 283). Exogenous institutions affect organizations from outside. They are imposed on organizations with little or no control from the organization itself. Endogenous institutions typically evolve within organizations, and may also change as a result of learning within the organization. In turn, endogenous change within an organization may change how an organization responds to exogenous institutions. In other words, the 'control' of the exogenous lies in the endogenous interpretation. This is then the explanation why an analysis of the legal text only may render results not consistent with actual practice understood as determined also by endogenous institutions.

Coriat and Weinstein's second institutional dimension essentially concerns the duration of the institution. These two types will be labelled 'long-term' and 'fixed-term', respectively. The long-term institutions rule the reproduction of the society as a whole, considered in the long run, whereas the fixed-term institutions are fixed in time. Put together, these two dimensions of institutional types form a taxonomy consisting of four distinct categories. Long-term exogenous institutions are manifested in organizations such as schools and hospitals and refer to the general rationale reflecting their existence, such as the general idea about citizens' education or criminals' punishment. Short-term exogenous institutions are universal and fixed in time. Examples of short-term exogenous institutions would be non-permanent policy programmes that attempt to change behaviour on the lower institutional levels. Long-term endogenous institutions include institutions stemming from organizational choices regarding modes of coordination within an organization. Fixed-term endogenous institutions consist also of choices stemming from within organizations and are thus 'local'. They also have a limited time span. Most contracts fall into this category. These four institutional types are displayed in Table 2.2.

Table 2.2   Institutional dimensions affecting innovative public procurement

	Long term	Fixed term
Exogenous	Law, Mission of public agencies	Public policies, programmes
Endogenous	Organizational choices regarding modes of coordination	Contract

The exogenous–endogenous dichotomy also acknowledges the existence of the institutional hierarchy or, at least, order. The focus is different from the mode of multilevel institutional analysis as discussed above. The starting point here is a specific context or institutional level or, to use Ostrom's terminology, a focal level (Ostrom, 2005, p. 12). For each such context there prevail endogenous institutions and exogenous institutions that co-determine outcomes. What to a certain focal context counts as exogenous institutions might also include institutions that are not strictly speaking superior in a hierarchical sense, but are just endogenous institutions for other contexts or ranges. For an organization, other organizations' endogenous institutions are exogenous institutions. Take a soccer game, for example: the members of a soccer team may play according to an agreed strategy. For the team such internally agreed strategy is an endogenous institution. The team will be affected also by the formal rules of the game, which is an exogenous institution in relation to the team. For the other (opposing) team in the soccer game the soccer rules will also be an exogenous institution. The other team will be affected by its (most probably different) endogenous institutions. This means that each team will be affected by its own endogenous institutions and two types of exogenous institutions: the formal soccer rules and the endogenous institutions of the other team. Thus two types of exogenous institutions are distinguishable: absolute exogenous institutions, in this case the soccer rules; and relative exogenous institutions, in this case the endogenous institutions of the other team. The exogenous–endogenous mode is useful, for instance, for analysis of the EC directives on public procurement in relation to the EU member states. For the member states, the directives are exogenous. Member states can choose how to implement the directives according to their endogenous institutional set-up, but they cannot directly change them. If the EU is the focal level, the directives are however endogenous and subject to change. The perspective also acknowledges that the same exogenous institutions may render different outcomes on 'lower' institutional levels owing to differences in the particular endogenous institutions on the 'lower' levels.

The exogenous–endogenous mode also provides an explanation in institutional terms for the success of public procurement contracts. In this light public procurement contracts emerge as the result of an institutional match between different exogenous institutions and endogenous institutions. Long-term exogenous institutions set the conditions for lower levels. To this level belongs the requirement to comply with laws and regulations, which universally affects all actors. Fixed-term exogenous institutions are for instance activities that help to induce change on other institutional levels. Examples of fixed-term exogenous institutions are policy programmes like coordination actions or funding schemes. These are set up in compliance with laws and regulations, that is, long-term exogenous institutions, but with the aim of changing behaviour at other endogenous institutional levels. Long-term endogenous institutions belong to the institutional focus level. For a firm, such institutions are long-term business concepts on which an organization is built, or the rationality behind an organization. Although endogenous choices are made within the organization, they are still affected by law, that is, long-term exogenous institutions. Organizations may also make certain decisions affected by fixed-term exogenous institutions such as policy programmes. Fixed-term endogenous institutions also belong to the focal context. Typically, instances of this type of institution can be derived from the long-term endogenous institutions in a particular organization. To some extent, one can think of these as the implementations of long-term endogenous institutions. The corresponding fixed-term endogenous institution to a tradition in an organization of having well-trained staff would be the course a staff member attends to upgrade his or her skills.

Although the exogenous and endogenous levels discussed above may correspond to organizational levels, it should be noted that this model is essentially an institutional model and not an organizational model. Still, endogenous institutions are often specific to an organization. They vary among individual firms, public agencies and other forms of organizations. If one wants to emphasize the dynamics in this, one could regard the signing of a contract as a situation in which a public buyer and a supplier have reached compatible institutional set-ups. Other organizations affected by the same exogenous institutions – in the same country, for instance – may have developed institutions that do not fully match a certain public agency's institutional set-up. In such cases of institutional mismatch, the probability of a contract's being signed between these entities is low. Or alternatively, if collaborating organizations actually reach a formal agreement, they might later on realize that they do not fully match. This line of thinking also underscores the role of institutional differences among organizations. A political organization for instance, as compared to a private firm, has different rationalities, where leaders of the former are driven by a wish to survive the next election, while the latter's most important goal is commercial success. This perspective provides an explanation of why collaborative public procurement of innovation may fail, if collaborating organizations' endogenous institutional set-ups vary too much and do not match. Another way of expressing this is to say that a certain organization is following a certain rationality. This is the third mode developed in this chapter.

INSTITUTIONS AS RATIONALITIES

Some years ago, by applying an institutional analysis, Gregersen (1992) regarded the public sector as a 'pacer' of private sector innovation. Focusing on a set of related activities including public procurement of innovation, she discussed how the innovative performance of public agencies can be affected by factors such as their specific rationalities and more general goal orientations, as well as relationships with their external environments. The starting point for such an argument is the assumption that any organization fulfils its purposes in conditions of scarce resources. This means that actions carried out by an organization are purposefully selected (Vanberg, 1997). This also implies that organizations must contain some kind of 'procedure for determining the action to be taken' (Nelson and Winter, 1982, p. 57) or, in the terminology used here, rationality. This rationality will affect the conditions for learning and the creation of organization-specific routines (Nelson and Winter, 1982), that is, an organization's endogenous institutions. More generally, learning is accomplished within an organizational context, and can be understood from an organizational perspective as 'those activities by which we create premises which are assumed, or are proven, to be valid and from which we draw conclusions about how to act' (Argyris, 1994, p. 7). Thus, learning is the outcome of the evaluation and possible alteration of pre-existing knowledge or premises, resulting from an action or a conjecture based on the pre-existing knowledge and premises (Schön, 1983; Rolfstam, 2001). Organizations are in this sense entities that 'can create conditions that may significantly influence what individuals frame as the problem, design as a solution, and produce as action to solve a problem' (Argyris, 1994, p. 8).

Van de Donk and Snellen (1989) distinguish between four different rationalities that may influence the actions and decisions in public administrations. These are political rationality, legal rationality, economic rationality and scientific rationality. This framework, slightly modified by Gregersen (1992), can be useful in helping analyse institutional mismatches, understood as differences in rationalities. The rationalities can briefly be summarized as follows.

Political rationality means essentially that the ruling group will act in such a way that it will remain in power. In order to do this it needs to address problems emerging in society, 'the problems of the collectivity' (van de Donk and Snellen, 1989, p. 10). This implies that 'government actions and decisions reflect the – at any time – dominating political and economic interest groups or coalitions' (Gregersen, 1992, p. 132). The solutions suggested by the ruling group will be sought in the direction which the ruling group finds most desirable, but also within the limits dictated by the integrity of society. Legal rationality refers to the law and thus to the legal establishment. Public policy 'must have its foundation in law, must honour the guarantee function of the law, and must ensure equality before the law and legal security' (van de Donk and Snellen, 1989, p. 10). Economic rationality refers to restrictions on public policy due to budgetary limitations. A public agency, for instance, is not supposed to waste taxpayers' money. The importance of economic rationality, following van de Donk and Snellen (ibid., p. 10), varies over time, as the economic conditions change. Scientific or, as suggested by Gregersen (1992, p. 132), 'paradigmatic' rationality refers to institutional specificity in for example specialist public agencies, that is, 'each sector in society recognizes its counterpart in a social-scientific discipline or technological discipline' (van de Donk and Snellen, 1989, p. 11). For instance, one can expect agents in contexts occupied with technical infrastructure such as the electricity or railway systems to give high priority to maintaining and developing further related technical skills, while the emphasis on medical, humanistic and social professionalism are expected in public welfare agencies and hospitals. The rationality notion also provides a starting point for explaining why certain public organizations are perceived as non-innovative. Most public agencies have been set up to deliver a certain service and have accordingly developed a rationality in compliance with that purpose. If a public organization after many years of exposure to efficiency policies is suddenly exposed to exogenous pressure emphasizing innovation and change, some institutional 'friction' would be expected. One could even argue that a public agency which does not face challenges in this policy shift has not been optimally adjusted to service delivery in the past.

The most interesting aspect of the model, however, is that it underscores a focus useful for an institutional analysis of cooperative public procurement of innovation, that is, where several different organizations may be involved in the same public procurement of innovation project. The actions taken by a private firm will rely mostly on economic rationality. A not-for-profit, non-government agency with a specific agenda of promoting a specific behaviour essentially follows a paradigmatic rationality. Although such an organization also needs funds to exist, the priority would be to get funds in order to carry on its paradigmatic activities. Earning money per se would not be the priority as would be the case with a private firm. Among organizations within the public sector, rationalities may vary. Actions taken by the political leadership in a borough council may be strongly determined by political rationalities and the wish to stay in power. A procurement unit within the same borough council might be much influenced by a paradigmatic rationality to comply with the directives and at the same time set up contracts that save taxpayers' money. If public procurement of innovation takes place as a cooperative project its success may depend on the ability among the participating organizations to harmonize their rationalities. The transfer of practices between organizations is often impeded by the lack of either 'a shared language across organizations' or the 'procedural memory' required to complete task routines adopted from other organizations, or both (Amit and Belcourt, 1999, p. 178). The four-rationality model thus becomes useful for analysing to what extent there is an institutional match between endogenous institutions among different organizations. In this perspective, institutional match could be said to occur because of compatible rationalities among collaborating actors. In situations of institutional match, similar problems can attend the adoption of common practices by separate organizations that are attempting to act in concert. It should be noted, however, that institutional match is unlikely to be the default situation. This is also the reason why it has been argued that cooperative public procurement of innovation involving multiple buyers may be more difficult to coordinate than its direct counterpart involving only one: 'A monopsonistic public agency pursuing its own priorities can behave quite differently from one that attempts instead to lead a group of buyer organizations with related but perhaps only partly overlapping agendas' (Hommen and Rolfstam, 2009, p. 17).

CONCLUDING REMARKS

The implication derived from the discussion of the Hommen matrix is that public procurement of innovation can be manifested in all phases of a product's life cycle and in different interaction modes. It is not a tool used exclusively to deliver radical innovation of products and services which 'did not exist'. The ingenious procurer will be able to find possibilities for delivering process innovation, replacing and destroying components, and transferring markets for depreciated products also at later stages in the life cycle. Innovation can occur driven in collaboration with others, or entirely from outside, where the role of public procurement becomes facilitating and responding in character, rather than initiated as an explicit 'demand'.

The starting point for the institutional analysis carried out in this chapter is the appreciation of the shift of focus regarding policy development for public procurement. Expressed in practical terms, this means that public agencies in member states might need to consider revising current practices in order to adapt to the new policies. The rules of the game of public procurement are in that sense undergoing a rather fundamental change. It may be argued that the old efficiency policies affected practice for many years, leading to procurers developing risk-averse behaviour, and adopting contract-awarding principles based on cheapest price rather than value for money, which one could argue reduced the likelihood of public procurers engaging in (risky) innovation projects. The recent complementary development of policies emphasizing innovation thus challenges currently institutionalized practices and skills, as public procurement of innovation may require a rather different set-up to that for the procurement of well-known products (Hommen and Rolfstam, 2009). In order to respond to this policy development, the ultimate challenge for public agencies in member states becomes to develop sound innovation policies and practices for public procurement of innovation. For the innovation research community the ultimate challenge becomes to provide support, critique and innovative ideas useful for policy and practice. The underlying assertion is that an institutional perspective as developed in this chapter provides a holistic tool prompting the 'search for relevant observable facts' (Chalmers, 1999).

It seems then that the three modes may provide some alternative to the 'old' approaches to understanding public procurement of innovation and could help to avoid some of the earlier shortcomings. The three modes – multilevel institutional analysis, endogenous and exogenous institutions, and institutions as rationalities – are partly intertwined and partly accessory modes that provide guidelines for the studying of public procurement of innovation in the sense that they provoke questions that may strengthen future research. The subsequent empirical chapters provide justifications for this framework in several ways. Chapter 3 deals with a case study initially set out to corroborate the general claim that the EC directives hinder innovation. It did however fail on that account, and instead gave reason to consider the role of lower institutional levels for achieving successful outcomes of public procurement of innovation projects. Chapter 4 develops this understanding further by looking into the interplay between different endogenous institutions in relation to an exogenously introduced innovation. In Chapter 5, a particular focus on institutions understood as rationalities among stakeholders is adopted. This perspective is developed further in Chapter 6, while also coming back to a discussion on the relation between exogenous and endogenous institutions. Chapter 7 extends the point that endogenous institutions are important by listing an array of factors that are essentially endogenous.

3. Legal institutions for public procurement of innovation

The interest in public procurement as a means to stimulate innovation provides one explanation of why public procurement law 'has moved from relative obscurity to become a subject of great legal importance' (Arrowsmith, 2005, p. iv). There is a clear need to understand how compliance with the EC directives on public procurement affects the possibilities for public agencies to procure innovation. The fundamental question to pursue is the following: do the EC directives hinder public procurement of innovation? This chapter aims at answering this question by discussing the case where Telenor A/S, the former state-owned telecom agency in Norway, acted as a public agency under the directives on public procurement and procured a new system for maritime radio communication. Without giving away the whole story at this stage, the chapter will provide justification for questioning studying the law as a *sufficient* way of providing the answer to this question. The underlying assertion developed here is that legal studies are central for institutional studies but, if institutions other than formal law are not considered, only subsets of the full answer are achieved.

The rationale for carrying out this study was a concern derived from the perceived tension between the interactive characteristics of public procurement of innovation and the implicit assumptions built into the public procurement directives that the possibilities for public agencies to procure innovations may be limited, as maintained by Edquist, Hommen and Tsipouri (2000). These authors claimed that there prevailed a lack of strategic concern in relation to public procurement, as reflected in how the legal framework might affect the possibilities for public procurement of innovations (ibid.). Their basic argument was that the interactive learning and user–producer interaction required for innovation would be inhibited by the rules. The International Energy Agency also quite early 'recommended to suggest clarifications in the existing public procurement rules, for example the EC Directives, in order to facilitate procurement efforts within innovation purpose' (IEA, 2000, p. 14). Other scholars had warned that '[t]he consequence of rigid procurement rules may be that procurement processes give rise to solutions that are price competitive, but do not spur innovation and the dynamic development for firms and society as a whole' (Nyholm *et al.*, 2001, p. 264). The empirical work started out with the aim of verifying these claims. As will be discussed below, it turned out that the evidence eventually collected prompted a revision of the assertion that the EC rules prevent innovation. To discuss this point further, there follows a brief summary of the legislative package regulating public procurement in Europe.

The EC directives on public procurement are transposed into national legislation among EU member states, but (as was discussed in Chapter 2) other, non-EU member states also comply with the same rules. Following the subsidiarity principle, member states should implement any regulations that concern them in the way they find most appropriate. In Sweden, for instance, since the time it became a member of the European Union the directives on public procurement have been implemented by amendments to the 'old' act on public procurement (SFS 1992, p. 1528, Lagen om offentlig upphandling) and to the latest version of the law (SFS 2007, p. 1091). Denmark has chosen to directly incorporate the directives 'telles quelles', that is, without further adaptation of the text. It should be noted here that, although Norway is not formally a member of the European Union, it has accepted compliance with the same procurement rules through its participation in the EFTA agreement (EFTA, 2006) and its membership in the European Economic Area (EEA) (Weltzien, 2005; Grønningsæter, 2010). In practice, this means that public procurement must be carried out in compliance with the public procurement directives within the institutional domain. Although there are some national variations, for instance regarding procurement below certain threshold values, the principle of institutional set-up is the same, that is, they follow the EC public procurement directives.

The directives coordinating public procurement have evolved since the first versions adopted in the 1970s. In the 1980s, as reported by research at the time, governments had adopted protectionist procurement policies; it was also perceived that preferential public procurement had led to inefficiencies and that significant economies would accrue from a competitive EC-wide single market (Uttley and Hartley, 1994; Arrowsmith, 2005, pp. 120–25). The aim with the directives was to remove these prevailing barriers to trade in public procurement practices. Through the adoption of these rules, the best bid, regardless of origin in the Union, would be awarded a contract tendered for. The intention was initially to exclude the utilities sector from coordination, because those activities were in some member states provided by public organizations and in others by private firms. As it turned out, the utilities sector eventually became regulated, but with less stringent rules than for the classical sector (Green, 1994). These rules also regulated private firms operating in the utilities sector on the basis of 'special or exclusive rights granted by a competent authority' (Directive 93/38, Article 2b). The public procurement directives in force at the time for the procurement project studied here were the Works Directive 93/37, the Supply Directive 93/36, the Service Utilities Directive 92/50 and the Utilities Directive 93/38 (see Arrowsmith, 2004b). The directive that was applied in this particular case was the Utilities Directive 93/38, regulating entities operating in the water, energy, transport and telecommunications sectors. On 1 May 2004 the new Utilities Directive 2004/17 was adopted to replace the old one (Arrowsmith, 2004b). At the same time a new directive for the classical or public sector was also adopted, Directive 2004/18. Telenor, today a private company, was at the time a public undertaking (Directive 93/38, Article 2), procuring technology for the provision of telecommunication services to be used on a market where it had a monopoly, the maritime radio network in Norway.

One central element of the directives is the specification of procurement procedures a public procurer can apply to award a contract. The procedures specified in the old Utilities Directive 93/38 are the open procedure, the restricted procedure, the negotiated procedure and the design contest. The procurement procedure applied in this case was the negotiated procedure with a contract notice. This means that the procurers first issued a notice calling for suppliers to submit their interest in participating. The procurers then sent the full specifications to selected tenderers, among which a subset was invited to negotiations. The negotiated procedure, as was used in the case studied here, remained in both the 2004 directives (R. Williams, 2004). One could therefore argue that the results of this study are also valid for the current legislative regime. The 2004 directives for the classical sector also included a new procedure, the competitive dialogue, developed to allow more flexibility for complex contracts (Arrowsmith, 2004b).

A CASE OF PUBLIC PROCUREMENT OF INNOVATION

The chapter continues as follows. After providing a brief historical background of maritime radio technology and an introduction to the procurer Telenor, it gives a description of the procurement project. Analytically, a distinction is made between the pre-procurement phase and the procurement phase. The pre-procurement phase is supposed to capture the events that took place from the time when ideas started to emerge and needs were identified, while the procurement phase started the day the tender call was published. A central element in the pre-procurement phase is the emergence of and the process of defining a need for the procurement. A central element in the procurement phase is the process of finding the supplier that best can satisfy the need. The chapter concludes with a discussion of the case study findings.

The Historical Background of Maritime Radio and Telenor

The most important engineer for the development of radio technology was probably Nikola Tesla (Brenner, 2009). Experiments conducted in 1897 by Guglielmo Marconi, where radio signals were exchanged between two Italian warships, have however become a more widely accepted starting point for modern marine radio communication. As the technological development progressed, there followed institutionalization, for instance through the establishment of requirements for radio operator certificates and standardization. Partly as a response to the *Titanic* disaster, a maritime safety conference held in 1914 resulted in the establishment of the International Convention for the Safety of Life at Sea (SOLAS). This convention is today maintained by the International Maritime Organization (IMO), which is an agency organized under the United Nations. The IMO manages several other conventions, for example the 1978 International Convention on Standards of Training, Certification and Watchkeeping for Seafarers (STCW) and the 1979 International Convention on Maritime Search and Rescue. In 1992 the implementation of the Global Maritime Distress and Safety System (GMDSS) was started. The GMDSS includes specifications and require-ments for transmitting and receiving distress calls, and other safety devices such as the use of emergency position indicating radio beacons (EPIRBs) (Isaksen, 2003). Since the late nineteenth century, when maritime radio communication consisted of sparks put together according to Morse code, a tremendous development has taken place, in which innovation has been a central feature. This development is of course also the result of innovation in supporting or generic technologies such as space technologies, ICT and so on. Modern terrestrial coast radio involves an array of services for the shipping trade, the fishing fleet and leisure craft. Examples of such services are the transmission of naviga-tional warnings six times a day (warnings about dangers in the area, such as beacons out of order), traffic lists (informing if ships have incoming telephone calls), medical advice, weather forecasts, general radio mon-itoring, rescue coordination, and the transferring of radio calls (from vessels) to the telephone network (Maritim Radio, 2005a).

The procurer in this case was a special branch of Telenor, Telenor Networks Maritime Radio, the unit responsible for providing these services in Norway. In addition to the services mentioned in the previous paragraph, Telenor also managed licences through its Radio Licensing Department and executed inspections of equipment installed on board ships through the Radio Inspection Branch (Maritim Radio, 2005b). Telenor Maritime Radio had at the time about 100 employees. The historical roots of Telenor go as far back as 1855, when Telegrafverket (the telegraph agency later to become Televerket, the public telecom agency) established the first telegraph connection between the two cities of Drammen and Christiania (Maritim Radio, 2005a). In the 1990s, the company was transformed from a public monopoly to a private company. In 1994 the public agency Televerket became a public company, Telenor, and in 2000 the company was introduced on to the Oslo Stock Exchange market. The developments of the last few decades have meant that the company has had to adapt to a competitive environment. Telenor today is active, on the international market, in satellite communication and telecommunication and, on the domestic market, in internet technologies (Maritim Radio, 2005b). In the case studied here the EC directives for public procurement applied. Today, in principle, Telenor acts like any private company, that is, without an obligation to comply with public procurement rules except in cases where the procurement concerns activities that are 'exclusive rights granted by a competent authority of a Member state' (Directive 93/38, Article 2, para. 1b).

THE PROCUREMENT PROJECT

The tender call for a supply contract that was eventually published, on equipment for Norwegian maritime radio communication, included the following items:

- approximately 30 operator positions, equipped with PCs/terminals in a Windows-based environment (standard office equipment);
- digital switches (eight–nine) with direct access to the public ISDN network, and interconnected via WAN and audio network.

One of these switches was to be set up on each coastal radio station. The switches were to be used to mediate communication between sea- (i.e. radio traffic) and land-based communication networks.

According to the tender document the system should support:

- distributed operational control of any radio channel to all coast radio stations within the network;
- radiotelephony on VHF, MF and HF, and calls to/from PSTN;
- automatic connections to/from PSTN using DSC signalling (VHF and MF/HF);
- the sending and receiving of text messages (telex, e-mail);
- the handling of Morse telegraphy on MF and HF;
- internet access to coast stations and possibly to/from ships;
- distress and safety recommendations, SOLAS-74 and SOLAS-88 from the IMO, to be fulfilled;
- accompanying databases;
- multiplexing and compressing equipment for data and audio;
- installation of the equipment to be part of the delivery.

Procured Innovations

An essential issue for case study research on public procurement of innovation is to establish what kind of innovation actually occurred in the case. With reference to the discussion on definitions of innovation in Chapter 1, one could say that innovations are commercially successful applications based on new knowledge or new combinations of existing knowledge. Innovations can also appear in different ways, for example as product innovations or process innovations. As will be discussed in the following, several types of innovation were achieved.

The procured system included a feature called distributed operational control (DOC). This meant that a radio system consisting of several radio stations in principle could be operated from one station. This particular system had not been built or used before and was different from other systems installed elsewhere at the time. In that sense, the system was a product innovation. The company that finally became the supplier to Telenor, Frequentis GmbH, had previously delivered a coast radio system to Lyngby Radio in Denmark, although the Danish version was not as technologically sophisticated as the Norwegian system. The most evident innovative component of the new system (distinguishing it from the Danish system) concerned new flexible ways to operate the different radio stations, located evenly all over Norway, through the use of DOC. In Denmark, the system consisted of only one station, Lyngby Radio, and thus there was not an obvious need for such features. Frequentis had however used the principles of distributed technology on one emergency response system procured for fire stations in Germany. They still needed two years of software development before the complete system was delivered to Telenor.

Another way of determining to what extent innovation has been delivered is to consider any organizational changes prompted by the introduction of the procured item. Such analysis in this case would draw attention to the fact that replacing the analogue system by the new digital technology developed in the project also meant changes related to the organization. With the analogue technology used before the procurement project, all stations operated individually and separately served their own geographical area. Through the application of DOC, it became possible to provide and maintain these services from remote locations. Basically this meant that one station could take over operations from another station, as all the coast radio stations in Norway in practice became interconnected. With the new technology installed, a small station can have one person on duty and, if something happens that requires the engagement of several radio operators, the operator can be assisted by other stations, either a neighbouring station or the main station. It is also possible to temporarily close down a station for the weekend or over-night, for example in low-peak periods. Given some minor changes in the new system, it would actually, in principle, be possible to serve the entire Norwegian coast from one location. In principle, these features have also made it possible to reduce the number of staffed stations and thus the number of operators without jeopardizing operations.

Another innovation concerned the automation of calls to land-based systems. Previously, this type of call was handled manually by operators. When a ship needed to make a phone call to the land-based network, it used to call the operator manually by using the VHF radio and ordered a telephone call, which was then administrated (and billed) by the operator. The new digital system automated this procedure. This automation could then be seen as a process innovation. If the proper radio equipment is installed on board, a ship can in principle dial the desired telephone number (and receive the bill) without interacting with an operator. The means to achieve this innovation mainly consisted of software develop-ment and, to some extent, configuration of hardware components. The hardware used was, at least as far as the subject matter of this study is concerned, existing products. At the outset Frequentis already had a switch upon which the solution was built, and standard personal comput-ers were used as platforms for the operator work stations. In that sense, the innovation can also be described as new combinations of existing knowledge.

Yet another characteristic of this project was integration. The procurers needed to take into account the variety of already existing communica-tion technologies. The customers of the services provided by the system would be all kinds of vessels, ranging between small leisure boats to commercial ships. The technology that needed to be supported included 'plain' VHF radio and, in order to be able to communicate with parts of the Russian fishing fleet, even Morse code. Requirements as specified for example by the GMDSS standard also had to be included in the design. This meant that a lot of effort had to be put into ensuring that all these technical standards and specifications of interfaces were adequately implemented in the system.

PHASES OF THE PROCUREMENT PROJECT

Some important dates of the whole procurement project are displayed in Table 3.1, which briefly summarizes the process.

Table 3.1 *Key events in the public procurement of an innovative maritime radio system.*

Autumn 1997	Work on definition of needs and specification
10 March, 1998	Tender call was published
14 April, 1998	Submission deadline for requests to participate
29 April, 1998	Request for quotation sent to qualified tenders
19 May, 1998	Refusal letter to participants
30 June, 1998	Deadline submission of bid
15 July, 1999	Contract signed
4 April, 2000	Final Design Review Protocol
End of 2002	System delivered

The procurement process started in the autumn of 1997 with preparation, and was published on 10 March 1998. The deadline for submitting qualifying documents, references and so on by interested tenderers was 14 April 1998. After being reviewed by Telenor, qualified companies were sent an offer, the request for quotation, on 29 April 1998, that is, the specification of the system to be procured. The deadline for submission of complete tenders was 30 June 1998. Then another process of selection followed, and Telenor initiated negotiations with a small number of tenderers.[1] Eventually, Frequentis, today a multinational supplier of communications and information systems, was awarded a fixed-price contract. Roughly one year after the deadline for the submission of bids, on 15 July 1999 the contract was signed.

THE PRE-PROCUREMENT PHASE

As was mentioned above, this study distinguishes between the pre-procurement phase and the procurement phase. Accordingly, this section covers the events that took place from the beginning, with the initiation of the procurement project, up to the point when the tender call was published.

The Need to Be Satisfied

In 1990, Telenor was prompted by the Norwegian government to introduce new technology that would make it possible to make rationalizations and reduce the number of employees working at the coast radio stations. The government also stipulated that such rationalization could only take place by implementing technology that had proven its capability. In a sense, this was a kind of risk management on the government level. Within Telenor Maritime Radio, ideas had been discussed about the possibilities that might be offered by the emerging new digital technologies. Some features of the system in operation today had been discussed by Telenor employees in the early 1990s. There was also an interest motivated by commercial considerations for pursuing a procurement project devoted to the development of new technology.

The technology that at the time existed within the organization was becoming inefficient, especially in the light of emerging digital technology that, if procured, would allow for the implementation of new services as well as automation of existing ones. It was also perceived that the new technology would offer flexibility in order to serve all Norwegian waters at all hours. The average age of the personnel staffing the radio stations had exceeded 50. Retirements and sick leave could potentially jeopardize operations in the future. A system allowing operators located elsewhere to take over some or all radio traffic previously earmarked for the closest radio station would reduce operational risk due to these workforce-related problems. As Telenor was in the process of being transformed from a public monopoly to a company on a competitive market, the need to consider new ways of making money was also emphasized. Some of the services, those handling safety and distress calls, were and are still funded by the state. Other services were included in the procurement project for commercial reasons. Examples of such services to be offered by the new system were automatic connection of calls by radio to the public telephone network and the transmitting of other forms of data such as e-mail and telex.

A Previous Project

Some years before the procurement project under study here was initiated, another procurement process was carried out (around 1995), with the aim of procuring new technology for the coast radio stations. This early project seems to have played an important role in providing knowledge and experience that contributed to the success of the second attempt under study here. The supplier that was contracted the first time used the name Garex. This company had delivered the analogue radio system that was in operation at the time at Telenor Maritime Radio. The digital switch which Garex intended to use in the new solution had also proven its ability in other areas, for example in providing radio communication solutions for airports. Another factor that may have played a role when Garex was awarded this contract was that Telenor owned parts of the company at the time. This first project ran for two years. As the project developed it started to encounter problems. Although some equipment was delivered and tested by Telenor, the development process was eventually terminated in 1998. The main reason for this was that it was concluded that the technology delivered by Garex would not be able to meet the specifications. In particular, the suggested solution failed to implement the DOC features that were central for the procurers.

In retrospect, it is possible to identify certain experiences from the first attempt that seem to have been very useful. For instance, the specifications for the system were too general. This generated several late changes and amendments in the design process. Project communication methods that were too unstructured eventually led to a situation where no one had control over the development of the system. The supplier that had been chosen had not delivered the same technology elsewhere before. Fairly late in the development, it was discovered that the technology intended for the implementation of the system was not capable of implementing the wanted DOC principle. All these problems in turn led to the project requiring more time and using more monetary resources than initially expected. It is not unlikely that these experiences exposed problems that the following procurement management could draw on, thus making sure they avoided them the second time. It was also emphasized by the procurement manager of the second successful attempt that, 'before appointing a supplier, we wanted to be sure that we had chosen one that would be able to deliver'. The learning and experiences from the first procurement project also meant that the procurers now were quite clear on the technical requirements of the system to be procured.

Specifying Needs and Finding Potential Suppliers

The pre-procurement phase of the procurement that eventually became successful started in autumn 1997. As was indicated above, the earlier experiences may have assisted this work, in terms both of knowledge about the system that was to be procured and of general procurement management skills. In this stage, more emphasis was placed not only on defining the needs but also on how to define needs in an open, technologically neutral way. Company policy within Telenor prompted use of specifications that were as open as possible in order to attain the highest number of tenders possible, that is, to stimulate competition and thus reduce the price. According to the interviews carried out in this study, this policy had been applied even without a requirement to comply with the procurement directives. In principle, the specification used in the procurement process was a functional specification (van Weele, 2002, p. 52). This means that, rather than specifying certain technologies and how functions should be implemented, the required function of the procured system was described. As the system involves communications between different standards and protocols, these interfaces were also described in the tender document. This means that the tender document was functional where possible, but specific (according to the interface specifications as used by other interacting systems) when so required. Many questions from the procurer to tenderers at later stages of the procurement process served to make the tender show that all these interfaces were to be implemented in the system to be delivered. Applying a functional specification, rather than a technical specification, will ideally make room for supplier-side innovation, as this gives freedom for the suppliers to utilize possessed knowledge and technology in the way they find most appropriate. In this case, the opportunities for the supplier to suggest alternative solutions were restricted, as the specifications were rather detailed. It should be noted that the procurer had not described how the supplier should adjust its technological platforms or use its capabilities in order to meet with the requirements. 'But we had described exactly what we wanted', as the project manager put it. The tender call was published on 10 March 1998.

THE PROCUREMENT PHASE

The publishing of the tender call marks the start of the second phase, that is, the procurement phase, which will be discussed in the following.

Diversity and Selection

The way Telenor went about this project can be summarized as follows. Initially, efforts were made to attract as many tenders as possible in order to establish competition and make sure that competent tenderers were participating. Once gathered, the tenderers had to go through a qualifying process, where the strongest candidates remained and those judged to be less competitive were excluded. Towards the end, Telenor initiated negotiations with a small number of tenderers, and eventually the contract was awarded to the tender that was most competitive technically and economically. The supplier finally awarded the contract was the Austrian firm Frequentis GmbH. Prior to the publishing of the tender call Telenor had surveyed the market globally for potential suppliers. Several intermediate organizations and sources were used for this purpose: the Japanese as well as the American embassy, the Australian Trade Commission, countries' 'yellow pages' telephone directories, and other public agencies using similar technologies. For instance (what was then called) the Swedish Civil Aviation Administration was consulted on this matter. When the tender call was published, Telenor notified the suppliers that had been identified in the pre-procurement phase and also encouraged them to participate.

Steps in the Qualifying Process

The first formal step in the qualifying process was the published tender call. The tender call listed a number of requirements, minimum standards that any bidder had to be able to demonstrate in order to qualify as a tenderer and be allowed to take part with the specification documents. These requirements were as follows:

- The tenderer should be able to show a certificate of enrolment on the professional or trade register under the conditions laid down by the laws of the state in which it was established and, where applicable, a statement of the register's classification.
- The tenderer should also be able to show that it had fulfilled obligations relating to the payment of social security and taxes in its country, as well as providing appropriate statements from bankers and presenting the undertaking's balance sheets or extracts from the balance sheets.
- Statements of the firm's overall turnover in respect of the services, works or supplies to which the contract related for the previous three financial years were required.

- Details were required of technicians or technical services available, whether or not belonging directly to the undertaking, with special reference to quality-control arrangements.
- Samples, descriptions and/or photographs of the goods were to be supplied.
- Certificates were to be drawn up by official quality-control institutes or agencies.

A special requirement was also formalized:

- Documentation was required that customer-adapted equipment within switches and radio telecommunication had been delivered and functioned satisfactorily at another customer.

As specified in the tender call, these requirements (and the corresponding documents) were used to select those candidates that later would receive the invitation to tender. At the beginning about 20 companies communicated their interest in the project. Fourteen companies eventually made a formal submission in order to become qualified as tenderers and thus receive the complete specification. These companies represented an array of different countries acting either from branches located in Norway or from abroad. Six companies situated in Norway submitted. Of these two were domestic and four international acting from local branches, representing Finland, France, Germany and the US. Participating nations represented by the companies acting from abroad were Austria (one company), Denmark (two companies), Germany (one company), Italy (one company), Sweden (two companies) and Switzerland (one company). Of the 14 companies that made a formal response, ten companies managed to become pre-qualified and were sent the complete tender specification.

The invitation to submit a full proposal, the request for quotation, was sent out on 29 April 1998. Of the ten pre-qualified companies, five finally submitted a proposal. Of these, not all companies submitted a proposal that was considered as a potential candidate for the contract. Eventually the companies that had been most successful in demonstrating their capabilities as well as their understanding of what Telenor wanted were invited to negotiations. In the general case, Telenor shortlisted two or three candidates for negotiations. The tenderers that eventually ended up on the shortlist offered solutions that required further development before it was possible to install the actual system. They also had in their possession the elements on which they could base this development. The deadline for submitting a bid was 30 June 1998, and the day when the contract was finally signed was 15 July 1999. This means that Telenor spent roughly one year negotiating with the remaining companies in order finally to select a winner of the contract.

The reason for awarding the contract to Frequentis was that the company outperformed competitors in an array of aspects of the project, as summarized in the following:

- date of delivery;
- profitability;
- technological assistance;
- services after delivery;
- price;
- operation costs;
- quality;
- technical value;
- aesthetic and functional values, which in this case mostly concerned functional values.

In retrospect, it is noteworthy that from the beginning Frequentis had distinguished itself as compared to the other competitors, in terms of its ability to demonstrate a clear understanding of what Telenor wanted to buy. Several of the other tenderers had written offers where, in the view of the procurer, they revealed a lack of such understanding. Frequentis had at the time some key people who possessed technical knowledge and skills as well as abilities to understand their customer's needs; they demonstrated an interest in delivering what the customer asked for. Frequentis also wanted to move into this market for strategic reasons. Winning this contract would provide a springboard for such a move. The negotiators on the procurer's side had to comply with an upper price limit of NOK 50 million, set by the management of Telenor. The total price for the system was not allowed to exceed this figure, but the functional requirements still had to be fulfilled. These two requirements were met in the agreement. The final price agreed upon was significantly lower than most of the competing tenderers had initially proposed.

Refining the Functional Specification

As indicated in Table 3.1, between the signing of the contract and the delivery, another document, the design specification, was produced by the supplier and accepted by the procurer, as noted in the final design review protocol. This meant that on 4 April 2000, that is, some ten months after the contract had been signed, Frequentis had arrived at a satisfactory and definite description of how the complete system should be implemented. The completion of the document marked the end of an intense period of interaction between the two actors. Over this period technical meetings were held every month either in Norway or in Austria, and an array of e-mails were sent between the organizations. The design specification suggested by Frequentis had gone through several review cycles characterized by interactive learning, leading to a preliminary design specification that was evaluated by Telenor. The review of the version of the design specification that eventually was accepted took roughly two weeks. The final design review documents were received by Telenor on 17 March 2000. Basically, the end result can be seen as the refined result of iterations of this cycle. In the time period 10 October to 12 December 1999, for example, there was a period characterized as 'exchange of technical documents with short time limit'. This meant that Frequentis required information from Telenor that was necessary to the development of the final design specification. A preliminary report dated 17 December 1999 concluded that some aspects of the design specifications were 'not satisfactory', and prompted the supplier to come back with a more detailed description, which it ultimately was able to do at the beginning of April.

THE DELIVERY

The delivery of the system was set up in different steps, whereby each one had to be finished and delivered before commencing on the next step. At each step several tests were performed, such as acceptance tests and functional tests. When the delivery of each step was found to meet the requirements, payment for the current part was transferred to the supplier. The contract also specified measures to be taken if something did not meet the time schedule written into the contract. If the supplier had not delivered parts according to the agreed timetable, it would have been forced to pay fines. This however was a clause that never needed to be invoked.

Project Management

On the procurer's side the project was managed by a relatively small team with clearly defined tasks. The team consisted of a project manager who had the overall responsibility for financial, technological and operational aspects of the project. The project manager also wrote the technical specification for the project. There was a project member responsible for ensuring the system's compatibility with GMDSS standards. For a limited time also an external consultant was engaged on this issue. Another project member worked with the database in the system. A fourth member of the team was a procurement expert who worked with the procurement process. When the tender process had been concluded and the contract awarded, this person was in principle released from the project.

In general the project was managed quite tightly. Although a functional specification was applied, the specification was still quite detailed. A lot of effort had also been made to get it right from the beginning. If something had been omitted in the specifications, and further amendments to the specifications had been necessary, this would have meant a severe increase in cost for the procurer. Thus, this illustrates the benefits of 'intelligent demand'. Clearly it was possibly for Telenor to produce a sensible specification because of existing in-house competence. Another feature of the project concerns the leadership in relation to the stakeholders of the new system. Although there was interaction between the intended users of the new system, the suppler and the procurers, a central policy was to stick to plans and agreed-upon decisions. Occasionally the project manager had to act in a very determined way to avoid potential delays associated with late changes because of new suggestions on how to do things. A point that further illustrates the tight leadership concerns communication between the procurer and the supplier. All communication between them went through the project manager. This helped to avoid the project reaching a state where coordination was lost. Here, the lessons learned from the first attempt to procure a new system contributed to the tight style of project management in the second attempt. In order to be successful, coordination was critical.

DISCUSSION

The discussion includes a number of sections briefly outlined as follows. Initially, for analytical purposes and also to validate the study, the innovative features of the project are discussed. This is followed by a discussion on the interaction an innovative process requires. Then follows a discussion on how the law affects the procurement process, followed by a discussion based on a comparison between the first unsuccessful attempt to procure a new system and the second, which turned out to be successful.

Establishing Innovation

As was discussed above, the public procurement project carried out by Telenor led to both product and process innovation. With a development time lasting from July 1999, when the contract was signed, to the end of 2002, when the system was finally delivered, this was indeed an example of public procurement of innovation in terms of both learning and outcome (Schumpeter, 1934 [1969]; Dosi, 1988; Lundvall, 1992). One could perhaps view the system as built on a new combination of existing knowledge, incorporating already codified maritime standards, based on in-house expertise and the supplier's technical capabilities. Although exactly the same system had never been built before and the project included R&D and technical change, the project corresponds to what is sometimes called adoptive public procurement (Edquist *et al.*, 2000). The fact that Telenor procured the system to satisfy an intrinsic need makes the project an instance of a direct procurement of innovation with a dyadic supplier relation (Hommen and Rolfstam, 2009). Having established that innovation actually occurred makes the case interesting, as it suggests that it is possible to achieve innovation through public procurement in compliance with the EC directives on public procurement. This would also mean that the necessary interaction between procurer and supplier actually could happen within the legal framework. If this was possible, questions arise regarding how that was achieved. A discussion of these and related matters follows.

Public Procurement of Interactive Learning

Conceptually, innovation and design are activities that concern the creation of new products, processes and/or services. This means that all aspects of a new product and/or service are not known in advance and that any innovative project involves different kinds of uncertainty and risk. One could then understand interaction with the supplier or other stakeholders as a way of reducing uncertainty in public procurement of innovation projects. This basic assertion also corresponds to how the case evolved. Through learning in the pre-procurement phase the procurer had gained the knowledge of the requirements, that is, what the system was supposed to do, what interfaces it was supposed to handle, according to what standards and so on. The supplier, on the other hand, had in its possession the knowledge and technology necessary for implementing the functional requirements and to solve any problems that might come up as they went along. This means that, at the beginning, neither of these two actors had in its possession sufficient knowledge to design, develop and install the system without input from its counterpart. What made the innovation possible was interaction that allowed transfer of the different kinds of knowledge and skills between procurer and supplier. Thus, from an innovation theoretical point of view, public procurement of innovation as it took place in this case can be seen as a special instance of innovation, characterized by learning and interaction (Dosi, 1988; Lundvall, 1992). In addition, viewed in this way, public procurement of innovation would by no means be considered a linear process, but a process where interactive learning and user–producer interaction take place (Kline and Rosenberg, 1986; von Hippel, 1988).

Although the emphasis on interaction is useful for analysis of innovative activities, there is a tendency to neglect the actual direction of the learning undergone. In this respect, design theory adds a useful complementary perspective for further analysis of the interaction that took place between the procurer and the tenderers. Design theorists would understand public procurement of innovation as a learning process driven by a vision that provides the direction towards a solution (Stolterman, 1991). The initial perception of the design task is determined by the designer's ideals and thought figures, that is, the designer's knowing or reasoning. To objectify the vision the designer develops an operative image from the vision. This is the result of the 'negotiating' mediated by the designer's thought figures between his or her perception of the design situation and his or her vision. The vision, so to speak, leads the development of an operative image at the same time as it is affected by it. At some point in time the development of the operative image becomes established as the design suggestion, that is, as some kind of artefact (Arnheim, 1962; Rolfstam, 2001). It is a reflexive process where '"the solution" does not arise directly from "the problem"; the designers' attention oscillates, or commutes, between the two, and an understanding of both gradually develops' (Cross, 1992, p. 49). The point to make however is that, although the outcome in the technical sense is unknown, the process is still guided by rationalities and visions that will help developers to determine when the intended outcome has been reached. This means that the design process, although uncertain, is a rational process (Stolterman, 1991).

Applied in this context, this perspective suggests that public procurement of innovation can be seen not only as interaction between collaborating actors in general, as an analysis based on innovation theory would suggest, but also as a design process guided by a vision pointing at an increasingly concrete goal. One way of identifying specific instances of such processes would be to indentify the corresponding goal. In this case it is possible to distinguish analytically between three distinct processes and corresponding visions aiming at: establishing the need; finding a supplier; and satisfying the need (by developing the actual system). The starting point of the first process is by nature vague, as it might be tracked back in time long before the first attempt to procure a new system was made. It did eventually manifest itself in the pre-procurement phase delivering the specifications of the system included in the documents sent out to the qualified tenderers. The second process started in the pre-procurement phase and was driven by the vision to find a supplier able to deliver. The issue was not at this stage primarily to develop the system, but to find a supplier that could demonstrate the best 'knowing and reasoning' among the competitors, in order to ensure the delivery of a working system once the contract was awarded. This vision to find a supplier that would be able to deliver based on technology that would work was quite explicitly formulated both by the Norwegian government and by the engineers working on the procurement project. The third process occurred in the procurement phase, that is, from the point in time when the contract was awarded, and continued to the successful final delivery of the procured system. This was a period of extensive interaction between procurer and supplier, where conjectures were evaluated and sometimes disapproved, to finally reach an acceptable quality. Thus, the interactive conditions in this third process correspond more closely to what innovation theory would predict for innovative projects in general. The user–producer interaction was as unrestricted as the interaction in developing pairs used to be (Fridlund, 1999), with the only difference that the duration of the interaction in this case was regulated by the contract. As this intense interactive learning took place between the procurer and the supplier after the contract had been signed, this was by no means a violation of the rules.

Another example of the interaction between different actors in the procurement project was the work towards reaching specifications of the graphical user interface (GUI) for the operators' work stations. The general ambition was to make a graphical user interface in such a way that the operators did not require long periods of training in order to use the system, and at the same time the new system should enable more efficient operation. Different suggested solutions were available. For instance, there was a choice between traditional PC monitors and touch screens. But there was also a need for decisions on what the design of the graphical forms displayed on the screen should look like. Decisions also needed to be made on 'where' in the system a user should enter when starting the computer and how the application should be structured, that is, issues concerning the interaction design of the program. The suppliers on the shortlist were allowed to study current workplaces that existed in the current system. These studies also involved working procedures, that is, how the work was carried out with the existing technology. Another reason for studying existing systems was to reduce the learning threshold for future users of the new system. A user group consisting of employees at the coast radio stations was also involved and contributed to the features of the new system. The procurers visited installations made previously by the shortlisted tenderers. Examples of such installations were control rooms for railway systems, systems for coordination of emergency services, and air traffic control systems. The procurers also studied installations that they themselves had delivered to (other) customers.

It may be argued that the procurement procedure used might have had implications for the possibilities of interactive learning and hence the possibilities for innovation. As mentioned earlier, the procurement procedures available in the old Utilities Directive are the open, restricted and negotiated procedures (Directive 93/38, Article 1, para. 7). If negotiations are allowed, procurers may gain knowledge useful for determining the winner of the contract. For instance, an offer that initially seems to be the most advantageous offer does not always come out as the winner. One reason for this is that tenderers might apply different pricing strategies. Some tenderers build in room for negotiations in their price offerings, while others submit a price that is from the outset very close to the lowest level they can possibly afford, that is, with very little room for negotiation. Another issue that may be revealed in the negotiation phase is related to technical aspects of the contract. One such issue may be the level of complexity in proposed solutions. One tenderer may specify a hundred lines of program code to solve a certain problem while another tenderer requires one thousand lines of code to solve the same problem. This difference is usually reflected in the price given by the tenderer. Complicated solutions are usually more expensive than smoother ones. Given the view of public procurement of innovations understood as an activity requiring interactive learning and user–producer interaction, the most relevant procedure for procuring innovation under the old Utilities Directive would be the negotiated procedure. The main reason for this is that in the negotiated procedure 'the contracting entity consults suppliers, contractors or service providers of its choice and negotiates the terms of the contract with one or more of them' (Directive 93/38, Article 1, para. 7c). In other words, this would be the procedure that to the greatest extent allows interactive learning between supplier and procurer. On those grounds one could tentatively argue that one reason for the successful outcome of the project was that the procurers used the negotiated procedure instead of the open procedure. This is however an argument that could be challenged.

Even if the negotiated procedure allows negotiation to a larger extent than the open procedure does, the case provides only ambiguous support for the general claim that the negotiated procedure is more conducive to innovation than any other procedure. This claim is supported by the observation that important interaction that enabled the actual development of the solution took place after the contract was signed. The central purposes of the negotiation phase were to reduce all uncertainty related to the project, that is, to reach clarity and to gain information in order to be able to select an adequate supplier that would be able to deliver. Subsequently, at a stage out of institutional range for any tender procedure, the procurer engaged in unrestricted interaction with the supplier aiming at ultimately developing the solution. The experiences from the earlier procurement project appear to confirm this reflection. Even if one can assume negotiation underwent relatively unrestricted, the first attempt failed to deliver a final solution.

INTERACTING ACCORDING TO THE RULES

In general, throughout a procurement process, the directives function as an exogenous limiting factor. There are things that a public procurer must do and there are things a public procurer may not do. What is noteworthy, as discussed in Chapter 1, is that the directives neither directly regulate the content, that is, what is procured, nor distinguish between public procurement of innovation and public procurement of regular goods. With reference to the case, this means that compliance with the law does not necessarily inhibit innovation. In fact it may actually increase the possibilities for innovation and a successful outcome in general. Typical obligations specified in the old Utilities Directive were the requirement to publish a tender call in the *Official Journal of the European Communities* (Directive 93/38, Article 21). The contracting entity was also obliged to base the contract award on certain criteria (Directive 93/38, Article 34). The tender eventually chosen had to be the 'most advantageous tender' or the offer with 'the lowest price' (Directive 93/38, Article 34, para. 1).

Non-discrimination is a central theme in the directives. 'Contracting entities shall ensure that there is no discrimination between different suppliers, contractors or service providers' (Directive 93/38, Article 4, para. 2). These principles were complied with in different ways throughout the project. A central conviction within Telenor was the importance of treating all tenders in the same way, in terms of the information that was distributed. If, for instance, a tenderer asked a question about the system to be built that required answers that had not already been made available to all the competing tenderers in shared documents, the answer was distributed to all tenderers. Especially in the negotiation phase, one can of course suspect that there could be a risk of information leakage, for example that one tenderer's suggestion would be revealed to any other competitors. In order to safeguard against such leakages, internal meetings were held for technical personnel to train them not to unintentionally reveal such tender-specific information to a competitor. In general, it may happen that tenderers try to formulate questions that may cause procurers to reveal information about other tenders on the shortlist. In such situations, it is important to strongly emphasize that it is against company policy to reveal such information, that is, it requires practical leadership at the negotiation table. In this particular case it was safeguarded by the presence of the procurement specialist in meetings with tenderers. What is noteworthy is the claim from the procurer that the transparency and disclosure policy would be applied even without legal requirement. The rationale for applying this policy was to signal trustworthiness and professionalism to the market.

In the first attempt, the contract was awarded to a company that at the time was owned by the procurer. It seems that the search for alternative suppliers had been very limited or even non-existent. In the second attempt, in accordance with the principle of stimulating competition, the procurers not only published the tender call, but also put significant effort into market research before publishing. In this regard, compliance with the directives encouraged a global search for suppliers, and selection of the most innovative company. Another difference between the two attempts concerns verification of the professional ability of the supplier. The directives specify that contracting entities which select candidates 'to participate in negotiated procedures shall do so according to objective criteria and rules' (Directive 93/38, Article 31). In the successful attempt, especially with the failure still in mind, finding a supplier that would be able to deliver was considered a critical issue. In the first attempt, the project had to run several years before it was discovered that the supplier would not be able to deliver according to specification.

Another issue that perhaps is not so much discussed nowadays concerns the requirement that procurers need to include a technical specification in the tender documents (in this case Directive 93/38, Article 1, para 8; Article 18). Sceptics saw a tension between specification and innovation. The argument was that the requirement assumes that the procurer knows what should be procured, a condition that might not be satisfied if the procured item 'does not yet exist' at the time of the submission of the tender call. Another 'problem' associated with this line of thinking was as follows. When dealing with (at least partly) unknown innovations, innovative projects may sometimes reveal new solutions to a problem as the project develops. If specifications cannot be changed as the project develops, it might not be possible to exploit the new solution, as tenderers that did not get the original contract might complain on the grounds that the innovation eventually delivered did not match the specifications made in the tender call. Although the use of functional specifications has been encouraged for quite some time now, for example in the context of green procurement (European Commission, 2004b), because '[f]ocussing on the outcome or functionality desired gives suppliers the opportunity to be innovative' (Central Procurement Directorate, 1994, p. 12), it might still be problematic to propose radically and previously unproven solutions in an ongoing project.

In this case the obligation to include specifications seems to have worked as an enabler rather than a constraint to innovation. The experiences from the first attempt reinforced the procurers' emphasis on producing a clear specification. The clear specifications developed in the successful attempt were also seen as a success factor for the project. Although new and alternative solutions emerged in the project, the priority from management was to stick to already agreed-on plans. This in turn is consistent with the vision set out by both the Norwegian government and the project manager. The goal was to produce a radio system that would work, rather than explore new opportunities. There is also a connection to organizational knowledge creation as developed by Nonaka and colleagues (e.g. Nonaka, 1994). Following Nonaka, 'innovation ... cannot be explained sufficiently in terms of information processing or problem solving. Rather, innovation can be understood as a process in which the organization creates and defines problems and actively develops new knowledge to solve them' (Nonaka, 1994, p. 14). In principle, what Nonaka describes is a reflecting process, where knowledge is created through conversion between tacit and explicit knowledge. Viewed as such, the actual process of writing the specification for the system to be procured forces tacit knowledge to become explicit knowledge. This means that the writing of a specification per se may be understood as a learning opportunity in itself. Writing a specification requires the author to learn about the system to be specified and therefore it should be understood as part of the innovation process. In that sense, the requirement of a specification actually becomes something that stimulates innovation (Directive 93/38, Article 18, para. 1).

Before close interaction was initiated in the pre-procurement phase, in line with the intentions of the directives to utilize market forces, extended worldwide market search was carried out, in order to maximize the number of submitting tenderers. The winning bid came from a firm previously unknown to Telenor, originating from another country. In a survey of public procurement in 1993 it was concluded that, in 88 per cent of the contracts awarded, the supplier had a local address in the country where the procurement took place. In 2004, the number of direct cross-border procurements still remained low (European Commission, 2004a). Although the majority of the bids came from foreign firms (which, one would assume, would increase the chances that a foreign company would actually win the contract), this case has actually developed according to the visions of creating a common European market. Furthermore, in this respect, complying with the directives did actually help in finding the supplier of the technology judged as being the most adequate for the context.

After the supplier had been identified, the interaction characteristics significantly changed in the project. Up to that point much effort had been spent on ensuring equal treatment of the tenderers. The interaction possibilities were also in general quite restricted by the procurement directives. The purpose of the interaction also changed at that point. Initially the primary task had been to find a supplier that was able to demonstrate its capacity to eventually deliver the procured system. Once the contract had been awarded the purpose of the interaction became to provide the supplier with information critical for the implementation of the system. The fact that it took a further nine months after the contract was signed to develop a design specification that could be used actually to build the system also suggests that it is possible to talk about two processes with different purposes, the process to find the supplier and the process to develop the product. When arguments are brought forward about the restricting effects the directives might have on interactive learning and user–producer interactions (Edquist *et al.*, 2000), making the distinction between the two processes may contribute with some clarity. Up the point when the supplier has been appointed, the directives *regulate* interaction. In the process leading up to the contract award the procurer needs to maintain transparency and avoid favouring any bidder. But, after the contract has been awarded, all the processes associated with 'free' innovation that enables the supplier to deliver the specified product may take place.

DISCUSSION

Among critics of the current legislative package for public procurement there prevails an implicit liking of and reference to the realm of private firms. The assumption is that, if public agencies were allowed to manage their procurement activities in the same way as private firms, everything would be just fine. The fact that Telenor had just undergone the transition from being a public agency to a private company at the time for the study offered a special opportunity to compare the events that took place in the context of the public procurement project and the actions taken dictated by procurement law, and what Telenor acting as a private firm would have done in a similar situation. Interestingly enough, the general view among the interviewees was that most things in the process would actually have been carried out in the same way even without the obligation to comply with the directives. Sometimes the processes around managing the tender calls become somewhat 'bureaucratic', as the public procurer is for instance required to publish information in a certain way. But in principle the procurement procedures at Telenor did not change after Telenor became a private company, although the formal requirement to comply with the EC procurement directives ceased to apply. According to the findings in this case, then, the directives do allow procurement to take place in the way a private firm would conduct such a project. This makes sense, as private sector procurement was an important source of inspiration when the directives were designed.

Still, it should be admitted that a general problem with the directives in force at the time of the procurement project studied here was that they were complex and needed to be simplified and become more flexible (Boyle, 1994). These problems were also taken into account when the directives were eventually modified (Arrowsmith, 2004b). This is however not the same as arguing that the directives would specifically hinder innovation, as some authors have claimed. A central point in their argumentation is the perception that the law in practice forbids long-term collaboration between a public agency and a national champion, sometime referred to as a 'development pair' (Fridlund, 1999). It is of course still possible to set up tender calls for the development of new technology, but the informal interaction possibilities between a national 'champion' and the public procurer are inhibited in the directives. Furthermore, the control of who will actually win a contract is also in principle lost, as a contract must be awarded to the tender that best meets the specified award criteria. These effects are quite in line with the underlying neoliberal policies on which the legislation is based: to prevent nationalistic, protected and (therefore) inefficient procurement and instead promote the creation of a common European market (Cox and Furlong, 1996). The legal framework does in that sense implement a balancing act between the ambition to avoid corruption and favouritism of national or local champions and at the same time the maintenance of competition. This set-up is also justifiable from an innovation theoretical point of view. Ideally any instance of public procurement of innovation should deliver the most innovative solution. Choosing inferior domestic technology before state-of-the art technology available elsewhere might satisfy political rationalities. In the long term, however, such a policy might increase the gap between domestic technology and state-of-the-art technology available elsewhere and potentially create a lock-in to depreciated domestic technology.

It follows from the general assumptions in innovation theory that, in order to enable innovation, the procurement procedure should as far as possible allow interaction between procurer and supplier. It may therefore be interesting to consider the different procurement procedures defined in the directives and discuss further to what extent the interaction possibilities vary among the procedures. Innovation scholars have expressed certain hopes for the negotiated procedure, as it 'seems to have been designed for highly innovative development projects' (Lundvall and Borrás, 1997, p. 131; see also Gavras *et al.*, 2006). The use of the negotiated procedure is however exceptional, and risk-averse public procurers have therefore nurtured reluctance towards its application. One concern has been the requirement to remain competitive throughout the tender process. This was not a problem in this case, as '[t]he negotiated procedure with both notice and competition … involve[d] competition almost to the same degree as open or restricted procedures' (Arrowsmith, 2005, p. 561), whilst at the same time it allowed the interaction between procurer and suppliers required to enable innovation. Interestingly, there seems to be a discrepancy between this attitude and what the directives actually stipulate. In the old Utilities Directive, a contracting entity could choose 'any of the procedures' among the procedures available (Directive 93/38, Article 20, para. 1). In the old directives regulating the classical sector, however, the use of the negotiated procedure was much more restricted. On the other hand, to allow more flexibility in certain situations, the competitive dialogue was introduced in the new Directive 2004/18 for the classical sector. The opportunities for public procurers to incorporate interaction in public procurement of innovation projects appear therefore to be rather well served, both in the past and today – by applying either the negotiated procedure or the competitive dialogue.

It is however hard to draw any particular conclusions regarding the relation between innovation-friendliness and a certain procedure. This case, for example, brings out the difference between the negotiated procedure with prior publication of a contract notice, and the negotiated procedure without publication of a contract notice (Arrowsmith, 2005, p. 559). The combination of these two elements was probably a part of the successful outcome. This in turn suggests that other variables are at play too. Public procurement utilizing the open procedure can also deliver innovation depending on the contextual factors that tend to be ignored in an analysis based on reading only the legal texts. The attempt to make links between specific procedures and the extent to which they enable innovation prompts therefore some reflection regarding the application of innovation theory. The innovation theory and design theory drawn on above emphasize primarily the interactive aspects. They focus less on the importance of a competitive selection process on a supplier market with several potential winners, which actually was a significant success factor in this case. Although interaction is essential, *who* is interacted with is essential too. Therefore, in order to identify the most suitable supplier, competition must prevail too. If the procurers had used the restrictive procedure, or the negotiated procedure without a contract notice, the chances are that the supplier actually selected would never have been identified.

CONCLUSIONS

The general conclusion that came out of this case is that the Utilities Directive did not prevent public procurement of innovation, as some authors would have expected. Instead, the case prompted attention to other factors than the directive. In order to be successful, as suggested by the case, public procurement of innovation projects needs certain specific competences attached to it – competences perhaps best referred to as public procurement of innovation expertise. Based on the lessons drawn from this case, three critical expertise areas can be mentioned:

1. Expertise on the public procurement procedures as specified in the directives. In the pre-procurement phase, there was a person dedicated to making sure that legal requirements were followed. For instance, this person made sure that the communication to tenderers was managed in an open and transparent way. The response to any question asked by one tenderer was also distributed to other tenderers. This person also instructed technical personnel on how to

act in for example meetings to avoid transferring competitive information between tenderers.

2. The vision and competence to be able to produce a specification. Another success factor that was emphasized concerns the technical competence Telenor possessed that enabled it to define and specify its actual need. Although it was different to the earlier attempt to procure a new radio system, there was a clear vision of the intended outcome of the project. This suggests that, although functional specification may allow room for innovation by procurement in general, it cannot be applied in combination with a weak vision of the outcome.

3. General project management skills. The way the procurement project was managed also significantly contributed to its success. The project was managed in a fairly tight manner, with a focus on sticking to the original plan, where for example late suggestions for alternative ways of doing things were not accepted.

NOTE

1. It has not been possible to collect information on the exact number of firms that got to the negotiation stage.

4. Public procurement of innovation diffusion

One single case study giving an anomalous result such as the one discussed in the previous chapter makes a weak foundation for reformulation of a theoretical proposition. One case is however still enough to falsify the general claim made in the past that the EC procurement directives inhibit innovation and the implications for innovation policy that comes with it. Demonstrating that it is possible to procure innovations within the legal framework raises questions to what extent revision of the directives might be adequate to facilitate public procurement of innovation. A case suggesting that public procurement of innovation is indeed feasible within the current EC directives also provokes some other questions. One set of questions would aim at understanding further the reasons for the success and if there are any more generic lessons useful for any instance of public procurement of innovation to be derived. It should be noted that the results do not suggest that public procurement of innovation is free from problems, only that the earlier attempts to reduce the discussion to a legal problem are inadequate. Still, if one assumes that the findings in Chapter 3 are valid beyond the case itself, one question in particular becomes interesting: if the EC directives are not hindering innovation, what is?

In order to pursue this question, it may be useful to reflect on the case discussed in Chapter 3 a bit more. The case study described public procurement that in compliance with the EC directives successfully delivered innovation. Essentially, the case provided the answer to a question that can be formulated as follows: how do formal, exogenous and regulatory institutions help or hinder public procurement of innovations? The answer to this question was that, given access to certain resources and skills, the exogenous institutions appear not to hinder innovation. On a general level, the analysis conducted to reach that result ascribed importance primarily to two variables: the formal institutions applied in the case, that is, the EC directives; and the outcome of the case, a new innovative maritime radio system installed and in operation on the Norwegian coastline. An interesting way forward would be to find a case with the same variables but with a different relation between them, that is, either a successful case of public procurement of innovation where the EC directives were not applied and/or a case conducted in compliance with the EC directives where the intended outcome was not attained. This chapter will analyse a case belonging to the second category.

Chapter 2 promoted an approach that considers the role of other institutional levels than exogenous laws. This was also the implication alluded to in Chapter 3. The reasons for success identified – access to expertise on the procurement rules, skills in coming up with a useful specification, and general management skills – are all activities that to a large extent belong to the endogenous institutional levels. They are all outcomes of endogenous learning processes reflecting organization-specific rationalities. Thus, even if the overall interest is the same as for the case studied in Chapter 3, that is, the relationship between the EC directives and the possibilities to procure innovation, the findings in Chapter 3 prompt for an analysis that also includes other institutional levels. This chapter discusses a case study useful to pursuing an answer to the following question: how may endogenous institutions affect the possibilities for public procurement of innovation?

The case summarizes certain events that emerged within the context of a study conducted in England and Sweden in 2006 involving multiple cases of public procurement of innovation. The idea was to include cases that did not deliver the initially expected outcome. This means that the current case was chosen through purposeful or theoretical sampling to fill a theoretical category (Eisenhardt, 1989, p. 537). The role of the public procurer in this case was mainly to facilitate adoption, that is, to procure an innovation that had been developed by the private sector but was new to the procuring organization. This means that the innovation existed elsewhere prior to the formulation of public demand. This situation also offered one interesting opportunity for an institutional analysis in the sense that some of the observer-independent institutional barriers encountered, related to the technical development, would arguably be removed. Interestingly, even if this case excluded the development phase, a lot of institutional phenomena were identified.

PUBLIC PROCUREMENT, INNOVATION AND DIFFUSION

As this case concerned adoption and not as such a project that in itself generated innovation, some theoretical considerations might be useful before dealing with the actual case. In the study, innovation was considered a process consisting of a series of activities, including diffusion (Maidique, 1980), thus stressing the point that, 'without diffusion, innovations have little social or economic impact' (Hall, 2005, p. 459). This study applied the definition of innovation as derived from the intersection of definitions made by Freeman (1982) and Rogers (1995). Freeman defines innovation as 'the introduction of a new product, process, system or device – to be distinguished from invention which is a new idea, a sketch, or model for a new improved device, product, process or system' (Freeman, 1982, p. 7). An innovative product does not however remain an innovation but eventually matures (cf. Utterback, 1994), corresponding to what Edquist *et al.*, (2000) refer to as 'regular' products. Rogers, on the other hand, defines innovation as 'an idea, practice, or object that is *perceived* as new by an individual or other unit of adoption' (Rogers, 1995, p. 11, italics added). This justifies inclusion of products in any stage of their life cycle in the understanding of what public procurement of innovation is, as long as the procured item is perceived as new.

Essentially, this point draws on the diffusion aspects of innovation. Diffusion, then, is the idea, practice or object 'communicated through certain channels over time among the members of a social system' (Rogers, 1995, p. 5). A basic requirement for diffusion in any social system is that the innovation has to be known. It is also likely that the innovation has 'at least some degree of benefit for its potential adopters' (Rogers, 1995, p. 13). This means an innovation can be developed in one social system and then be exposed to another social system. Also, and therefore, what is perceived as an established item in one social system might be considered an innovation in another. In this light the dichotomy distinguishing regular from innovative public procurement suggested by Edquist *et al.*, (2000) becomes ambiguous. A procurement of what these authors would call 'regular' goods, that is, already existing products developed elsewhere, might actually be perceived as 'new' when introduced into another social system. This means that, from the potential adopter's perspective, some off-the-shelf products may be considered as public procurement of innovations. This also gives reason to expect interaction between stakeholders and rules of the game affecting these interactions to be a central part of the story for public procurement of already developed innovations.

The decision to adopt an innovation is generally determined by how it is perceived by adopters. It may sometimes be hard to distinguish conceptually between diffusion and adoption, as both these concepts try to capture how an innovation is received. One way of achieving such a distinction is to think of diffusion as something that takes place in a population, for example a sample of firms or adopting units among which adoption would take place. Adoption studies understood in this perspective focus on the individual unit, for example a person, and try to further understand the individual adoption behaviour (Lissoni and Metcalfe, 1996). The characteristic features of diffusion and adoption processes occurring within organizations may be considered through employing a social systems approach. Rogers defines a social system as 'a set of interrelated units that are engaged in joint problem solving to accomplish a common goal' (Rogers, 1995, p. 23). Units of such a system may be individuals, informal groups, organizations and/or subsystems (ibid., p. 23). There are some fundamental differences between individual consumers' adoption of an innovative end-consumer product and an innovation adopted by an organization. Following Rogers (ibid.), individuals within an organization may sometimes not be able to adopt an innovation before the organization, that is, somebody with authority over the organization, has decided to facilitate or enforce the adoption. In addition, the decision made by an organization to adopt a certain innovation does not by necessity mean that an individual within the organization will comply. Thus, within an organizational context, the decision to reject or adopt an innovation is not as straightforward as it might be elsewhere (ibid.).

Diffusion understood strictly as a process relying on decisions made by potential adopters is, therefore, somewhat insufficient in the light of institutional theory. Determinants of diffusion and adoption of innovation in a social system, as emphasized by systemic approaches to innovation studies (Dosi *et al.*, 1988; Lundvall, 1992; Hollingsworth, 2000), underscore the role institutions play during the process of innovation. In other words, implementation of decisions may be affected and potentially hindered by institutional barriers. Thus, institutional theory acknowledges that decisions are required but still not sufficient for diffusion to take place. The assertion that institutions manifest themselves on different levels in society, as was discussed in Chapter 2, also has a bearing on diffusion analysis. Super-national institutions such as the EC directives on public procurement, transpositions of these laws into national public procurement law, specific directives and policies for specific public agencies, endogenous institutions or rationalities among potential suppliers or collaborators, and individual habits and values are all relevant for analysis of public procurement of innovation diffusion. Again, the argument brought forward in this chapter is that it is very problematic to make any general statements based on formal and exogenous institutions only. Therefore focus in this analysis is set on endogenous institutional levels.

The case study deals with a British attempt to introduce an innovative catheter into hospitals. To map the entities in the case with the institutional dimensions discussed in Chapter 2, one could say that a hospital with its role to provide health services for citizens is a long-term institution. One example of a short-term endogenous institution would be a contract between a hospital and a supplier of medical equipment where the contract would regulate certain behaviour from the actors involved over a defined time span. What makes it endogenous is the limited range of the contract. It is essentially an agreement exclusive to the stakeholders signing the contract. A decision from central hospital management that all wards should adopt a certain technology would to the individual wards be an exogenous institution. Such a decision would manifest itself as directives or instructions working effectually over a limited time frame, and could therefore be considered to be a fixed-term institution.

A certain endogenous institutional set-up in an organization may prevent the adoption of a specific item and its diffusion throughout the organization. An innovation new to an organization may or may not be institutionally matching with, for example, existing technology, current and existing standards, established ways of working, perceived values, strategic decisions, rationalities, or established budgets. The prevailing institutional set-up within an organization will also affect how the introduced technology will be used (Orlikowski, 1992). The success of an exogenous decision aiming at diffusing a certain item into an organization is thus determined to the extent such a match is established. Institutions typically evolve slowly and reactively following, at least for endogenous institutions, an internal logic. This creates the illusion that institutions sometimes lag behind technical change. This divergence is manifested as mismatch problems 'which prevent the full realization of the productivity potentials of technical innovations, which forestall the reallocation of resources and efforts from mature to emerging technologies, and which generally favour established technological trajectories to new ones' (Edquist and Johnson, 1997, p. 55), which suggests that institutions may also sometimes act as barriers, preventing the diffusion of innovation throughout an organization. From this follows the importance of considering the institutional aspect of introducing an innovation into an organization. Some kind of institutional coordination may be required for successful diffusion of new technology. This requires an understanding of how the institutional set-up affects innovation processes, which requires an analysis of the interplay between different kinds of institutions conceived as coordination mechanisms or governance structures (Hollingsworth, 2000). In other words, if institutional barriers are not negotiated, projects involving public procurement of innovation may have to be terminated without delivering the intended result.

Equipped with the sensitizing terminology outlined above, the chapter continues by summarizing the empirical material gathered in the study. Initially there is a description of the procuring organization, the National Health Service (NHS), and the context in which the procurement activities took place. Then follows a summary of different supply routes and the measures that were taken to fast-track the diffusion of the catheter. The remaining parts of the chapter discuss some institutional barriers that had to be negotiated to enable diffusion.

THE CASE OF THE SILVER-COATED CATHETER[1]

The NHS was established after the Second World War to provide healthcare for everyone resident in the UK. The NHS is one of the largest organizations in the world, employing roughly 1.3 million people (Lister, 2004). The cost of running the NHS at the time of this case was estimated at £100 billion, coming entirely from tax money. The NHS consists of an array of different healthcare providers and administrative functions. The healthcare providers are organized into different types of trusts, for example primary care trusts, NHS hospital trusts (or acute trusts) or NHS hospitals. One organization that played a part in this case was the central procuring agency at the time, the NHS Purchasing and Supply Agency (PASA). NHS PASA's role was 'to ensure that the NHS in England makes the most effective use of its resources by getting the best possible value for money when purchasing goods and services' (NHS PASA, 2008).

In many countries healthcare providers struggle with patients coming to the hospital with one problem and contracting yet another disease while hospitalized. This case concerns one solution offered to a particular problem in this category, namely catheter-associated urinary tract infections (CAUTIs). In the last decades of the twentieth century the NHS had to deal with increasing problems with healthcare-associated infections, that is, those infections transmitted to patients seeking care at NHS facilities. Urinary tract infections belong to a group of four problem areas, including surgical-wound, lower respiratory tract, and skin infections (Emmerson *et al.*, 1996), where the most common of these are urinary infections (see also Department of Health, 2003). Thus, in 2002, healthcare-associated infections were identified as 'a major problem for the NHS' (Department of Health, 2002, p. 62) and therefore listed as one of the key areas that should be prioritized in order 'to combat the present as well as the possible future threat posed by infectious diseases' (ibid., p. 22). Apart from the suffering imposed on individual patients, healthcare-associated infections are also costly for the healthcare system. Costs for these infections were estimated at £930 million per annum in England, with £124 million imposed by urinary tract infections (Plowman *et al.*, 2001).

Many factors drive the increase of healthcare-associated infections. Factors include the increased number of patients with severe illnesses in the healthcare system, as patients in a serious condition become more vulnerable to infections; but it can also be therapeutic factors, that is, that indwelling catheters need to be used to help cure patients, organizational factors, for example a poor staff-to-patient ratio, or behavioural factors such as poor compliance with hygiene standards (Department of Health, 2003). Guidelines were also developed to address these areas (Pratt *et al.*, 2007). These guidelines were also made accessible to NHS employees through an award-winning e-learning project (Pratt and O'Malley, 2007). Interestingly, what this chapter deals with is another category of means to battle healthcare-associated infections, namely adoption of new technology. In general, promoting the adoption of innovation within organizations appeared to be a rather underdeveloped area. In the NHS guidelines for healthcare-associated infections, the topic was relatively recently still listed under 'Areas for Further Research' (Pratt *et al.*, 2007).

Supply Routes for Innovation

One starting point in the study was to establish how products generally are sourced in the NHS. For consumables, there was not a single supply route but a variety of options, which all had different characteristics. Any NHS trust could utilize available supply routes in the way they found appropriate. In principle (for the purposes here) three routes for supply of consumables to an NHS hospital were identified. Products could be ordered through an electronic ordering system, Logistics On-Line (LOL). The products included in this electronic catalogue were supplied from one of the six regional stores managed by the NHS Supply Chain. A second option was to order directly from a supplier through a framework agreement negotiated centrally. These products were available online through the NHS E-Cat. These orders were placed directly with the suppliers, with a reference to the framework contract number, and the supplier would deliver directly to the specified address and invoice the trust directly. It was also possible to order from contracts set up through public procurement on the local level. Similar to ordering from framework agreements provided centrally, the supplier would deliver the ordered products to a specified address and send the invoice directly to the trust.

These three supply routes differed in terms of administrative complexity. Procurement through the NHS Supply Chain was the most straightforward way and executed essentially as an office routine, by placing an order in the LOL order system. Buying products included in the NHS PASA framework agreements as published in the E-Cat required awareness of the specific contracts as well as interaction with the supplier and was therefore slightly more demanding and time-consuming. The third option, to manage the complete procurement process locally, was the most complex, as it required development of contract specification and going through award procedures to find suppliers. The first supply route would be the normal way for sourcing catheters to an NHS ward. For a nurse with responsibility for replenishing the stock of catheters on a ward, ordering a new catheter would be a routine task accomplished through the use of an electronic system. Deliveries would come once a week in appropriate packages, and the invoice would typically be handled by the supplies department at the hospital. Ordering a product not in the system would possibly require the submission of a (paper) requisition and also interaction with the hospital's supplies department. This would probably require more time, especially if the order was for something different. It might be the case that the wanted product was on a framework agreement administered by the supplies department. This is however also a longer and more complex process than just ordering from an electronic system.

There are obvious advantages with central procurement agreements or central procurements in general. From the perspective of the daily operations on a hospital ward, supply of catheters can take place as straight rebuys. These are routine transactions requiring a minimum of new information and consideration of new alternatives (Robinson *et al.*, 1967). For wards where the primary concern is providing care for patients, this would enable staff to go about executing their core duties and minimize resource allocation to administrative tasks. On the other hand, for a new product not in the system and therefore more difficult to access, the same routines become an institutional barrier, as they may reduce both trialability and observability for an innovation. It becomes a little bit of a catch-22 problem. How can you test a new product that is not in the system to make decisions whether or not to include it in the system if the product needs to be included in the system before you get access to it? From an institutional perspective these three supply routes altogether appear to have a conserving effect. The option associated with lowest transaction cost is the one facilitating sourcing of products that are already in the system. A new alternative product that is not in the LOL system may face difficulties in competing with existing products, as it may be difficult to make people switch away from an easy supply route.

The NHS did not however leave the diffusion of the silver-coated catheter to these routines. One such non-routine activity was the establishment of the Rapid Review Panel, an organization essentially exercising some kind of institutional coordination to help innovations enter the supply chain. The Rapid Review Panel was set up in August 2004. Run by the Health Protection Agency on behalf of the Department of Health, the panel had the purpose of encouraging industry to come up with ideas that would tackle the problems related to healthcare-associated infection. The panel's task was to 'assess new and novel equipment, materials, and other products or protocols that may be of value to the NHS in improving hospital infection control and reducing hospital acquired infections' (Health Protection Agency, 2006). One of the first products submitted to the Rapid Review Panel was the Bardex catheter. The suppliers claimed that the risks of acquiring an infection with the Bardex catheter would be much less than with conventional catheters. The Rapid Review Panel agreed that it was a good product, it was new, it had antibacterial activity and there was evidence that it would reduce the number of catheter-associated infections if used in patients needing catheterization for more than 48 hours. As one of very few products, the Bardex catheter received the top mark, that is, the judgement was that it had 'shown benefits that should be [made] available to NHS' (ibid.).

As a response to the result of the Rapid Review Panel, NHS PASA fast-tracked the Bardex catheter into the NHS Supply Chain. When the Bardex catheter was introduced in England in 2002, initially the only supply route available was the most complex one, that is, it was not available on contract and neither was it in stock. When it became available from the NHS Supply Chain, in September 2005, roughly a year after the Rapid Review Panel had published their results, the use of the product increased. In 2006, about 30 NHS hospitals were using the Bardex catheter. The estimated market share for products in its range was at the time 2–3 per cent. In the US the same catheter had a market share around 40 per cent.

It should be noted that, from a clinical point of view, the Rapid Review Panel had a strictly indicative function. The task of the panel was to make statements based on evidence taken into account on whether or not a product did what it said it did, as reported from other studies. The panel neither recommended nor provided mandatory directives as to whether or not to use a certain product. In this case, the decision to use the Bardex catheter was made by clinicians. What did happen as a result of the panel's judgement was that the Bardex catheter was brought into the NHS supply chain by NHS PASA more quickly, which meant that any clinician in a hospital championing the Bardex catheter could just order it from the system rather than going through a complete procurement process.

The Role of Endogenous Institutions

An expectation that actions taken to fast-track a product into an organization's supply routes would increase the use of the product within the organization appears at first glance a reasonable one. In spite of the work carried out by the Rapid Review Panel and NHS PASA, the use of the silver-coated catheter was modest. Different endogenous institutions played different roles in achieving this outcome. Some worked as endogenous barriers that impeded diffusion. Some measures designed to overcome them were also identified. The endogenous barriers and some of the means evoked to negotiate them are discussed in the following sections and summarized in Table 4.1.

Organized scepticism
In the first years of the diffusion process of the Bardex catheter, scepticism regarding the evidence base prevailed among NHS clinicians, infection control staff and continence advisers. NHS staff did not necessarily subscribe to the view that the silver coating used on the Bardex catheter would help reduce healthcare-associated infections. Although no studies appear to challenge the assertions made by the suppliers of the Bardex catheter, concerns have been raised regarding the limitations of the studies referred to. Within the time frame of this study, the Rapid Review Panel's grading of the Bardex catheter did not lead to an increased rate of diffusion. The organized scepticism illustrates well the double aspect of institutions discussed by Coriat and Weinstein (2002). An institution works both as a constraint and as a resource (ibid., p. 283). The requirement for evidence of an innovative product's claimed properties is central to any organization providing healthcare. From a diffusion perspective these requirements tend to work as a barrier to diffusion.

Technology champions
What is often emphasized as a significant element in the diffusion processes is the role of innovation champions. These are typically

'powerful individuals' (Rogers, 1995, p. 398) who promote the innovation within an organization, or implementing leaders enabling collective learning (Edmondson *et al.*, 2001). What has been suggested as a problem in the case of catheters in general relates to the way catheters are used within healthcare organizations. The problems related to catheters are different from for example wound infections, which much more clearly fall under the responsibility of surgical units, and are not as easily connected to a specific unit. Catheters are used in operating departments, in accident and emergency services, and post-operatively in any medical unit or ward. This means that ownership of the problem becomes less clear, and the emergence of innovation champions specifically devoted to catheters is not promoted.

Decentralized decision structure
As was discussed above, the perceived need for an innovation is central to its diffusion. What seems to be common among the early adopters of the Bardex catheter is that within these hospitals a clear perception of the need to prevent and control healthcare-associated infections prevailed. Comprehensible business cases were developed displaying the current level of catheter-associated infections, their cost, and the expected benefit from introducing the Bardex catheter. What also seems to be a common theme is that the decision to introduce the Bardex catheter for a hospital was often made centrally, perhaps by the overall financial budget holder for the whole organization. Some of the hospitals that were among the first in England to introduce the Bardex catheter did that through an authority innovation decision (Rogers, 1995, p. 372). When introducing the order codes for the Bardex catheter in the ordering system, they excluded the possibility of ordering traditional catheters.

Silo budgeting
One issue related to the diffusion of the Bardex catheter was the problem of evaluating the economic benefits of using the product. Compared with traditional catheters, the Bardex catheter was more expensive. Studies indicated however that, although the Bardex catheter would be more expensive per unit, it would still save money in the end, as it would reduce the risk for patients of contracting healthcare-associated infections, and avoid unnecessary hospitalization. Arguing for using a new catheter that is more expensive than the ones currently in use also touches upon a generic problem of public healthcare and the nature of 'saving' by improving healthcare. Although the use of the Bardex catheter might mean that unnecessary hospitalization could be avoided, the savings are not clearly visible. The reason for this is that it is hard to

measure the value of what is not spent. In addition, what is unavoidable for new products is that independent studies of economic benefits are not available (I. Williams and Bryan, 2007). One way of attaining evidence of economical benefits is through historical studies of the same care unit, where comparison between usage of conventional catheters and Bardex catheters is possible (Rupp *et al.*, 2004). It is however in the nature of such studies that they take time.

Another problem relates to the way budgets are organized. In some cases the potential benefits of the introduction of the Bardex catheter would not be visible in the budget affected by the increased spending on a more expensive catheter. Although total cost would be lower for the hospital, the incentives for a financial manager responsible for a budget to accept a cost without gaining anything would be low. Similar experiences have been made by other companies attempting to introduce innovations to the NHS. '[T]here is a major problem in gaining acceptance into the NHS due to budget silos – where the purchasing department bears the brunt of the cost while the savings are passed onto another department' (Levinson, 2006, p. 10). These problems related to the 'separation of appraisal and resource allocation functions' have also been brought up by researchers (I. Williams and Bryan, 2007, p. 2127). Even if it were possible to establish the economic benefits (supported in for example Rupp *et al.*, 2004) from using Bardex catheters, it would still be impossible for a procurement department which had not been provided with the means to cover the excess cost associated with the adoption of the Bardex catheter. One way of removing this barrier, as reported in the interviews, was to fund the increased cost internally. This means that resources were put aside to cover the extra cost associated with procuring the Bardex catheter with a higher per-unit price in order to save money as a result of the reduction in total hospitalization time.

Pricing, budget changes and existing contracts

In one sense existing framework agreements also work as institutional barriers that are endogenous and fixed-term. Even if an adopting unit would like to change catheter, it would generally wait until current contracts were about to be renegotiated. One interviewee highlighted that the evaluation is not only about the Bardex catheter versus traditional catheters. In an economic organization there might also be other priorities or potentially beneficial activities to consider that would improve the health service. This issue, more generally formulated, concerns the importance of changes to budgets. Even in situations where there are sufficient levels of evidence verifying that a new product is beneficial, the question remains as to what other item should be removed from the budget in order to allow for the introduction of the new (I. Williams and Bryan, 2007, pp. 2125–6). In that sense, diffusion has its own version of creative destruction, which in turn justifies the inclusion of destruction in the extended Hommen matrix, as discussed in Chapter 2.

Endogenous Institutions and Coordination

Table 4.1 summarizes institutional barriers to the diffusion of the Bardex catheter in the NHS, as found in the case study. The rightmost column in Table 4.1 lists suggestions of coordination activities to negotiate the institutional barriers identified. These suggestions came out of the study, either through the interviews or through further consultation of related literature. The list includes three institutional barriers where no clear-cut corresponding coordination activity was found. The fact that catheters in general lack a natural champion is not easily remedied. Making changes to the budget is also a problem that is not easily resolved. Related to the second barrier was the problematic situation caused by earlier commit-ments inhibiting reallocation of spending from the old to the new. The study also failed to produce any good solutions to this problem. Dealing with existing framework agreements becoming barriers for new emerging products is however probably in principle doable. It would require contract clauses giving the procurer the right to abrogate agreements at the point where the supplied technology becomes inferior to other products available on the market. Such a contract would then add a continuous incentive for the supplier to stay innovative. To what extent this is feasible in practice however remains to be seen and addressed in future research.

Table 4.1   Institutional barriers to adoption identified and corresponding coordination activities

Institutional barrier	Description	Coordination activity identified in the case
Getting into the supply chain	A product available in existing supply systems will be favoured before products not available in existing supply systems.	Rapid Review Panel set up to evaluate solutions suggested by industry and to fast-track into the supply chain those found to be useful.
Organized scepticism	Clinical staff requiring a high level of proof before an innovation can be adopted.	Conduct clinical studies that confirm supplier's claims.

No technology champion	In comparison to other healthcare technologies, there appeared to be no clear champion catheters.	N/A.
Decentralized decision structure	A centrally made decision to make certain technologies available may not necessarily lead to adoption in lower layers of the organization.	Authority innovation decision. Removing existing alternative option (conventional catheter) from the supply chain.
Silo budgeting	Spending and gains from spending do not affect the same budget, which removes spending incentives.	Additional funds allocated by central hospital management to cover additional cost.
Price	An innovation may be more expensive per unit (although less expensive over its life cycle) than already existing technology.	Additional funds allocated by central hospital management to cover the additional cost.
Problems with demonstrating the value of the innovation	Problems in showing the value of the innovation (and hence justifying adoption) never tried out before in a practical setting.	Conducting long-term historical studies. Development of a business case.
Altering budgets	Although proof supports the value of innovation the question remains as to what should be removed from the budget to allow the adoption of the innovation.	N/A.
Existing agreements with the supplier of current technology	Commitments made in current contracts prevent the reallocating of resources.	Contract clauses enabling contract termination of depreciated technology.

Wards primarily provide care for patients; other tasks, such as procuring supplies, are given relatively less attention and are conducted in a routinized way. Procurement activities leading to innovation would in practice be exceptional. This makes perfect sense if a ward is considered as a provider of health services only. Understanding the ward as an adopter of innovation gives reason for some further reflection. Routinization of the procurement activities means that products already in the digital order system, that is, regular products, will benefit from some kind of de facto preference in comparison to products not included in the system. Unless some event occurs, for example a contract expires or a new item enters the system after a procurement process has been carried out, the range of available products for wards is in principle static. Thus, unless something happens that challenges the prevailing institutional set-up, the chances of adopting new products are low.

From an institutional perspective, the setting up of the Rapid Review Panel was an attempt to create the necessary change, that is, to redesign the institutional set-up defined by the NHS Supply Chain. This was also achieved. However, even if making the Bardex catheter available in the digital order system was necessary, it was not fully sufficient for diffusion, as other institutions were also at play. One example of what worked as an inhibiting institution was the organized scepticism among physicians. The benefits from organized scepticism are obvious for patient safety in relation to the introduction of new, untried technology. Assuming that a certain technology is actually safe and good, organized scepticism does work as an institutional barrier. A clear technology champion could have helped to negate the scepticism, but owing to the way catheters are used in the organization such champions are unlikely to occur spontaneously.

The case provides lots of examples on institutions with a different range (Jepperson, 1991, p. 146). The institutional range of the Rapid Review Panel was for instance relatively limited, as any hospital or trust could choose itself whether or not to follow the advice given by the panel. Apart from the decentralized decision structure, other institutions in the organizations also contribute to the institutional set-up. Many of these institutions stem from a general concern from public agencies to be accountable for spending taxpayers' money. The prevailing incentives structure that comes with that concern does not encourage managers to overspend their budgets or buy products with higher per-unit prices than existing options. It could also be seen that institutional redesign by central management, in the form either of authority innovation decisions or of additional allocating of funds, was common among the earlier adopters of the Bardex catheter.

Although some examples of institutional coordination and redesign identified here were quite concrete, the case also includes institutional barriers that do not have a clear-cut countermeasure. Organized scepticism, for example, regarded above as an institutional barrier for innovation, is in general a good institution that should not be destroyed. One way forward for public procurers of innovation is probably a negotiation game, where one potential move would be to allocate resources for local clinical tests of new products. Making changes to budgets and the problem of getting out of existing contracts for depreciated technology are other examples that appear problematic. To overcome these problems, one general way forward for public agencies would be to emphasize further long-term innovation planning and technology forecasting. This could help to create awareness of situations when existing technology is coming close to the point when consideration of alternatives is critical. This requires in turn a rather fundamental shift in how to look at public agencies in general. Public agencies must take on the role of competent buyers and drivers of innovation. In other words, they need to see public procurement of innovation as a way towards improved performance of the public services they are set up to deliver. A 'hospital' should be understood not only as an instance of health provision, but also as an entity driving innovations for health provision.

CONCLUDING REMARKS

The chapter focuses on a relatively neglected area, namely adoption and diffusion of innovations in public procurement. There are three main justifications for countervailing that tendency. First, a better understanding of diffusion processes in relation to public procurement of innovation may help to stimulate innovation, especially in those markets operated by innovative suppliers mainly addressing public needs. Second, a better understanding of diffusion processes may help managers to sustain a more efficient service by adopting new and better products. Public procurement of innovation does not, however, end with the contract being signed. Success is ultimately achieved when the procured item is adopted and used.

The empirical findings discussed here underscore the importance of adopting a more holistic view of public procurement of innovation. The case study revealed an array of institutional barriers that had an inhibiting effect on the diffusion of the procured item. These were barriers that had to be dealt with in order for the procured item to diffuse into the organization. One basic implication of the case concerns the understanding of the practice of procuring innovation as different from the procurement of well-known regular goods. The understanding of public procurement of innovation cannot be limited to setting up the tender procedure and awarding a winner. Resources must also be provided to coordinate and negotiate the institutional set-up into which the procured innovation is diffused. The value of an innovation may be considerably underutilized if no attention is paid to the diffusion of the innovation into the organization.

Theoretically, this chapter deals with innovation and diffusion as essentially a social and interactive process, determined by institutions, which may or may not enable diffusion. Therefore, institutional coordination may at times be necessary in order to achieve diffusion. Although the perception of institutions as elements working on different societal levels is well established in the literature, the chapter also attempts to counteract the tendency to limit institutional analysis of innovation to exogenous levels. Often this means that the institutional analysis of public procurement of innovation boils down to analysis of the procurement law. By pinpointing barriers hindering innovation and diffusion on other institutional levels, the limitations of such narrowly focused approaches become evident. In principle, all the institutional barriers discussed in this case belong to the endogenous level. This in turn justifies the claim that institutional coordination and redesign should also take into account endogenous levels.

Thus, the position taken here, as argued also by Uyarra and Flanagan (2010), is that the application of public procurement as a means to stimulate innovation does not involve only public technology procurement where a public agency formulates demand for products that do not currently exist. There is also a need to acknowledge the supply side, that is, situations like the one described in this chapter, where private sector suppliers approach public procurers with unsolicited offers of new, innovative products. In order to fund future innovations, suppliers need to secure returns of investment in research and development. In sectors dominated by the public sector, suppliers offering unsolicited innovative products or services may be dependent on public agencies' ability to adopt innovation. What also makes this an important issue is the common use of framework agreements in public procurement. Although centrally negotiated contracts may exist, diffusion will not take place until call-offs (i.e. actual purchase) are made from these contracts by departments within the organization. Thus, understanding public sector adoption of innovations may be critical for stimulation of innovation in a long-term perspective.

NOTE

1. The study was conducted with two colleagues at the time working at the Centre for Research in Strategic Purchasing and Supply, School of Management, University of Bath, UK and is available in the form of a journal article (Rolfstam *et al.*, 2011).

5. Public procurement of innovation as collaboration

The analysis in the previous chapter essentially considered the whole NHS as an organization containing different endogenous institutions. The exogenous component consisted of the ambition to diffuse a certain innovation while different endogenous institutions at play effectively provided 'resistance' to the envisaged change. Little attention was given to the extent to which any of these institutions could be considered as embedded in specific organizational sub-units within the NHS. The institutions themselves, rather than the organizational connection with specific organizations within the NHS, were at the core of the analysis. Such an approach is convenient, because it enables a discussion on institutions not clearly associated with a specific organization. One institution that belongs to that category is organized scepticism among physicians. Regarded as an institution, organized scepticism is more strongly connected to the medical community of physicians than to a specific organizational unit, such as a ward. It is an institution that transgresses formal organizations. To have a look at the other option, then, this chapter develops a perspective on endogenous institutional set-ups where the focal level is organizational. The underlying assertion is that organization-oriented institutional analysis may be particularly important for understanding how institutional factors may affect the success or failure of multi-organizational collaborations in public procurement of innovation. Although the basic theoretical foundations are the same as in previous chapters, the starting point here is an understanding of organizations as containers of a certain institutional set-up or rationality. The underlying idea is that any organization would undertake actions reflecting its rationality, which does not necessarily correspond to actions undertaken by any other organization. When different organizations interact, their respective rationality and to what extent these match will determine the outcome of the interaction.

The chapter discusses a case that evolved in the administrative district of Bracknell Forest, England in which the Borough Council, in collaboration with a number of other organizations, tried to procure a woodchip-fuelled power plant intended to deliver sustainable energy to a renewed

part of Bracknell town centre. This procurement project was part of a
larger urban development initiative. The project did not however achieve
the intended result. At the end of the procurement process, there were no
suppliers interested in obtaining the contract and the project was terminated without finding a supplier. The chapter attempts to explain this
outcome by analysing the interaction of the organizations involved in the
project, focusing especially on endogenous organization-specific rationalities. In other words, the case is treated as an example of how the
interplay of endogenous institutions may prevent collaborating organizations from innovating through public procurement.

A CASE OF PUBLIC PROCUREMENT OF INNOVATION TERMINATED

This case evolved in Bracknell, one of several towns in the UK that were
developed after the Second World War, in itself a story of the times that
was characterized by elite decision making, effectually paying less
attention to local democracy (Dunleavy, 1981). Situated within a 30-mile
radius of London, Bracknell Forest locates several major companies'
national offices, including BMW, 3M UK, Waitrose, Hewlett-Packard and
Panasonic (BRP, 2006a). The case emerged however as one element in a
rather grand attempt to avoid economic decline in Bracknell. Increased
population and new developments around the town centre, in combination with relatively limited development in the town centre itself, had
created stagnation and decline, and people had begun to do their
shopping and other leisure activities elsewhere. The town was designed
and constructed in the 1950s and 1960s, and town developers realized
that a major renewal scheme would be required to guarantee sustainability. As a response to this situation, activities were initiated in the late
1990s 'to transform Bracknell town centre into a culturally self-confident
centre that is mature, vibrant and truly mixed-use, hosting a wide range
of shopping and leisure activities which are accessible to all' (Bettison
and McCormack, 2002). This appreciation manifested itself in a rather
impressive £750 million regeneration scheme. The plans included the
development of 56 000 square metres of new retail space, 15 000 square
metres of new bars, cafés, restaurants, and entertainment and leisure
facilities, 1000 new homes, 3500 new parking spaces, up to 62 000
square metres of new and replacement business space, a 4000-square-
metre food store, extensive public spaces, transport improvements, a
large health centre, a new library, a new bus station, better CCTV, a new
police station, a new magistrates' court and a new borough office (BRP,

2006b). Concerns regarding sustainability and energy efficiency were also incorporated into the development plans. The town planners perceived that Bracknell had a great opportunity 'to show itself as an innovator and leader in this area by making the town centre demonstrably energy efficient' (*Bracknell Town Centre Masterplan*, 2002, p. 13). Opportunities and/or challenges mentioned were: renewable energy technologies such as solar, wind and biomass energy; energy efficiency built into the design of the buildings; and issues concerning waste and transport (ibid.). Among these opportunities was the idea to develop a renewable energy centre that would supply the new town centre with sustainable energy based on woodchips.

Eventually the formal procurement process started, and Bracknell Forest Borough Council published a contract notice in the *Official Journal of the European Union* in order to find a supplier and an operator of the power plant. The procurement procedure used was the negotiated procedure with a contract notice. This meant that only suppliers that managed to become pre-qualified were eventually allowed to submit a bid. In order to gain this status, bidders were asked to fill in a pre-qualification questionnaire to be returned to the procurer for validation. This questionnaire included questions on technical, economic and financial capacity. The tenderers also had to show their sound legal position, that is, demonstrate that their businesses operated in compliance with the law. The tenderers that successfully passed the evaluation of the questionnaire and became pre-qualified would then be asked to submit a complete proposal. The procurers expected ultimately to invite to tender between two and five suppliers. The notice was published on 8 January 2005, specifying that the winner of the contract was to form an energy service company (ESCO) to 'commission the design, construction, installation of the facilities ... and manage the commercial activities, maintenance and operation of the facilities and the distribution network over its economic life' (TED, 2005). Four organizations became pre-qualified out of the dozen or so suppliers that initially responded to the contract notice. Many of the bidders that did not pass the evaluation wanted to deliver (small) parts to the project and not a complete energy centre. There was also a category of bidders that had prior experience in the technology required, but on a much smaller scale. As the supplier was supposed to finance the project as well, and thus accept a big commercial risk, the procurers judged that only bidders with prior experience both of projects on that scale and of financing such projects would become pre-qualified.

This project would have brought about innovation if the initial intentions had been realized. The actual outcome was that the procurers eventually had to terminate the procurement process without awarding a contract. The energy centre, if built according to the initial intentions, would have implemented woodchip energy technology on a scale never before attempted in the UK. The idea was also to get local farmers to grow fast-cropping timber that would be used as fuel for the power station. If successful, the project, at least as the Bracknell Forest Borough Council perceived it, would also have had a positive impact on an underdeveloped UK market for renewable energy in general. With reference to Schumpeter, as discussed in Chapter 1, this project clearly was innovative. It involved, at least on the national level, the introduction of a new good and a new method of production; it would have opened up a local market for fast-cropping timber and, consequently, it would have meant the creation of demand for new raw materials. The 'good' refers here to the physical plant, that is, the energy centre, which was based on technology applied on a scale never before seen in the UK. At a later stage, when finally delivered, this energy centre would in turn also be delivering sustainable energy, which in itself was an innovative energy form. One could then say that some great ambitions were abandoned on 11 April 2006, when the notice was published announcing formally the cancellation of the project. The reason given by the public procurers was that the scheme had been judged 'commercially unviable' (TED, 2006), ultimately because the procurement process had not generated a supplier willing to sign the contract.

At first glance the developments in this case appear to have a straightforward explanation: the reason for terminating the project was that there was no guaranteed market for the new energy centre. The ESCO that would have committed itself to building and running the energy centre could in theory have ended up in a situation where town centre tenants were securing their energy supply from elsewhere. In that sense, the project failed to deliver an innovation owing to the second aspect of innovation discussed above, the requirement to be successful on a market. This observation could essentially be seen as the lesson learned from the project, and all involved could then just move on with their lives. However, although the analysis that follows will not change these factual circumstances, it will provide a more profound understanding of how organization-specific endogenous institutions played a role in this case. In fact, the apparently obvious conclusion that there needs to be a market for an innovation may not be the most critical observation that this case has to offer.

COLLABORATING FOR INNOVATION: A RATIONALITY DRAMA

Any student of scriptwriting for film or theatre will sooner or later be exposed to the thesis that 'All drama is conflict.' This is the principle on which any narrative play or film is based. In any good drama there should be a protagonist, a hero of some kind who wants to achieve something. There should also be an evil character, an antagonist who for some reason wants to prevent the hero accomplishing his or her desires. The protagonist's struggle against the antagonist is what makes the story go forward until the final scene when the hero after hardships and adventures eventually reaches the goal. If the tension between the protagonist and his or her desires and the antagonist did not exist there would be no story. Leaving aside an attempt to identify the heroes and the evil ones in the current case, the parallel to rationalities among actors collaborating in public procurement of innovation should be clear.

The analogy to drama and thinking of the 'character' of an organization finds a foundation in the innovation literature, as summarized in Chapter 2. The chapter outlined the view of organizations as entities with scarce resources making any actions purposefully selected (Vanberg, 1997), where each organization develops a specific 'procedure for determining the action to be taken' (Nelson and Winter, 1982, 57), which in turn sets the conditions for learning (Argyris, 1994) and the creation of organization-specific routines (Nelson and Winter, 1982). The result of this recursive evolution is here captured by the rationality notion – which would correspond to the character notion any drama student has to work with in order to write great scripts. With reference to van de Donk and Snellen (1989) and Gregersen (1992), Chapter 2 also discussed different types of rationalities: political rationality; legal rationality; economic rationality; and scientific (or paradigmatic) rationality. Chapter 2 also drew on Coriat and Weinstein (2002), distinguishing between long-term exogenous institutions, fixed-term exogenous institutions, long-term endogenous institutions and fixed-term endogenous institutions. The drama studied here occurs as interaction between organizations with different organizational rationalities. The project of developing an energy centre for the new town centre to be built involved an array of different kinds of organizations: Bracknell Forest Borough Council, regional public agencies, national agencies, private companies and organizations, universities, and temporary organizations funded by the European Commission. In the following section, a selection of these organizations is briefly described. A discussion of each organization's rationality is included.

Bracknell Forest Borough Council was the public agency that administered the public procurement process. For the purposes of the present analysis, it is important to distinguish between two different bodies within the public agency. One is the political side, that is, the elected leadership of the Borough Council. The other is the professional entity consisting of public officers administering the procurement process in the more practical sense. These two categories did not have the same rationality. For the political leadership, political rationality was more central than for the procurers. The good publicity a successful project would render was clearly in the minds of the political leadership. Bracknell Forest Borough Council's chief executive, Timothy Wheadon, expected that the project would 'add to Bracknell's profile as a high performing local authority and will make us stand out as a high quality town centre' (University of Reading, 2004). Political leaders obviously need to run their borough council within budget, according to law and in agreement with expert knowledge, in a way that the general public will find appropriate, if they are to be re-elected. The assumption here is however that the political rationality is strongest; politicians strive to stay in power. The professionals, that is, the public procurers in the Borough Council, did not have the same requirements to satisfy political rationality. As employees they are not as dependent on public opinion to keep their jobs. Instead, the ambition among procurers was to achieve a good outcome in compliance with the EC procurement directives. Thus, one could say that the procurers were driven mainly by paradigmatic rationality.

Bracknell Forest Borough Council developed the town centre plans in collaboration with the Bracknell Forest Regeneration Partnership (BRP). The BRP was set up as a private joint venture formed in April 2003 by the town's two major landowners, Legal & General and Schroders Exempt Property Unit Trust. The BRP also brought in a consultancy firm, Stanhope Plc, from London. The underlying purpose of the establishment of the BRP was to counteract the ongoing decline of commercial activities in the town centre, in other words to pursue the development and regeneration of the town centre. If the decline continued and commercial life were completely taken over by shopping malls situated outside the town centre, the consequences for property owners in the town centre would obviously be negative. As a commercial entity, this organization had a rationality that was primarily economic, to secure income to the landowners in the future. The essential business of this organization was property. Thus, it is also possible to distinguish a paradigmatic rationality embedded in the BRP.

One organization that played an important role early in the process was Thames Valley Energy (TV Energy). TV Energy was a not-for-profit regional renewable energy agency working on local, regional, national and international levels with 'matters relating to the understanding, promotion and delivery of renewable energy projects', funded by different organizations in the UK as well as the European Commission (TV Energy, 2005). TV Energy was not paid directly for carrying out its activities, as a private company would be. Neither was it dependent on public elections to conduct its activities. The inclination to prioritize a legal rationality was also quite low, in the sense that it would not be its responsibility to comply with for example procurement laws. This organization was driven mainly by a paradigmatic rationality, that is, to contribute to the diffusion of renewable energy. It played a significant role when it came to attracting funding for the development of the project.

Funding rarely comes without expectations from the funder on how the funds should be utilized; it typically reflects a certain rationality the beneficiary should endorse in return for the funding. The funding attracted in this case was no exception to that general rule. The project benefited from grant funding coming from two sources, the European Commission through the CONCERTO initiative, and a national source, the Energy Savings Trust (EST). The CONCERTO initiative was funded by the 6th Framework Programme for research, supervised by the Directorate-General Energy and Transport of the European Commission. The purpose of the initiative, to be endorsed by the beneficiary, was to proactively address 'the challenges of creating a more sustainable future for Europe's energy needs' (CONCERTO, 2006a). In principle, the programme was set up to work in two ways, as a promoter of the development of new knowledge and as an agent for diffusing this new knowledge to others. The initiative supported local communities in forming strategies and development towards self-supply of sustainable energy and energy efficiency, currently in nine projects involving some 30 communities. A central idea for the projects included in the initiative was also to offer 'a platform for the exchange of ideas and experiences' between the participating communities, as well as with other cities committed to introducing similar strategies (CONCERTO, 2006b). Among the projects in the CONCERTO initiative, Bracknell Forest Borough Council became involved in the Renaissance project (Renewable ENergy Acting In SuStainable And Novel Community Enterprises).

In addition to Bracknell Forest, the communities of Lyon in France and Zaragoza in Spain were active participants in the project. In addition, an array of communities in Europe were affiliated as 'observer communities' (Renaissance, 2006). The Bracknell Forest Renaissance team included regional partners in addition to the Borough Council: the University of Reading, the Bracknell Forest Regeneration Partnership, TV Energy, Waitrose, South East England Development Agency (SEEDA) and Slough Heat and Power (University of Reading, 2004). The main rationality governing this organization was paradigmatic in the sense that it had a clear ambition to promote a certain paradigmatic idea, namely renewable energy.

The final category to be defined here consists of private firms that would respond to the tender call, to build and eventually operate the energy centre on a commercial basis. These companies were governed by essentially two rationalities. For commercial entities depending on making a profit, the economic rationality was central. This takes place through utilizing their organization-specific knowledge in energy technologies. Thus, it is possible to discern within these organizations a paradigmatic rationality as well. This paradigmatic rationality might also vary with the profiles of the individual companies, suggesting that each company would strive towards supplying the specific technology it had supplied before. For all commercial companies it is the case that the paradigmatic rationality could be followed only if it complied with the economic rationality, that is, the activities resulted in income for the company. This condition, then, is quite different from that for a not-for-profit organization, where funding is not as directly coupled with a certain activity. Table 5.1 displays a summary of the organizations and rationalities discussed.

Table 5.1   Organizations involved and their main types of rationalities

Organisation	Primary Rationality
Bracknell Forest Political Leadership	Political
Bracknell Forest Public Officers/ Professionals	Paradigmatic, legal
Bracknell Forest Regeneration Partnership	Economic, paradigmatic
Thames Valley Energy	Paradigmatic
CONCERTO/ Renaissance project	Paradigmatic
Energy Service Companies/ Tenderers	Economic, paradigmatic
Suppliers	Economic (paradigmatic)

PUBLIC PROCUREMENT OF INNOVATION AS COORDINATION OF RATIONALITIES

Being a public agency procuring something above threshold levels, Bracknell Forest Borough Council had to comply with the EC procurement directives, as transposed into national legislation. As was discussed in Chapter 1, these directives serve to guarantee competition and transparency and to prevent corruption in order to economize with public spending (European Commission, 1998). The directives stipulate, for instance, that the public procurer should publish tender calls, diffuse knowledge and deal with award criteria, together with the principles that should apply for awarding contracts (Arrowsmith, 2005). In reality, however, compliance with these rules has historically been problematic. One could see this as a diffusion problem related to these rules being an exogenously imposed legislative package that might not settle in national contexts too easily. Lack of familiarity with the rules, the perception that the rules are inefficient, and risk averseness are examples of factors brought up as reasons why procurers might not apply the tender procedures as stipulated by the directives (Gelderman *et al.*, 2006). Even if it appears as if the general awareness of the directives is growing and some of the negative perceptions have been gradually removed, compliance might still not be self-evident among all potential actors in procurement projects. In the light of what at the time were prevailing attitudes (see Boyle, 1994), the decision to apply the EC directives was not a self-evident one, as reported by one of the interviewees. There was a similar project evolving at the time in a town nearby where the procurers had chosen not to apply the EC directives. The public procurers in Bracknell Forest Borough Council had stronger faith in the benefits of the EC directives, however. They thought that by complying with the directives – rather than seeing them only as a hurdle to get over – they might bring something more to the scheme. For instance, compliance with the directives and the obligation to advertise might attract suppliers previously unknown to the procurers. To the procurers, the project offered an interesting possibility to see the procurement directives at work.

TV Energy was the organization emphasizing renewable energy. Before the formal public procurement started, TV Energy helped Bracknell Forest Borough Council conduct a feasibility study funded by the Energy Savings Trust. TV Energy also played a significant role when it came to attracting funding to the project and in developing the renewable aspects of the specifications of the new energy centre. One funding network was, as described above, the CONCERTO initiative, funded in turn by the European Commission. The main concern of TV Energy was the technical aspects involved in promoting the development of renewable energy rather than the administrative procedures implied by the public procurement rules. To some extent, this tension became more apparent owing to the fact that the champion of sustainable technology and leader of the Environment Group in Bracknell Forest Borough Council, Councillor Terry Mills, died at a pivotal moment of the project. In the initial stages of the project, TV Energy felt that all the stakeholders were supportive of sustainable technology. This changed after Terry Mills's death. The perception of TV Energy was that the 'courage' required to undertake innovative projects vanished, and the focus shifted towards more conventional technology in order to avoid the risks associated with innovation. They also felt that the project was slowed down further as a result of what they thought were unnecessarily bureaucratic procurement procedures. TV Energy did not emphasize the virtues of complying with the directives to the same extent as did the procurers at the Borough Council.

The different views on the public procurement process created friction between TV Energy and the procurers at Bracknell Forest Borough Council, and this condition contributed to the delay of the project. After the first step in the procurement procedure and the shortlisting of four bidders, the project started to lose pace. The project was affected by a conflict between the legal rationality among the procurers and TV Energy's paradigmatic rationality. Altogether, the delays meant that the procurers had to work in a tight time window in order to keep up with the development of the town centre. This further reduced the possibilities of coming up with innovative solutions in the interaction with the suppliers. This also put pressure on the BRP, as it needed to know how the new buildings in the town centre should be configured in terms of the energy supply. The concern was that there would not be time enough to work with the winner of the contract to guarantee that there would be an ESCO and an energy centre in place on time. For the BRP, essentially an organization in the property business, the priorities were the regeneration of the town centre and the commercial aspects of the whole project. Although the BRP participated in the work to develop sustainable solutions, this would not be its first priority. The BRP required that the proposed energy centre scheme should be able to deliver energy six months before the new town centre was to open. If this could not be achieved, the BRP feared ending up in a situation where the completed, renewed town centre would be without an energy supply. Such a situation, if it occurred, would be very costly to the BRP.

The different rationalities were also manifested in the way the specifications for the tenderers were written. Here, what can be seen as a conflict between the public procurers' paradigmatic rationality and TV Energy's different rationality becomes evident. Although the importance of this particular feature of contract designing is sometimes given too much attention compared to everything else that is important for public procurement of innovation, the use of functional specification (van Weele, 2002, p. 52) is often seen as a means of allowing innovative ideas to be submitted. Specifying outcomes rather than a specific technological implementation may create room for the submission of creative and innovative solutions that would otherwise become disqualified in the evaluation stage of the tender process. On the other hand, if a procurer is confident about exactly what item to procure, the use of functional specification may seem unnecessary. As was remarked in the interviews, 'TV Energy put in quite a lot of detail what they wanted to see, because they thought it should be based on renewable technologies.' This meant that the specifications became '[t]oo prescriptive'. The effect of the tight specifications was that potential tenders involving existing technology or technology with ambitions that were not as high when it came to sustainability were excluded. Solutions based on proven commercially viable gas-fired alternatives that would still have meant energy savings in the new town centre could not be submitted. Another issue related to the set-up of the contract was the decision to allow only bids involving one (big) supplier. This excluded solutions delivered by consortia of smaller and potentially more innovative firms. One view reported was that the public procurers should have encouraged supplier innovation, asking suppliers what they would propose to deliver for the town centre. According to this view, instead of explicitly demanding renewable technology, the public procurer should have settled for encouraging and allowing submissions of such solutions. By adopting such an innovation-friendly approach, the procurer would also have allowed conventional solutions. This would have increased the chances of getting a supplier at all, even if that might have required a lower ambition concerning sustainability. Consequently, the ambitions regarding sustainability were reduced in later energy plans for the new town centre, opening up the possibility of considering already available solutions. The envisaged capacity of the power plant was reduced to one-quarter to one-half that of the initially intended energy centre.

The CONCERTO initiative and the Renaissance project essentially promoted the use of renewable energy, that is, it was also a project devoted to knowledge diffusion. It provided a platform for knowledge sharing among the project members as well as funding aimed at contributing to the development of the individual members' projects. In that sense, the underlying paradigmatic rationality originated from these two activities, the promotion of certain behaviour (i.e. implementing sustainable technologies) and the diffusion of information. In order to get the funding to develop the renewable energy centre in Bracknell, the participators had to sign an agreement. In the view of the BRP, the practical conditions provided by the CONCERTO agreement were not adapted to the conditions of commercial reality. The CONCERTO project involved some 30 communities in Europe. The grant was shared by these different organizations that were all developing renewable technologies in their respective regions. In the way the agreement was written, the whole grant could be revoked if one of the participants failed to deliver its part. Although the European Commission had informally communicated that it would not implement those terms, the existence in writing of such a possibility led the BRP to refrain from signing the agreement. The pre-qualified suppliers thought the requirements connected to the funding made participation 'too complicated'. In addition to actually delivering the technology, they were supposed to share their experiences through written reports and by participating in training events across Europe. The position among suppliers was that their business was about supplying energy, not about tasks related to knowledge diffusion. These other tasks were also perceived as vaguely defined. In the view of the suppliers, they were being forced to make a more or less open-ended promise in return for the funding. Another problem was related to the time schedule of the funding provided by the CONCERTO initiative. The allocated money had to be spent within a certain time frame, which was incompatible with the course of events for the regeneration project. All in all there appeared to be a mismatch between paradigmatic rationalities embedded in the EU funding and the commercial actors in the project.

A claim that economic rationality for suppliers was not achieved is substantiated by the fact that all the pre-qualified suppliers withdrew from the competition and the public procurement process was therefore terminated. One important circumstance contributing to this development was the stipulations placed on the winner of the contract. The selected supplier was supposed to form an ESCO and build and run the energy centre on a commercial basis. In order to borrow money to do this, a supplier would have been required to produce for potential financiers a proposal demonstrating that there was going to be demand for the energy supplied by the new energy centre. As the planned buildings remained to be built there were no tenants to make any commitment to rely on the energy centre. This situation made it impossible for the BRP to provide guarantees that several years on from the completion of the whole regeneration scheme the tenants would be using the energy supplied from the energy centre. The BRP also wanted to avoid a scenario in which it would have to turn down a large potential tenant because the latter had secured a supply of renewable energy from elsewhere. One possible action Bracknell Forest Borough Council could have taken would have been to help create demand. There are lots of examples of public agencies that were able to use public procurement to create incentives for firms to engage in innovative activities they might otherwise have been reluctant to, for instance in telecom (Palmberg, 2002; Berggren and Laestadius, 2003), in the building sector (Westling, 1991), in health technology (Phillips *et al.*, 2007) and in 'eHealth' and 'eEnergy' (Turkama *et al.*, 2012, pp. 57–78). A commitment from the Borough Council, as a public agency and also a fairly significant future tenant in the renewed town centre, to buy energy from the energy centre could have worked as a catalyser to create the initial market required for the renewable energy centre. One of the stakeholders suggested that such a commitment could have been included in the tender call. The view of Bracknell Forest Borough Council was, however, that restrictions in the procurement law made such a commitment impossible. The argument brought forward was essentially related to the requirement to achieve 'best value' for money at all times. Making a commitment to a certain energy supplier before the energy centre was built could have led to a situation in the future where the Borough Council was unable to choose any cheaper alternatives offered by other suppliers. According to this interpretation, such an advance commitment could not guarantee that the Borough Council would get value for money at all times. Instead, the supplier of energy for the public premises in the new town centre would be appointed through a separate public procurement process. It is not the purpose here to determine this specific legal issue. It was indicated in the interviews that such commitments had been made elsewhere in the UK, which might suggest that it would have been doable in this case as well. It is also noteworthy that the UK has been pioneering in developing public procurement methods emphasizing 'forward commitment' (Environmental Industries Unit, 2006). Another issue that had required some reflection concerned the Council's capability to procure innovations in general. 'It is not the Council's core business … it is not part of its everyday business, and it doesn't have the experience. So the Council is always considering risk regarding the innovation as well. And the Council will always choose the least risky strategy.' Risk aversion is an interesting phenomenon, as it fits analytically into several rationalities. In a way it can be seen as a political rationality, as risk-averse behaviour will help avoiding exposure to events that can threaten a powerful position. It can also be perceived as an economic rationality, as it may be regarded as a sound policy to avoid jeopardizing taxpayers' money. Given the perception of a procurer as risk averse in general, it is also a paradigmatic rationality, as it would then be seen as a norm within a given prevailing institutional set-up.

Essentially related to the fact that the Council has limited experience in procuring innovations was the perceived lack of clearly defined goals for the project. Council staff stated that they 'were drawn along by the agendas of ... some of the other partners. ... We didn't really take control and say "This is what we want; this is how it is going to be."' To some extent this, too, may be explained by the death of the project leader at Bracknell Forest Council, Terry Mills. It may have been difficult to find a replacement able to maintain the high ambitions regarding renewable energy within the time frame of the project. This development in turn provides an explanation of why the procurement was managed in a relatively poor manner (e.g. unclear goals, time delays, and eventual termination of the project). The ideas and visions seem essentially to have come from the private sector and, more specifically, the two major property owners, Legal & General and Schroders (Bracknell Forest Borough Council, 2007). In addition came the different requirements as embedded in the rationalities of TV Energy and the EU funding schemes. In the middle of everything were the Council's procurers, caught in the crossfire of different ambitions and rationalities.

In sum, it appears as though the procurement process at Bracknell Forest Borough Council was guided by political rationality responding to external initiatives. This was indeed an attempt to commit to public procurement of innovation. The characteristics of the project diverge however from the idealized situation envisaged, that is, where the procurer acts to formulate demand that drives private sector innovation. That reflection brings the discussion back to the purpose of public agencies. No one can really argue against the assertion that the long-term institutional justification for the existence of public agencies is the public service they are set up to deliver. This reflects also how procurement activities are conventionally set up, namely as a sourcing mechanism that in a rather static way supports the delivery of public service. Given the risk averseness discussed above and the lack of determination observed when the champion was no longer there, one could say that the public procurers got stuck in a paradigmatic battle between old, traditional efficiency rationalities and those required for innovative activity. In that light, one could say that the champions of this project challenged the long-term rationality of Bracknell Forest Borough Council as a supplier of public service by pushing it towards becoming a public innovator. A

list of some identified rationalities among the involved actors is displayed
in Table 5.2.

*Table 5.2   Collaborators and their specific efforts indicating their specific
rationalities*

The Political Leadership → **'Beacon for green energy'**
The Council Procurers → **Comply with the rules, Time for
developing tender call**
BRP → **Energy on time**
TV Energy → **Strict specification on sustainable technology**
Funding Schemes → **Required sustainable technologies**
Renaissance project → **Diffusion of knowledge**
Suppliers → **Deliver and operate energy centre for commercial
reasons**

IMPLICATIONS AND CONCLUDING REMARKS

This case study dealt with a procurement project involving a set of actors
where the ultimate aim was not reached: to build and operate a
sustainable power plant. The 'drama' that evolved in the project can be
summarized as follows. One benefit the political leadership appreciated
was the 'beacon effect', that is, the prestige the building of an innovative
sustainable power plant would render. The priority for the BRP was to
have a(ny) solution available on time. The potential supplier and operator
needed to make sure there would be a market once the power plant was
built. The council procurers wanted to comply with the rules and
undertake a good procurement process. Being a promoter of renewable
energy, TV Energy was quite specific regarding requirements for sustainable technology. The EU funding schemes also required sustainable
technologies. There was also attached an information diffusion programme that would require certain efforts from the winner of the
contract. Viewed in isolation from each other, all these ambitions are
quite straightforward and unproblematic. The problem is that a rationality
understood as a selection mechanism for an economic organization also
implies deselection. This means that certain competences evolving within
an organization take precedence at the cost of others, which are downplayed or completely ignored. Even if the ability to excel in one area in
itself might not pose a problem, the absence of other abilities might.
Rationality, like any kind of institutional entity, is therefore 'good' or

'bad' depending on the situation. For example, in general any striving towards developing sustainable technology is good. The same goes for the ambition to follow the EC procurement rules. In a situation where sustainable technology is to be procured, problems might occur when one of these aims reflect a rationality that downplays or ignores the other. The 'drama' encountered in this case evolved when these different rationalities were forged into one common activity, to build a new and innovative sustainable energy centre. The 'story' was essentially about how a set of organizations had to adapt their behaviour 'to a joint regime, which requires a transformation of culture, mode of organizations, work and management of the parts involved' (Nassimbeni, 1998, p. 545). The extent to which this was achieved was determined by the differentiated rationalities among the participants (Lundvall, 1992, p. 46).

The advantage of the institutional perspective developed here is that it not only allows for explanations of innovation that take into account exogenous institutions such as public procurement law, but also prompts a search for explanations of behaviour due to endogenous institutions, for example institutions stemming from within an organization. As was stated earlier in this chapter, the analysis of this case could have led to rather 'straightforward' conclusions, expressed in terms of events, their consequences and maybe also the identification, and potentially blame, of actors that caused effects that undermined and eventually terminated the project. Such an analysis would help to identify problems and allow for suggestions as to how to remedy them on an operational level. One outcome could be a checklist of things to take into account for future attempts to engage in public procurement of innovation. Even if the importance of dealing with such issues is not downplayed, thinking of stakeholders in terms of their rationalities, as was endeavoured here, may offer a more profound analysis, where the focus is not so much on the single events as they occurred but on their underlying reasons for occurring. Looked upon as isolated entities, all the involved stakeholders actually acted according to their own rationality and, in that sense, did what they were supposed to do. The problems occurred as institutional clashes in the interaction with other actors with incompatible rationalities. Given the assertion that collaborative public procurement involving innovation manifests itself as the result of the extent to which there prevails an institutional match between collaborating actors, the case can be seen as an instance in which such a match did not occur. For public procurers this perspective raises issues concerning how public procurement of innovation projects can be set up in a way that aligns with the rationality of commercial firms or any other stakeholders involved. For suppliers aiming at winning public contracts, this perspective raises issues concerning building awareness of the underlying principles on which public procurers act. Although most instances of public procurement of innovation probably occur as collaborative projects where several stakeholders are involved, as partners in a consortium, as sub-suppliers or as contributors in consecutive tender processes, this assertion would also be relevant in cases where there is only one procurer and one supplier involved; in order to be successful, there needs to be an institutional match between involved rationalities.

Thus, the case studied here proposes that public procurement of innovation may be affected by endogenous organization-specific institutions encapsulated by the organizations that participate in a specific procurement process. This suggests that one necessary condition for a successful public procurement project seems to be that there is an institutional match between the organizations finally selected as supplier(s) and the public procurer. Also, if the procurement process does not achieve such a state, one could expect that the possibilities for a successful project in public procurement of innovation would be diminished. The understanding of endogenous institutions as evolutionarily determined and therefore organization-specific in turn underscores the specificity of public procurement processes involving several different collaborating organizations. Depending on the composition of organizations which participate in a specific procurement project, the constitution of institutions required to achieve an institutional match may therefore vary. A general implication of these assertions, which also finds support in earlier research, is that 'co-operative technology procurement is especially problematic, compared to other types, in terms of external governance, the management of technological risk, and the articulation of demand' (Hommen and Rolfstam, 2009, p. 28).

This analysis suggests an alternative route of doing research aiming at informing public procurement of innovation policies. If the reasons are sought as to why public procurement of innovation sometimes fails, the endogenous institutions embedded in collaborating actors need to be taken into account. This approach contrasts with the old tendency to view the relation between law and public procurement of innovation as a single variable causality. If the failure is explained by a mismatch between long-term endogenous institutions among the collaborating organizations, the justification for an exclusive focus on the directives weakens. It is also very hard to find any incident in the case, where the directives themselves worked as a barrier to innovation. More important were the different rationalities regarding the *perceptions* of public procurement law. On that account Bracknell Forest Borough Council followed its own paradigmatic rationality, as did the other organizations.

The procurers saw a challenge in making the directives work, while several of the other actors thought of them as something unnecessarily bureaucratic making things more complicated. This disinterest was a central feature among organizations with a very strong paradigmatic rationality emphasizing sustainability. In other words, this outcome would justify a focus on further studying, in order ultimately to undertake institutional amelioration of the rationalities that produce these types of clashes.

This case also illustrates the relation between long-term exogenous institutions and long-term endogenous institutions. Technically speaking, the public procurement directives are universal, that is, they affect procurement activities carried out by any public actor. Still, the implications of the legal framework, its virtues, the degree to which it is useful, and so on depend also on the rationality of any organization attempting to apply them in practice. Bracknell Forest Borough Council concluded that it could not guarantee demand for the sustainable energy because of the procurement rules. The view of the public procurers at Bracknell Forest Borough Council was that the rules might support the process in general. For TV Energy, in possession of a clear view of the expected technical properties of the energy centre, the procurement procedure was a cumbersome element causing delay in the project. Here there emerges a temptation to become contrafactual. Had the 'antagonists', instead of effectually resisting the application of the rules, maintained a corresponding view thinking of the procurement procedure as a competitive race that would enable the selection of the best supplier, the outcome might have been different. Similarly, had the whole set-up been designed with a greater emphasis on the commercial aspects of the project, maybe the interest among suppliers would have remained all the way to the point where a contract could have been signed. Rather than trying to extend this list of possibilities, one naive point to make here is that the outcome of the project might have been different if the participating organizations had acted in other ways from how they did. From an institutional perspective such an implication becomes problematic, however. If actions reflect endogenous set-ups and organizations' rationalities then an organization's 'good' actions will potentially be complemented with 'bad' actions. The challenge that emerges is how to attain an institutional change where the good actions remain and the bad ones are polished to a state where institutional match can be achieved.

If one for a short while becomes hierarchical, the essential purpose of fixed-term exogenous institutions is to induce change or strengthen a certain behaviour on lower institutional levels. In situations characterized by disparate views stemming from a mismatch between long-term endogenous institutions, as in the present case, the function of fixed-term exogenous institutions becomes discernible. One example we saw in Chapter 4 was the Rapid Review Panel, a device set up to fast-track the silver-coated catheter into the NHS supply routes. Many examples are also to be found on the EU level attempting to impose change among the member states. Different kinds of studies or expert groups are set up, perhaps not so much to produce completely new knowledge, but instead assigned to emphasize and elucidate, ultimately to promote a change of behaviour. An array of such initiatives have been made over the last decade to promote public procurement of innovation. One early study that attracted some attention was conducted by a consortium led by the Fraunhofer Institute (Edler *et al.*, 2005). In 2007, within the Open Method of Coordination framework, a two-year initiative including partners from ten EU countries was set up to create awareness and to diffuse knowledge about practical tools for 'innovative public procurement' (Bodewes *et al.*, 2009). Another example was the expert group devoted to summarizing knowledge on risk management in relation to public procurement of innovation (Tsipouri *et al.*, 2010). The current emphasis on pre-commercial procurement is one of the latest attempts to promote one way of procuring innovation (Turkama *et al.*, 2012). The setting up of funding opportunities for pre-commercial procurement or other forms of public procurement of innovation also belongs to this exogenous fixed-term category. What follows from the institutional framework developed in this book is however that all exogenous initiatives should be understood in the light of the endogenous contexts they are targeting, which are conditions that vary from case to case. Endogenous institutional variation is probably one underlying reason why certain initiatives, such as the promotion of pre-commercial procurement, has had an uneven up-take among EU member states.

When the case was discussed in this chapter, the CONCERTO initiative and the Renaissance project were analytically dealt with as participating organizations. From the perspective of Bracknell Forest Borough Council and the institutional perspective outlined here, this network can also be treated analytically as a fixed-term exogenous institution. The CONCERTO programme clearly manifested an ambition to change behaviour at lower institutional levels. The participating organizations were encouraged and also given incentives through the funding to have high ambitions for the renewable aspects of the technology to be used. In terms of this specific public procurement project, however, this behaviour came partly into conflict with a generic ambition to secure energy supply under commercial terms. Had the specifications been more functional and less specific, there would have been a possibility for tenders based on technologies which, although not fully renewable, would still have been better options than just connecting to the grid. It is not the aim here to develop further a discussion of the priorities and choices in relation to environmental issues in general. What is of interest in this story is that it can be understood as a goal conflict between two fixed-term institutional targets, innovation in general and the promotion of renewable energy. This, in turn, underscores the need for cross-sector and interdisciplinary councils of innovation and competence building as suggested by Lundvall and Borrás (2005). Such organizations could possibly contribute to a more harmonized fixed-term exogenous institutional set-up if the practical requirements of the public procurement process were taken into account. Still, as was seen in this chapter, coordination is not easy.

In writings on public procurement of innovation there prevails a preference for success stories and best practices. Problems are reported to the extent that there are also solutions provided. Often, attempts to study less successful cases are associated with problems in getting access to data and also sometimes venues to publish the acquired results. Neither practitioners nor managers in the public sector want to be associated with failure. This is problematic, as projects that do not evolve as intended can be very useful, for many reasons. Although a specific project fails, the knowledge gained in trying might be useful in other contexts. That happened for instance in Sweden some years ago when public agencies made an attempt to develop a computer to be used by public schools. Although the project had to be cancelled because of competition from emerging DOS-compatible computers, the knowledge gained was useful for other developments within ICT in Sweden (Kaiserfeld, 2000). One reason why the maritime case discussed in Chapter 3 eventually became a success was the initial failure some years before, which produced some good experiences regarding what to avoid in the second attempt. Another successful case, which is discussed in Chapter 6, also included an initial failure. For the researcher, failures often offer an interesting starting point, namely to figure out why there was a failure. To explain why something went perfectly according to plan is typically much trickier (Rolfstam, 2001). Promoting an understanding of failure as a natural part of innovation, and also design contexts where failure is tolerated and expected, would therefore be useful.

This chapter thus aligns with the position that 'successful public sector pacing [of innovation] requires both maintenance and renewal of learning processes' (Gregersen, 1992, p. 144). The analysis done here also contributes to some insights in that regard, especially in the light of the increasing interest among policy makers in the EU in promoting public procurement as an innovation policy instrument. Such initiatives have typically had a tendency to target public agencies only. Following from the case discussed here, learning should involve not only public agencies but also other organizations that may in practice affect the outcome of public procurement processes. Efforts to assess the need for institutional redesign and harmonization of rationalities as well as increase understanding of other organizations' rationalities should be considered. One central target group would be private firms aiming for public contracts for innovation projects. These recommendations reflect the view that, in order to understand how to be successful in public procurement of innovation, a wider perspective should be adopted. If public procurement of innovation is defined strictly as something that occurs 'when a public agency places an order for something which does not exist yet', many important components of what happened in this case will be missed out. One should however not leave the association with the ability to learn and successful public procurement of innovation unchallenged. One interesting question derived from an institutional perspective is: can learning actually save a project when too diverse rationalities are involved? Assuming that the public procurers at Bracknell Forest did the right thing when they terminated the project discussed in this chapter, the answer to that question is 'yes'. This question is taken up further in Chapter 6.

A final remark concerns the design rationale for the EC directives. The rules for public procurement must strike a balance between preventing fraud, maintaining transparency and promoting competition in order to save taxpayers money, on the one hand, and allowing for interaction, negotiation and uncertainty, which is critical if innovation is to take place, on the other hand. The position maintained here is that the current directives do in many ways achieve this balance. The case discussed in this chapter, also supports the general claim that the reasons for any problems are not primarily to be found in the directives. This claim is also supported by the fact that pre-commercial procurement has been launched as a way of procuring innovation within the rules. This package does not contain any new legislation, but is entirely a scheme set up to demonstrate that public procurement of innovation can be done within the existing directives. This is not the same as saying that public procurement of innovation works smoothly within the EU. Problems do occur, but often as a result of (for instance) lack of procurement competence, lack of legal competence, lack of resources, lack of political support, lack of understanding for stakeholders' needs, lack of supplier understanding of the procurement process, risk averseness and lawyers' inadequate interpretation of the possibilities given by the directives. These success factors are discussed further in Chapter 7. Another often neglected aspect of the institutional set-up a public procurer needs to deal with is captured in the case discussed here, the rationalities of participating organizations.

6. Public procurement of innovation as endogenous–exogenous knowledge conversion

The previous chapter discussed a case of public procurement of innovation where alignment and coordination of the involved rationalities did not happen to the extent required for a successful outcome. In the sense that the role of the procurers was mainly to facilitate the procurement on behalf of the future operator of the power plant the project was also catalytic. The fact that the project ended in the way it did is interesting, as it is implied in the Hommen matrix that coordination is a much more important success factor for cooperative public procurement of innovation than for public procurement of innovation involving a single procurer aiming at satisfying an intrinsic need. In that sense the outcome of the case is consistent with what is implied by the Hommen matrix.

Another implication of the case is that any attempt to develop more knowledge on this topic must be based on an understanding of public procurement of innovation as a phenomenon that incorporates many aspects that go beyond the technical procedures related to the tender call and the award process. Thinking of public procurement of innovation as a process where 'a public agency places a bid' is simply not enough, as it may neglect many important determinants for success. This chapter attempts to develop this wider perspective further by comparing the case discussed in the previous chapter with another case of public procurement of innovation that took place in Sweden just a few years before the English case. In the Swedish case the aim was also to procure a power plant based on renewable energy, although the technological solution involved biogas instead of woodchip. Another difference was that, in the Swedish case, the procurers were able to find suppliers that were willing and able to deliver a solution.

Two relatively similar cases with diverging outcomes provide interesting opportunities for comparison. By comparing, a researcher may be able to reject competing explanatory variables (Ragin, 1987, p. 38). For a single-case analysis one might draw conclusions based on identified phenomena caused by certain stimuli. A cross-case analysis might strengthen the initial conclusion if the same phenomenon occurs caused by the same stimuli as in the other case. On the other hand, if a certain phenomenon is caused by the presence of certain stimuli, this does not imply a causal dependence if the same phenomenon occurs in another context without the stimuli being present. That is at least the general advantage with comparing two cases. One hazard the researcher needs to be aware of however is multiple causation, that is, the possibility that a certain outcome may be caused by several different factors. The general claim that the EC procurement directives impede innovation is one good example of such a mistake. Such a claim cannot be made unless even the most fundamental analysis of projects like the ones discussed in this chapter is ignored. One way of improving the rigorousness and helping avoid repeating such mistakes is the method of difference, that is, checking also for absence of causes leading to the absence of the studied effect. One could say that the generic strategy should be, as far as is possible, to consider the specificities in the case under study. The rigorousness will be achieved by taking into account context specificity for any given identified cause.

Thus, the empirical material drawn on in this chapter consists of two cases, the case that evolved in Bracknell Forest ('the woodchip case'), as discussed in the previous chapter, and a similar case that evolved in Sweden ('the biofuel case'), which will be introduced here after just a brief reminder of the woodchip case. As was discussed in the previous chapter, the project would have led to different types of innovation had it eventually been finalized. However, as things developed the procurers eventually came to a stage where there were no suppliers interested in submitting a bid. The fundamental reason for this outcome was the institutional set-up as given by the different stakeholders' rationalities that came to affect the evolution of the project. The biofuel case was about a project that at least at first glance appeared to be similar. It included a set of different organizations collaborating towards building an innovative power plant envisaged to supply sustainable energy. There were also some differences, as will be discussed in this chapter.

The biofuel case concerned the public procurement project that led to the development and finalization of what at the time was a state-of-the-art facility in Sweden, the biogas and upgrading plant in the Swedish town of Västerås. The procurement project was carried out by a public company, Svensk Växtkraft AB, in turn owned by several public agencies and NGOs. Attached to the procurement project was a consultant with vast experience of similar procurement projects, Lennart Björkman. The outcome of the project, the energy system, came into operation in 2005 as the result of a process beginning some 15 years earlier when local farmers began to consider abandoning increasingly less profitable food production and instead turn to production of green energy (see Table 6.1). The procurement project was included as one component in a larger European project called Agroptigas, gathering nine partners from different EU countries (Bengtsson *et al.*, 2006). The biogas and upgrading plant was built to produce bioenergy from organic waste generated by citizens in the region, ley crops grown by local farmers and grease trap removal sludge from restaurants and institutional kitchens in the area. The biofuel that came out of the process would be used in buses in the region, waste collection vehicles and cars. At the time, the system produced fuel-quality biogas corresponding to 2.3 million litres (traditional) petrol every year. Biogas that was not upgraded to fuel quality was used for production of electricity and heat. The residuals remaining in this process were used as high-quality fertilizers by local farmers. In the initial years the system received 14 000 tons of source-separated waste from households, 4000 tons of grease trap removal sludge and 5000 tons of ley crops grown by local farmers.

Table 6.1.   Milestones and events leading to the establishment of the biogas and upgrading plant.

Year	Milestones and/ or events
1990	Initial ideas by farmers
1995	The first ideas of combined biogas plant and waste and ley crops
1998	Main planning for bio gas plant starts
2001–2002	Procurement process
2003	Contracts signed
2004	Production of vehicle fuel
2005	Bio gas plant in operation

Different Schumpeterian types of innovation came in the wake of the project. Although similar systems had been built outside Sweden before, the facility meant a new way of producing energy in Sweden, that is, an innovation in the Swedish context. The project delivered organizational adoption (new ways of organizing) in the sense that a complete system for handling waste was integrated with a production facility for biofuel. The system relied on process innovation among different local stakeholders. Local farmers were contracted to supply ley crops; households had to incorporate routines to separate bio-waste from other waste; and consumers had to make commitments to buy the biofuel the plant would produce. The system also enabled substitution of conventional technologies. The system would produce bio-methane to be used in buses, which would replace conventional diesel, and the bio-fertilizers produced would help to reduce the need for NPK fertilizers (Baky, 2006). The project thus both created new markets and also relied on the creation of new markets in order to become successful. As a direct consequence of the procurement project, local public agencies could introduce vehicles running on biofuel, as the system would be able to provide enough volumes of supply of biofuel. One could therefore talk about a catalytic effect in the sense that the project generated infrastructure that enabled diffusion of vehicles running on biofuel in the local area. The biofuel case also included examples of the Dosi kind of innovation. Different dissemination activities came with the project. Information was published on a dedicated website (the now closed-down www.agroptigas.com). One of the project partners was assigned to diffuse information about the project to Eastern European countries (Bengtsson *et al.*, 2006). Information about the project has also been diffused through production and distribution of booklets and through participation in an array of events, presentations, workshops and so on. Study visits to the plant have also been a regular activity.

The system included several different subsystems or components delivered by different suppliers from different countries: the actual biogas plant for treating organic waste and agricultural material was supplied by Ros Roca International, Germany; the plant for upgrading the biogas to vehicle quality for filling stations was supplied by YIT, Sweden and Finland; storage for silage and a system for harvesting and handling ley crops was supplied by METAB, Poland; and gas pipes and liquid digestive storage facilities were supplied by Lindesbergs Grus och Maskin AB and Styrud, Sweden. Financially, the project benefited from subsidies from the Swedish state (*c.* €7 million) and funding from the European Union (*c.* €2.5 million). The remaining capital was allocated through ordinary bank loans. The total cost for the system was SEK 170 million (*c.* €17 million).

A comparison of the two cases reveals at least the following. Both projects intended to achieve some kind of sustainable energy solution. Both projects also envisaged the creation of local supply markets. In the biofuel case, a market for ley crops was initiated. In the woodchip case, the energy production would have relied on the local supply of energy wood. The level of innovation the two projects had in mind appears also to be similar. In both cases the envisaged systems would have manifested state-of-the-art technology in the respective countries. The delivery of sustainable energy instead of energy based on conventional technologies would then in itself constitute a new way of production, that is, a process innovation in energy supply.

Some elements appear in both cases, but were implemented in different ways. For instance:

- In both cases public procurement served to satisfy demand from a group of different actors. The way this was organized varied between the projects. In the biofuel case, a jointly owned company was established to procure the system. In the woodchip case, the procurement was conducted by public procurers at the Borough Council, in collaboration with an array of organizations.
- In both cases different rationalities were represented in the group that constituted the procurer side. The rationalities represented varied between the projects.
- Both cases included different kinds of stakeholder interaction in the pre-procurement phase. The categories of stakeholders interacted with varied between the cases.
- Specifications played an important role in both cases. They way specification played a role varied between the two cases.
- In both cases the role of champions played a role for the outcome. The way champions played a role varied between the cases.
- The endogenous institutional set-up within each project in relation to the external environment played a role in both cases. The way the endogenous institutional set-up played a role varied.
- Both projects involved requirements to diffuse information. The perceptions of this requirement varied between the projects.

There are also some other differences that emerge when the cases are compared:

- In the biofuel case the procurers acted in different ways to secure different types of commitment, while in the woodchip case the procurers refrained from making any commitment.
- This in turn has some implications for the understanding of how risk was handled in the two projects.
- The cases give reason to scrutinize further the mechanisms of demand. Both cases do in different ways deviate from an idealized view of public procurement as something 'that occurs when a public agency places an order for something which does not exist'.

These points are discussed further in the following sections.

ORGANIZING MULTIPLE RATIONALITIES IN PUBLIC PROCUREMENT OF INNOVATION

Both projects consisted of an array of different organizations that each had a stake in the process. In the biofuel case several public agencies and NGOs were involved: VAFAB miljö, a public environment (waste handling) company in turn owned jointly by the municipalities in Västmanlands County and two other municipalities; Mälarenergi AB, a public utility owned by Västerås municipality; Lantbrukarnas Ekonomi AB, a company owned by the Federation of Swedish Farmers (LRF); and Odlargruppen, an association of local farmers that later would become the supplier of ley crops and buyer of fertilizers. Identified actors in the woodchip case were the Borough Council procurers, the BRP, the political leadership, TV Energy, the two EU projects, and the future operator of the power plant. As was discussed in the previous chapter, these organizations all influenced the project in certain ways. In that sense, the situation was rather similar. Both projects also consequently had to engage in a certain level of coordination in order to attain rationality alignment.

The way this coordination was set up was however different. In the biofuel case the procurement was dealt with by a jointly owned company, Växtkraft AB. In the woodchip case the public procurers at the Borough Council managed the procurement process in collaboration with the other stakeholders. One could argue that the way the biofuel case was organized, where rationalities were translated into a jointly owned company, helped to reduce the coordination challenges from the procurement project. Once cleared with its board, Växtkraft AB could essentially conduct an intrinsic procurement. Any coordination required between rationalities among the different owners of Växtkraft AB would at least to some extent be hidden from the procurement activities. In the woodchip case, no such formalization was applied. This meant that the public procurers were continuously exposed to, and had to negotiate, any contrasting rationalities that prevailed among the actors. This situation, as was described in Chapter 5, created some challenges that in turn reduced the possibilities of reaching the intended goal.

It would be tempting in a comparison on this account of the two cases to conclude that the endeavour in collaborative procurement projects should always be to form some kind of organization assigned with the responsibility of conducting the procurement on behalf of all involved rationalities. Such a measure would change the project from a collaborative project to an intrinsic one, which would then help to reduce the need for coordination within the project and make it possible for the procurer to act with coherence and consistency towards suppliers. This was the situation in the biofuel case. There, procurers created a situation similar to the one in the maritime radio case discussed in Chapter 3, where the procurer could work with the suppliers based on a clear and unambiguous understanding of what they wanted to achieve. It is however uncertain to what extent forming a procurer organization in itself would have changed the outcome in the woodchip case. From an institutional perspective, the differences regarding the rationalities of the stakeholders would not automatically go away merely by encapsulating them in a formal organization. In that sense, the forming of a public company, as happened in the biofuel case, should be understood more as an outcome, or a possibility that emerged in a situation where the co-owners' rationalities were already aligned. Another difference is the revenue models applied. In both the biofuel case and the maritime radio case, the procurers would pay directly for the delivered system, while the suppliers in the woodchip case would rely on future operations to earn their revenue. It may be assumed that having access to funding would increase the chances of making the suppliers and other stakeholders work towards the same goal. Such purchasing power would not however be sufficient unless the procurers also had access to adequate competence to coordinate and specify demand. Given the institutional mismatch that prevailed in the woodchip case, especially after the death of the project champion, it is uncertain to what extent such competence existed. Several of the non-competitive stakeholders affecting the evolution of the project were at the same time autonomous, in the sense that they were not economically dependent on the success of the project. Thus, even in a situation where direct funding would have been available, this might not have changed the actions of the non-commercial stakeholders.

ORGANIZING RATIONALITY REPRESENTATION

The two cases prompt a discussion on what stakeholder to include on the procurer side in public procurement of innovation projects. In the biofuel case, stakeholders that would become future users of the final system were included from the beginning, while the procurement side in the woodchip case consisted essentially of all rationalities apart from future users. In the biofuel case, the future operator of the facility, Växtkraft AB, carried out the procurement project. Stakeholders that would be a part of the system once in operation, as co-owners of Växtkraft AB, were also indirectly included. One example is the farmer members of Odlar-gruppen, interested in finding a market that would enable a shift from growing food to growing crops that could be used for energy production. The woodchip case, on the other hand, evolved as a catalyst and in a way also a distributed procurement process, where the role of the public procurers at Bracknell Forest was to facilitate the process, not to operate the power plant. Instead, the builder and future operator was to be allocated through the procurement process. In the woodchip case the procurer side included rationalities that were relevant for promotion of secondary rationalities that would not have a direct operative interest in the power plant once it was built. TV Energy and the BRP, for instance, as was discussed in the previous chapter, represented primarily other rationalities: in the case of TV Energy the promotion of sustainable technology in general, and in the case of the BRP the ambition to build a new town centre.

The observation that the rationalities of the future operations were included on the procurer side in the biofuel case but excluded in the woodchip case is noteworthy. In the biofuel case, any critical requirement from the future operator could be integrated into the project from the beginning. As will be discussed further below, several other issues related to the operations of the future power plant were also dealt with before the actual tender call was published. One example of such foresight was the securing of commitments by certain target groups on which the future operation would rely. In the woodchip case, such operator access would have been established only after identification of the supplier/operator, that is, after the contract had been awarded. This means that the whole pre-procurement phase where the project was defined lacked a stake-holder that would advocate the operator's rationality. One can only speculate what would have happened if the operator perspective had been included in the pre-procurement phase of the project. Maybe what were now given as reasons for not submitting a bid at all could, if incorporated and dealt with, have helped to produce a different outcome.

INTERACTION FOR INNOVATION

The previous section tried to compare the two cases in terms of involved rationalities in relation to how the two projects were organized. The concern was with who was involved on the 'inside' of the two projects, which turned out to be an exercise transgressing formal borders. The analysis reflected an awareness of the distinction between endogenous rationalities and exogenous organizations. One could otherwise on formal grounds claim that the public procurers at Bracknell Forest were the procurers in the woodchip case and then ignore the fact that several other actors played important roles for the outcome of the project. One could as well claim that Växtkraft AB was the sole procurer in the biofuel case and then ignore that this company encapsulated other rationalities that also played important roles for the outcome of the project. Thus what would essentially be a formal or exogenous analysis would probably fail to notice that organizations may embed different rationalities and also have different means to deal with them. A discussion on interaction shares the same challenge. The assertion that innovation requires interaction between users and producers is well established, but is also, as will be argued here, an assertion in need for clarification. The inferred idealized understanding of public procurement of innovation as a demand-side tool, where the procurer places an order that is satisfied after interaction with the supplier, becomes especially problematic. First, as was alluded to above, the cases raise concern regarding how to determine what actor belongs to what side, the procurer side or the supply side. Second, situations may occur when interaction per se is still not sufficient, for instance in situations of institutional mismatch, as seen in the woodchip case.

Both the cases included interaction with different stakeholders such as public agencies, suppliers and other forms of organization. The problem as revealed in the two cases is that establishing what actors belong to the procurer side and to the supplier side is not a completely straightforward task – at least not if one assumes the sides to be distinct from each other. As we saw in the biofuel case, the farmers as represented by Odlargruppen were part of the procurer side as members of the Växtkraft board, and at the same time were a part of the future solution; they were the future suppliers of ley crops as well as customers paying for the fertilizers. In the sense that the whole project emerged as a response to the endeavour to develop an alternative to conventional farming, one could say that the farmers provided demand as well as parts of the supply, if not to the construction, then at least to the operation of the innovation to be built. In the woodchip case, the starting point for the whole project was the perceived need for a completely new town centre in order to sustain economic growth. In addition there was also pressure from paradigmatic and political rationalities emphasizing sustainable energy. The procurers at the local council facilitated in that sense a procurement process driven by demand from others. Although they were formally in charge of the procurement process, they did not fully play the role of demand-side agent placing a bid to stimulate private sector innovation, as envisaged in the idealized understanding of how to conduct public procurement as a demand-side innovation tool.

INTERACTION WITH THE EXTERNAL ENVIRONMENT

Up to this point the discussion has evolved mainly around interaction between endogenous stakeholders in one way or another connected to the procurement process. Another difference revealed in the comparison between the cases concerns interaction with the external environment, that is, stakeholders that do not fit neatly into the procurer–supplier dichotomy. This was especially pertinent in the biofuel case, where procurers extended their interaction to include stakeholders not directly involved in the contract. Over the years several different meetings were held with organizations and groups that could affect or be affected by the project. The procurers interacted with environmental authorities, city planning authorities, the Swedish food industry, the KRAV (environmental labelling) organization, voluntary environmental organizations, public consumer organizations and the Swedish Association of Waste Management. The way stakeholders (other than the procurer and the suppliers) were utilized was not only in terms of discussions or the sharing of information. An array of these external stakeholders played a concrete role in relation to the risk management and the decision to go ahead with the project (see Table 6.2). It appears that this interaction with external bodies was significant for the success of the project. Without the consent of these stakeholders, the project would not have been able to proceed. Long-term agreements with local farmers were set up to ensure sufficient supply of ley crops to be used by the bio-plant. Long-term agreements for buying biofuel were set up with the local bus company to guarantee a supply market for the product biofuel. Required legal documents, for example related to environmental laws, had to be in place. There was also an issue regarding the fertilizers the system would generate, and its intended role in relation to production of human food. Before commencing with the project, the procurers obtained an approval document from the food industry verifying that the fertilizers that would come out of the system could be used for food production. People who lived near the location for the planned system were also consulted.

Table 6.2.   Summary of identified target groups and purpose of interaction in the bio-fuel case (Agroptigas, 2005).

Target group	Purpose of interaction
Households and real estate companies	Anchoring the goals of the project, get input for choice of collecting system
Gas customers	Raise interest for the project, get input about users' demand on a fuelling station
Municipalities and other suppliers	Anchoring the goals of the project, establish a business relation
Food industry (dairy associations, grain association, meat association, ecological farming association)	Quality assurance and establish acceptance of technology, agreement on use of digestate.
Farmers	Involve a sufficient number of farmers.
Politicians, authorities, interest groups	Anchoring the goals for the project. For the environmental legislation; get permit according to environmental legislation

In the woodchip case, as was discussed in the previous chapter, different organizations were also allowed to influence the project in significant ways. In that sense, the public procurers in the woodchip case were open to any stakeholders presenting themselves with opinions on how the project should evolve. There were however some stakeholders not included in the woodchip case that were included in the biofuel case. As the buildings in the new town centre were yet to be built there were no tenants available. Any ambition to interact with future tenants in the pre-procurement phase was therefore impossible. The situation was the same for interaction with the supplier and future operator and any stakeholders that the supplier and future operator considered it important to include. It could be argued that in order to make sense such supplier–stakeholder interaction would take place only when the operator had won the contract, that is, when the supplier knew it would build the energy centre. The problem was that the commitments ideally coming from such interactions would be required to establish the commercial feasibility of the project, which was a requirement for being able to place a bid in the first place. Without them, the suppliers were not prepared to take the risk. In this sense the project in its own 'absolute simplicity' created its own institutional barriers that reduced the possibilities for interaction (Heller, 1994). Thus, there is an institutional explanation as to why this interaction did not take place in the woodchip case: the institutional set-up of the project did not allow it.

In sum, six categories of rationalities, or institutional ranges, emerge that appear to be worth considering in public procurement of innovation projects of this kind. All these played a role either to enable a successful outcome or, when they were not sufficiently formed or taken properly into account, to help to spoil the project. They are displayed in Table 6.3. The procurer category would essentially refer to the ability to formulate and, to the extent it is required in the given situation, coordinate demand. What appears to be a central component is a clear understanding of what is the intended outcome of the project. Supplier rationality refers to the need to design a procurement procedure to meet commercial rationalities for the suppliers that build the procured system. This can be achieved by being able to offer a price that corresponds to the suppliers' efforts associated with delivering the requested innovation. A procurement project does not end when the procured item is built and/or delivered. Success might be determined by the proceeding operations. Therefore the rationalities of the future operators should also be taken into account. In catalytic procurement where the builder and operator are the same entity, this would mean helping to organize the procurement process in such a way that uncertainties and operational risks could be managed to the extent that the commercial feasibility of operations is already attained in the pre-procurement phase. Another post-procurement rationality to consider is future suppliers to the operations. Especially when the innovation requires the opening up of new supply markets, certain support activities may be required in order to make sure that such supply markets exist when operations commence. Both the cases discussed here relied for example on the establishing of markets for the supply of fuel (e.g. bio-waste, ley crops, woodchip) to the power plant. Another category is operational customers, in the cases discussed here, for example, tenants buying energy, operators of vehicles running on biofuel, or farmers using bio-fertilizers. The final rationality, other institutional actors, was mostly seen in the biofuel case. Examples are the agreements and certificates obtained to enable the use of the fertilizers coming from the power plant for food production. Another example would be the households situated close to where the new power plant would be built. If the new power plant would lead to increased noise levels, bad smells and other potential environmental impacts, this would potentially produce problems for the operations.

Table 6.3. Rationalities to include in interaction for public procurement of innovation

Procurer
The supplier of the technology
The operator of the technology supplied
The suppliers to the operations
Customers of the operations
Other institutional actors

THE ROLE OF SPECIFICATIONS AND OTHER REQUIREMENTS

In both projects, specifications had an impact on the outcome. The way specifications were used varied between the two projects. In the biofuel case, the tender call was set up following the principles of performance-based procurement (PBP) (Wade and Björkman, 2004). In practice this meant that the procurers defined how much biogas the intended system should be able to deliver, not specifically how that should be achieved. This approach is an alternative to traditional design–bid–build contracts, where a design is produced followed by a tender process for building the facility based on the design. Instead, PBP is an integrated process where both the design and the building or implementing are integrated into the same contract. Rather than giving detailed technical specifications for how the procured item should work the procurer specifies the function wanted, leaving it to the supplier to figure out how the function should be implemented. One consequence of such a set-up is that the supplier is free to develop a solution that best fits its own capabilities. The principle applied in the woodchip case was also different from a design–bid–build set-up. The winner of the contract was supposed to build and operate the power plant. What was different from the biofuel case was the rather explicit demand for renewable technologies, which worked to restrict such freedom of action and also therefore to reduce the variety among bidders. As was discussed in Chapter 5, in retrospect one could argue that formulating a specification that would have encouraged innovative solutions while still allowing more conventional solutions might have been a better option. *Ceteris paribus*, such an innovation-friendly approach would also have failed to find a supplier delivering state-of-the-art sustainable technology. It would have been possible though to find a supplier working with conventional technology. This point of course raises a question outside the scope of this book of what would be the second-best option: if no sustainable solution were to be offered, would a solution based on existing non-sustainable technology be better than no solution at all?

Another aspect of the specification concerned the configuration of the bidding side. Here the two projects applied two different approaches. In the biofuel case, the finalization of the complete system relied on several different suppliers, where each supplied a component of the system. The size of the supplying firms was not an issue. The contracts awarded included only construction of the facility, not future operations. In the woodchip case, on the other hand, smaller firms and firms that could not document technological experience on the scale corresponding to the intended system were excluded. The tender call in the woodchip case was also set up with a financial requirement. As the future ESCO would have to be able to finance the project, the procurers assumed that this would imply a fairly large firm. The specific requirement of size, however, prevented the possibility of an ESCO to be formed by a consortium of smaller firms.

THE ROLE OF CHAMPIONS

Several of the cases discussed in this book justify a discussion on the role of technology champions understood as 'powerful individuals' (Rogers, 1995, p. 398) who act to pave the way for the introduction of an innovation. It could be argued that the rationalities of the champion should ideally converge with the rationalities of the procurer. This would typically occur in intrinsic public procurement of innovation. In such situations the role of the champion becomes less visible, as institutional alignment has already occurred. This at least was the situation in the maritime radio case, as discussed in Chapter 3. The technology champion may also play a role to promote the procurement and use of an innovation, although the procurement process is carried out elsewhere. One example is the case of the patient briefcase, discussed briefly in Chapter 7, where the head physician played an important champion role, especially in the early development stages of the innovation. The importance of technology champions in general is emphasized further if one looks at situations where no such person is available. One of the problems in the case with the silver-coated catheter, as discussed in Chapter 4, was that the use of catheters in general lacked a champion that could have promoted the diffusion of the innovative catheter. The two cases discussed in this chapter also offer similar insights.

In the biofuel case Lennart Björkman, an engineer with vast experience from similar projects, was attached to the procurement project. Although he was an external person, one could consider his role as a champion of the project, perhaps not as a provider of the intrinsic vision and justification for the project itself, but for the belief and skills required to pull through the procurement project. For the woodchip case, the individual who played this role until his death was Terry Mills. Some of the coordination problems encountered may be explained by the champion void that occurred. Studies of firms exposed to unexpected death in the top management also suggest that this leads in general to 'disruptive shock', where negative effects are lower in more stable and routinized organizations (Gjerløv-Juel, 2012). If a project is thought of as a relatively 'unstable' environment, it could be argued that without the technology champion any public procurement of innovation project will succumb to the prevailing institutional mismatch. In the wood-chip case this effect manifested in delays, unclear goals and eventually pre-procurement termination without finding a supplier interested in the contract.

DIFFUSION OF INFORMATION

Both projects were exposed to the requirement to diffuse information of the projects to others. Although other factors considered in this chapter are more central for the outcomes of these projects, this particular requirement still affected the projects in different ways, and the analysis of its role reveals some institutional phenomena. In both cases the requirement of knowledge diffusion essentially came with the EU funding from which both projects were benefiting. One difference between the cases was how this requirement was perceived among different actors. The stakeholders in the biofuel case appear to have complied with this requirement rather well. There was, for instance, a website set up displaying all kinds of information on the project. Although one could argue that the woodchip case did not reach a point where similar actions would make sense, it is still noteworthy that the perception of the knowledge diffusion requirement was not received very sympathetically

among some of the stakeholders. There is also an institutional explanation for this difference. In the biofuel case, many of the information
diffusion activities were placed upon the public procurer. In the woodchip
case, the suppliers and future operators of the energy centre were
supposed to play a larger role. As we saw in the previous chapter, the
suppliers did not appreciate this assignment, which in turn reflects the
difference between the political and paradigmatic rationalities of public
actors and private firms. The suppliers put more emphasis on the
technical and economic aspects of building and operating the energy
centre and less emphasis on the political rationalities associated with
knowledge diffusion. This appears also to have been the case with the
suppliers in the biofuel case. As far as this study goes, the suppliers did
not play an important role in diffusing information about the project. The
procurer in the biofuel case, acting on behalf of an array of public
agencies, was more appreciative of such political rationalities. So,
although both projects identified the builder/operator as a central agent
for knowledge diffusion, the difference was that in the biofuel case this
concerned a public agency, while in the woodchip case it was a private
firm. For the woodchip case, it could perhaps be argued that a better
choice would have been to assign the information diffusion tasks to the
local council. However, although the propensity to take part in such
diffusion activities would probably be higher for the public agency, it
would not have access to the profound knowledge of operations the
operator would have.

PUBLIC COMMITMENT ...

Commitment is a central notion in public procurement of innovation.
Public commitment expressed in a tender call can convince a supplier to
engage in R&D activities in an otherwise risky and uncertain situation
(Fridlund, 1999; Palmberg, 2002; Berggren and Laestadius, 2003). Public
commitment can manifest itself in different forms, where the most basic
form is the promise to credit the supplier against the delivered innovation. The procurer can also act to establish commitment from others, as
was seen in the biofuel case, discussed above. In general, public
commitment was an issue in both cases, but in different ways. In the
biofuel case, the procurers made an effort to establish commitment not
only through the procurement contracts but also through an array of
different stakeholders not directly involved in the procurement project
although still critical for the future operation of the power plant. In the
woodchip case, one could argue, the project could have increased its

commercial viability and chances of success if the importance of commitment had been emphasized more.

In the biofuel case the procurer essentially performed an intrinsic procurement, offering a contract to the supplier proposing the best solution to the specified problem. This commitment meant that the builders of the different parts of the power plant could engage in their development work with the expectation of getting duly rewarded for their efforts. As was described above, the procurer also secured an array of commitments from other stakeholders. These secondary commitments were important not primarily for the builders of the power plant but for the future operator, that is, in this case for the procurer itself. Examples of this kind of institutional commitment were the clearance from the food industry to use the fertilizers that would come out of the system for food production and the acceptance from households to adjust their waste handling routines. Thus, one point to make here is that it was the procurer, acting as the future operator, that took on the role of establishing these commitments. A second point is that it undertook all these arrangements before the tender call was published. The project would then be relatively secured from encountering problems stemming from the external world. The set-up in the woodchip case was different. The contractual arrangements required the bidder and future operator to agree to form an energy service company, that is, not only design and bid but also commercially operate the power plant without knowing whether any commitments from other institutional actors could ever be achieved.

On the general level the future or potential operators were in both cases exposed to the same challenges, but the cases differed in terms of the ability of the problem owners to deal with them. A primary reason for the lack of commitment in the woodchip case, as was mentioned above, was that some of these institutional actors did not exist at the time for the procurement project. One suggestion brought forward was that the local council – a fairly significant future tenant in the renewed town centre – could, if it had wished to make such a commitment, have worked as a lever to create the initial market required for the renewable energy centre. The position held by the local council was however, as discussed in the previous chapter, based on its interpretation of the procurement law. The argument made was that such an advance commitment could not be made because it might jeopardize the requirement to secure best value for money at all times. The other possibility, as was seen in the biofuel case, would be to make the future operator facilitate the establishment of such commitments. Given the set-up of the project, this would have required suppliers to be willing to engage in quite demanding pre-procurement activities without knowing whether or not they would eventually win the contract. Thus, even if all the potential institutional actors had been available and willing to participate, the expectations of any such pre-procurement activities appear to be rather unrealistic.

... AS RISK MANAGEMENT

The discussion on commitment has a tendency to digress into a discussion on risk and risk management in relation to public procurement of innovation, an issue that has increasingly gained attention (Aho *et al.*, 2006). Even if risk management in public procurement of innovation is sometimes hard to distinguish from 'good' management in general, a few comments on the cases in the light of risk management thinking might be useful. One type of risk emerges in a societal or organizational context. For instance, '[n]ew products and services applied by public administrations to deliver services to society may meet an unforeseen lack of social acceptance (within or outside the administration), lack of compatibility with existing products and institutional routines, lack of absorptive capacity (skills, awareness, readiness to take on switching costs) in administrations, unfavourable regulatory and institutional framework conditions or unforeseen changes thereof' (Tsipouri *et al.*, 2010, p. 33). The way the procurers in the biofuel case managed interaction with stakeholders to secure commitments before the actual project was initiated provides one example of how such risks were managed. Corresponding pre-procurement establishment of commitment could not happen in the woodchip case because of the set-up, where the operator would be identified through the tender process. Instead the procurement process itself worked as a distributed form of a de facto risk management that prompted potential bidders to consider the risks they could identify in the project. The decision ultimately to refrain from bidding was essentially based on risk considerations made by the suppliers, where the most important one was the uncertainty regarding the extent to which there would be a sufficient future customer base for the energy centre once in operation.

The importance of taking early measures to deal with risk is acknowledged in the literature. The notion of early supplier involvement underscores the importance of interaction early in the design cycle as a way of managing and minimizing risk. 'With better exchange of information comes knowledge of the situations surrounding the dynamics of a supply relationship, and with that knowledge comes greater potential for detecting, averting, and managing supply risk' (Zsidisin and Smith, 2005, p. 51). What is also interesting is that 'potential for product failure is minimized by problem prevention rather than through remediation' (ibid., p. 54). Early supplier involvement in the context of public procurement has also been discussed (van Valkenburg and Nagelkerke, 2006). The way the project was designed in the biofuel case gave the procurers the opportunity to take such early measures. Making agreements with other institutional stakeholders is also an example of preventing problems that could potentially emerge once the operations were commenced. The project set-up in the woodchip case left much of the risk management to the suppliers and future operators of the power plant. This might not in itself be a problem as long as the bidder could add costs associated with risk to the price offered. In this case, however, as the revenues were to be collected through the future operations, the situation was different from that in the biofuel case, where the bidders were guaranteed a certain price as agreed with the procurer. The bidders in the woodchip case were thus left to consider the market risks themselves. Again, any ambitions to take early measures such as establishing commitments were also reduced for the suppliers, partly because of the contract design, but also because of the fact that the future customers were not available at the pre-procurement stage. Thus, in terms of risk, the analysis here underscores the importance of other relations than strictly the classical procurer–supplier relations, as even other actors may significantly affect the outcome of public procurement of innovation projects.

EFFECTIVE AND EFFICIENT PUBLIC PROCUREMENT OF INNOVATION

Here emerges a possibility for a contrafactual discussion. One could ask what would have happened if the woodchip case had followed a similar approach to stakeholder interaction as was applied in the biofuel case. It would be tempting to suggest that the procurers in the biofuel case emphasized much more the interaction between different stakeholders and therefore became more successful than their British colleagues in realizing their demand for sustainable energy. To assume a linear relationship between how much emphasis is placed on interaction and successful outcomes of public procurement of innovation projects is however problematic. Such a claim would fail to take into account the different institutional levels and rationalities that may not be easily changed merely by interacting. One side story in the biofuel case provides a case in point. The biofuel case involved an attempt to build a power plant that was never realized. Building the biogas facility in Västerås was just a solution to a critical problem that emerged in the

Agroptigas project, namely that Växjö, a Swedish town situated some 450 kilometres south from Västerås that initially was intended to host the new facility, stepped down from the project. These developments, captured by Bengtsson *et al.* (2006), are summarized in the following.

Around 2000, Växjö worked together with two neighbouring towns, Alvesta and Ljungby, to develop routines and technology for waste handling and recycling of bio-waste. These towns, with Växjö as the leading partner, got funding to build a facility similar to the one eventually built in Västerås. The plan emerging from the project was to have the bio-waste fermentation facility in Växjö and then burn non-biological waste in a facility in Ljungby. However, there emerged various uncertainties that came to completely alter these initial intentions. A common waste handling method in Sweden at the time was simply to burn the waste without separation of bio-waste. This was also the principle followed by the waste handling facility operated by the town of Ljungby. Pressure from the EU prompted for the removal of fossil-based fuels. Many operators feared that they would be forced to adapt to waste handling systems where separation of bio-waste was carried out. After intense lobbying from Swedish towns and waste management authorities, the Swedish environmental authorities eventually interpreted the message from the EU level in such a way that it made it possible for Ljungby to commence operations without separation of bio-waste. To Ljungby, sending the bio-waste to Växjö instead of burning it at their own facility would mean a reduction of half of their revenue. The result of these developments was that Ljungby withdrew from the project. This situation prompted a search process that eventually led to the localization of the biofuel facility in Västerås. There were also other signs of the problematic situation that led to the change of localization of the facility. There was local political disagreement about the project. There were also doubts concerning its economic viability. The support from local farmers was also, at least initially, ambivalent. The fact that it was an area with large forests and that the Ljungby facility was already relying on woodchip as one of the fuels used for operations is further indication of the institutional mismatch between the project and the endogenous institutional set-up. The Ljungby situation was rather different from that in the biofuel case, where farmers for many years had worked with the idea of finding alternatives to food production. Another difference between the two Swedish cases pinpointed by Bengtsson *et al.* (2006) concerned the fundamental rationalities behind the projects. The work in Västerås was much more driven by a belief in the necessity to adjust to sustainable technologies, while decision making among its southern Swedish colleagues was mostly affected by economical rationalities.

The issues that emerged in Ljungby are to some extent similar to the situation in the woodchip case. In both cases doubts prevailed concerning economic viability. Both cases also suffered from a lack of stakeholder alignment. It could be argued that both the Ljungby case and the woodchip case were initiated by exogenous rationalities that did not fully match with the respective endogenous institutional set-up prevailing in the context in which the intended innovations were to be introduced. For Ljungby, the exogenous aspect came with the Agroptigas project and the emphasis on biofuel, which contrasted with economic endogenous rationalities and its tradition as a forest region. The exogenous starting point for the woodchip case was private landowners' initiatives to defeat town centre decline as well as exogenous pressure for sustainable technology. In the sense that end consumers were not identifiable, an essential part of the endogenous set-up was missing at the time of the tender process. The supply market for woodchip appears also to have been quite underdeveloped in comparison to the biofuel case, where ley crop producers were part of the procurer side. The Ljungby case and the woodchip cases are therefore interesting, as they help to qualify the understanding of the virtues of the different measures and steps taken by the procurers in the biofuel case. Even if the whole spectrum of measures to interact and establish commitments from stakeholders that was taken in the biofuel case had been set in motion in the woodchip case, this might not have changed the final outcome.

This gives reasons to re-evaluate the importance of the interaction. For local farmers in the biofuel case growing ley crops to be used for biofuel production would produce an alternative source of income. The realization of the biofuel plant was in that sense the manifestation of ideas discussed over many years before the procurement project was initiated. From that perspective the formal tender call was more the crowning of an endogenous process that had been ongoing for more years than the origin of the demand itself. This also casts new light on the interaction that took place between endogenous stakeholders in the project. If the project was seen as manifesting endogenously evolved demand, the institutional change required among actors to achieve an institutional match might have been relatively small. The interaction the procurers facilitated in the context of the tender process perhaps did not so much change the fundamental rationalities prevailing among actors as made endogenous institutions exogenous through formal agreements. It is in that sense possible to talk about efficient versus effective public procurement of innovation. This refers to the difference between doing the right things and doing things right. One could argue that among the success factors the procurers in the biofuel case could enjoy was the fact that they were doing the right thing in relation to the endogenous institutional set-up. One factor creating problems for the procurers in the woodchip case was that to some extent the project attempted to do the wrong thing in relation to the endogenous institutional set-up.

PUBLIC PROCUREMENT OF INNOVATION AS KNOWLEDGE CONVERSION

The typical contribution of institutional theory in relation to interaction is the focus set on the role of institutions as regulator or facilitator of the interaction. When it comes to the *outcome* of the interaction expressed in terms of institutional changes among the actors interacting, the implications are however problematic. An institutional analysis of the outcomes of interaction has sometimes the tendency to downplay the role of agency and imply a deterministic view of change (cf. Beckert, 1999; Coriat and Weinstein, 2002; Nelson and Nelson, 2002). The same tendency has also become embedded in the idealized thinking of public procurement as a demand-side tool, emphasizing purchasing power, as a means to make suppliers respond and change towards certain exogenously specified behaviours. This chapter gives reason to challenge such a dogmatic understanding, especially if the distinction between endogenous and exogenous institutions is taken into account. The dichotomy implies that an exogenous change imposed on an endogenous institutional set-up is for the endogenous institutional set-up a matter of adjusting to the exogenous change to avoid remedies, but as far as possible leaving the long-term endogenous institutional set-up unchanged. Although there is a risk of taking this point too far, one could argue that the implication for such an institutional understanding of interaction reduces the expectations of what interaction can achieve. The point would be that interaction attained to deliver innovation can be successful only if there already prevails an institutional match between the endogenous and the exogenous institutions involved. In other words, no matter what interaction tools and techniques are applied, claims about the virtues of certain interactions in a given case should be made only with caution, as successes could be explained by the prevalence of institutional match rather than any attributes ascribed to the interaction. Similarly, reasons for failure might not necessarily be found in the interaction attempted, but in the institutional mismatch among interacting agents. An attempt to set up a power plant running on ley crops in a region with a large forest industry might be such an example.

The distinction between endogenous and exogenous institutions has implications for the theoretical understanding of public procurement of innovation. Neither of the cases discussed here can be explained well by an analysis based on the understanding of public procurement of innovation as something that happens when a public agency places a bid for something which does not exist. Such a snapshot perspective may lead to an analysis that fails to take into account important developments evolving before the formal tender process is initiated. This is bad, as some of these processes might be important precursors to the context in which the formal procedure is initiated. The biofuel case gives a good example. Taking account the events that evolved before the formal procurement process, it was a project spanning 15 years (Table 6.1). Local farmers had nurtured the basic idea of growing fuel instead of food a decade before the tender call was published. In the woodchip case there was a mismatch between certain endogenous institutions and exogenous ambitions included in the tender call. The level of 'non-existence' of the technology to be procured was also similar in the cases. Neither was the level of non-existence a central reason for the termination of the tender process in the woodchip case. The result here confirms earlier conclusions that cooperative types of public procurement 'may involve more complex patterns of interaction and more complicated processes of interactive learning on the "buyer" side than does "Direct Procurement"' (Gavras *et al.*, 2006, p. 188). The question emerges therefore as to what extent there are complementary ways of analysing public procurement of innovation. To make an attempt to pursue an answer to that question, there follows here just a brief discussion on what perhaps could be labelled public procurement of innovation networks.

Although the notion of 'network' is well established both as part of normal conversation and as an academic concept, all annotations of networks may not be applicable for the purposes here (see Rolfstam, 2009b for a discussion on public procurement of innovation as network governance). Networks may establish and evolve through different drivers and within different contexts and may therefore also display specific characteristics. Public procurement of innovation networks would belong to those configurations that are neither (anonymous) markets nor hierarchies, but something in between. Building on existing literature, Sørensen and Torfing, for example, define governance networks as:

> [a] stable articulation of mutually dependent, but operationally autonomous actors from state, market and civil society, who interact through conflict-ridden negotiations that take place within an institutionalized framework of rules, norms, shared knowledge and social imaginaries; facilitate self-regulated policy making in the shadow of hierarchy; and contribute to the

production of 'public value' in a broad sense of problem definitions, visions, ideas, plans and concrete regulations that are deemed relevant to broad sections of the population. (Sørensen and Torfing, 2009, p. 236)

This definition is also fairly consistent with what Rhodes (2007) refers to as 'Policy Networks', which are 'sets of formal and informal institutional linkages between governmental and other actors structured around shared interests in public policymaking and implementation' (Rhodes, 2007, p. 1244). A central notion in Rhodes's network understanding is the dominant coalition that 'influences which relationships are seen as a problem and which resources will be sought' within the network (ibid., p. 1245). There is an interesting institutional aspect of governance networks that comes from the tendency of these networks to develop structural embeddedness (Jones *et al.*, 1997). One real-life implication of this tendency would mean that at any time already existing members of a network are favoured (in relation to the network) in comparison to those who are outside the network. It has also been taken into account in the literature that networks can sometimes exist in relation to other networks, where one network can exercise some kind of influence over the other. Such metagovernance:

> refers to higher-order governance transcending the concrete forms of govern-ance through which social and economic life is shaped, regulated and transformed. Hence, if governance is defined as a both formal and informal process through which a plurality of actors regulates a multiplicity of social, political and economic practices in accordance with some predefined goals, metagovernance can be defined broadly as 'the governance of governance'. (Sørensen and Torfing, 2009, p. 245)

One of the benefits with a network approach as outlined above is that it can be connected to theories of knowledge creation. Following Nonaka (1994, p. 14) 'innovation ... cannot be explained sufficiently in terms of infor-mation processing or problem solving. Rather, innovation can be under-stood as a process in which the organization creates and defines problems and then actively develops new knowledge to solve them.' Nonaka describes knowledge creation as interactive processes that take place in two dimen-sions, the ontological dimension and the epistemological. The ontological dimension refers to the interaction between individuals, groups, organ-izations and interorganizational interaction. The epistemological dimension refers to the interaction between tacit knowledge and explicit knowledge. Organizational knowledge leading to innovation is created from an idea that is allowed to transform between tacit and explicit modes and evolve throughout and across organizations.

Applying the Nonaka model in the analysis, drawing on an institutional framework, paves the way for an understanding of public procurement of innovation cases such as those discussed in this chapter as ideas evolving in endogenous networks eventually to become the target of formal procurement processes. In that light public procurement of innovation becomes a way of facilitating endogenous knowledge conversion (Figure 6.1). This perspective fundamentally alters how the formal procurement process should be understood. Rather than being a sign of 'demand', the formal procurement process becomes instead an interface between different networks. Examples of such networks in the cases discussed here are the farmers in the biofuel case, and the landowners and the NGOs promoting sustainable energy in the woodchip case. The fundamental implication that crystallizes from this perspective is clear. The challenge for policy makers interested in promoting public procurement of innovation is to establish an institutional match between idea-generating endogenous networks and exogenous networks. Thinking of public procurement of innovation as demand or a 'command' for innovation might lead to the risk that important underlying mechanisms are ignored, which in turn reduces the chances of successful implementation of these policies.

7. Success factors for public procurement of innovation

The initial empirical chapters of this book consisted of single-case studies. Chapter 6 then compared two cases. To complete the spectrum of possible case study designs there follows here a discussion based on eight cases. Looking at a set of cases of public procurement of innovation, each evolving in a specific context with a different degree of success, helps one to 'understand the similarities and differences between the cases' (Baxter and Jack, 2008, p. 550). Such an analysis could mimic Daniel's (1961) collection of success factors, in his case for remedying the information crisis prevailing among expanding American firms in the middle of the twentieth century. In a similar spirit, by comparing eight cases of public procurement of innovation, the current chapter explores to what extent it is possible to establish a set of success factors for public procurement of innovation projects.

The notion of 'success factors' might to some appear somewhat popular and simplistic, and therefore deserves some elaboration. 'Success factors' in this context are understood as conditions that if met in a particular case appear to work to contribute to the success of public procurement of innovation projects. These conditions can be established by the public procurer, any other stakeholders beyond the control of the public procurers, or, expressed in general terms, the context. Success factors have in that sense a dual role. In the same way as Boolean variables, they may, if met, increase the expectations of success for a project. They may also work to reduce the chances for success if they are not met. On the other hand, even if several success factors are satisfied, a project might still fail in situations where yet other success factors are not met. The importance of a specific success factor might also vary with the specific context.

CASES DRAWN ON

The cases drawn on are displayed in Table 7.1 and summarized below. Some of them are treated elsewhere in this book and will therefore not be described in detail here, while others are introduced for the first time in this chapter. The maritime radio case concerned the procurement of a new coast radio system in Norway, as was dealt with in Chapter 3. The case with the silver-coated catheter concerned the attempt to introduce an innovative catheter into NHS hospitals. This case was discussed in Chapter 4. The woodchip case dealt with the ambition to procure an innovative energy centre that was terminated without finding a supplier, as was discussed in Chapter 5. The biofuel case also involved the procurement of a power plant, but instead running on bio-waste and ley crops, introduced in Chapter 6. The case with the patient briefcase concerned the development of a communication device that allowed patients to receive consultation without being physically present at the hospital. The patient briefcase project evolved from an initially informal collaboration between a physician and a local engineering firm in Denmark. The innovation also attracted international customers. The e-ambulance case concerned the procurement of an electronic patient booking system in the Czech Republic. The procurer managed to acquire state-of-the-art technology from Taiwan, and was also able to develop some new features that would increase user value. The public safety radio case concerned a procurement project conducted by the Norwegian authorities of a radio system to be used by all emergency agencies in the country. Finally, the passive houses case summarizes events that took place in Sweden, leading to the development of innovative eight-storey passive houses built in wood.

Table 7.1   Cases of public procurement of innovation.

Case	Description
The Maritime radio case	A digital maritime radio system that would implement
The Silver-coated catheter	An attempt to procure an innovative catheter reducing risks of hospital acquired infections.
The Wood-chip case	An attempt to procure the development and operation of an energy centre.
The Bio-fuel case	A bio-gas and upgrading plant that would produce bio-fuel, distributed heating and fertilisers.
The Patient briefcase	A communication device enabling distributed health service.
The eAmbulance case	A system for electronic patient handling.
The Public safety radio Project	A shared radio system for emergency response agencies.
Passive houses	8–floor passive houses built in wood.

The Maritime Radio Case

The first case, dealt with in detail in Chapter 3, concerns how Telenor A/S, at the time the state-owned telecom agency in Norway, procured a new digital system for maritime radio communication. The project started in the late 1990s and ended with the final delivery of the system at the end of 2002. The procured system facilitated: communication between ships and land-based entities; automatic connection to land-based telephone networks; transmission of text messages (telex and e-mail); internet access; and Morse code telegraphy. Through implementation of distributed operational control (DOC), the new system made it possible to operate one radio station remotely and thus increase flexibility for operators. From the beginning of the project an expert on public procurement law was assigned to the project to monitor and safeguard compliance with the procurement directives. The project also invoked the technical expertise necessary to adequately specify what should be procured. The project leadership maintained strict policies to ensure that information exchange with the supplier always went through the project manager at Telenor. In a similar fashion, the decision procedures applied were strict, meaning that decisions were kept once they were made.

The Case with the Silver-Coated Catheter

This case study, dealt with in Chapter 4, summarized an attempt by the National Health Service (NHS) in England to procure and diffuse a new catheter throughout its trusts. This was a catheter originally developed and sold on the US market. What distinguished the silver-coated catheter from conventional catheters was anti-infective properties achieved through the use of a silver coating. The diffusion of the catheter, however, was exposed to an array of institutional barriers. One such barrier was organized scepticism among clinical staff and their requirement of a high level of proof before adopting an innovation. In comparison to the case with healthcare technologies more closely associated with specific specialities, there appeared to be no clear champion for catheters. The NHS is a relatively decentralized organization where centrally made decisions to make certain technologies available may not necessarily lead to their adoption in lower layers of the organization. Spending and returns from spending did not affect the same budget, which removed spending incentives. There were also problems in showing the value of the innovation (and hence justifying adoption). Another issue was the question of what should be removed from the budget to allow the adoption of the innovation. Commitments made in current contracts prevent the reallocating of resources.

The Woodchip Case

Also in England, Bracknell Forest Borough Council initiated a project with the intention of building a sustainable power plant running on woodchip, discussed in Chapters 5 and 6. This case involved an attempt to procure a woodchip-fuelled power plant intended to deliver sustainable energy to a renewed part of the town centre. As things developed, the procurers eventually had to terminate the project without awarding the contract. The basic reason why the project failed was that the project did not manage to negotiate the differences between rationalities and organization-specific institutional set-ups among the stakeholders. The stakeholders in the project were: Bracknell Forest Borough Council and the political leadership of the town; the Bracknell Forest Regeneration Partnership (BRP), a joint venture consisting of the major local land-owners; Thames Valley Energy (TV Energy), an organization devoted to the promotion of green energy; two EU-funded energy development projects, one of which was the CONCERTO initiative, with the purpose of promoting and diffusing new knowledge on green technologies; and potential suppliers, that is, private firms.

The Biofuel Case

This case study concerns the public procurement project that led to the development and finalization of a state-of-the-art biogas and upgrading plant in the Swedish town of Västerås. This case was discussed in more detail in the comparison exercise conducted in Chapter 6. A significant feature of the procurement project was the interaction between different stakeholders and the success in managing different stakeholders' interests and needs. Examples of organizations involved were environmental authorities, city planning authorities, the Swedish food industry, the KRAV organization, voluntary environmental organizations, public consumer organizations and the Swedish Association of Waste Management. Many of these external stakeholders played a concrete role in relation to the risk management and the decision to go ahead with the project. The original idea of developing some kind of biofuel facility came from local farmers. For them the ley crop production to be used for biofuel production would make an alternative source of income in an area where food production was not profitable. Switching to farming for biofuel production would also then be a way of keeping farmers active and therefore maintaining an open farm landscape in the area.

The Case with the Patient Briefcase

This Danish project concerns the development of the patient briefcase, a device that enabled communication between a patient and medical staff developed for patients suffering from chronic obstructive pulmonary disease (COPD), a disease that leads to a limitation of airflow to and from the lungs, often caused by tobacco smoking. The system consisted of two components: the patient briefcase supporting audio or video communication; and a work station for medical staff. The system also transferred bio-data from the patient, such as heart rate and/or blood pressure, captured by devices that could be connected to the briefcase. The new system meant that patients could be sent home from hospital within 48 hours instead of the six to seven days that would be normal hospitalization time for these kinds of patients. This would in turn free beds and reduce workload for hospital staff. It was also expected that providing out-of-hospital healthcare would in itself have positive effects on the treatment as well as quality of life in general for patients. The project involved business model innovation. The exchange mechanism eventually chosen was to lease the service enabled, not to procure the product. The rationale for leasing rather than procuring the product was that this would enable access to improved future versions of the product. For the supplier the contract offered an opportunity to move into a new market in which it lacked previous experience. The project was initiated in 2006, and the first trial patients were treated at the end of the same year. The supplier was awarded a contract by the regional authorities in 2008. By the year after, 975 patients had used the system. In 2010 the system became available through centrally procured framework agreements. The system has also attracted interest from outside Denmark. Other versions of the patient briefcase developed for other types of patients have been considered (Medisat, 2011). The budget for the project was DKK 6–10 million. DKK 1.2 million came from public project funding, and the rest from the supplier.

The project came out of discussions within a hospital unit about possible solutions for healthcare supplied outside the hospital. The first concrete event in this story was the head physician contacting a supplier active within IT, who was given what was basically a functional specification. The system was supposed to be handled by elderly patients; it should not look like a computer, and it should be water (and coffee) safe, mobile, robust and hygienic. The first version developed from this specification was revealed and modified after user evaluations, conducted initially by letting patients use the patient briefcase at the hospital, and later on by letting patients use the device from their homes. One issue for medical staff was to learn how to appear in front of the camera, that is, to be able to communicate with the patients at the same time as they operated the device. Technical aspects such as the quality of picture and sound had to be established. The response time for setting up the communication the system relied on was initially three weeks. An agreement with a telecom service provider was established that meant that a new connection for a patient briefcase would work within three hours.

The initial stages of the project appear to have run smoothly mainly because of the well-functioning collaboration between the supplier, medical staff and patients. This was an informal stage of the project conducted without any formal contracts. It could not have happened without a high level of trust prevailing between the champion of the project and the supplier. The project also attracted a lot of attention in the media. For national politicians the project harmonized well with the prevailing healthcare policy discourse in Denmark, which included reducing staff input and finding ways to deal with the emerging demographical challenges characterized by a larger share of elderly people needing to be taken care of by a decreasing pool of young people. The next step of the project envisaged by the developers was to diffuse the patient briefcase to other hospitals in the region. It was here, however, that the project stalled. The regional officials could not see how funding from the regional level could be allocated to the project. An illustrative point is that the developer's first commercial contract was not with the health authority that had hosted the initial developments, but with health authorities in Norway. The supplier, used to conventional business-to-business interaction, perceived the public partner to be slow.

Although the project delivered an innovative device, the most problematic challenges appear not to have been technical but concerned instead how to extend the project beyond the local hospital. The regional authorities lacked an organization able to support the further evolution of the project. There were no natural resources for advice on legal and other formal aspects of the development project. The first months of the project evolved with a strong focus on the technical aspects of the project. After a while, however, there emerged an awareness of issues such as intellectual property rights, contracts, patient data integrity and so on. The developers struggled to find advice on these issues in-house, within the region or among the universities. Ultimately DKK 1 million was spent on lawyers' fees to draw up a contract. It might be argued that, as the medical staff provided input and were heavily involved in the usability aspects of the development of the patient briefcase, a royalty for the hospital would be reasonable. This was also a part of the initial agreement. In the second agreement negotiated (after the expiration of the first one), however, the contract between the supplier and the hospital was reduced to a service contract, and intellectual property rights were to remain with the supplier. In this case, the firm that carried out the pre-commercial development also became the supplier of the commercial solution. This could be done if no one else was able to deliver something similar. The intention to sign the contract was officially communicated in the national media, and any competitors were given three weeks' response time to challenge this intention. If any competitor firm had come forward, a commercial tender call would have been issued. As it did not happen, the contract was awarded without a formal tender procedure.

The E-Ambulance Case[1]

In 2010, in the Czech Republic, the Vysočina Region and Jihlava Hospital initiated the e-ambulance project, aiming at procuring a system for electronic patient handling. The system was supplied by the Institute for Information Industry (III), a Taiwanese NGO established in 1979, through the joint efforts of the public and private sectors, supported by the Taiwanese Ministry of Economic Affairs. The idea of the project was to increase the efficiency and quality of the registration service provided by the hospital to the region's citizens through the introduction of an innovative online registration system. The solution that was selected built on an existing system, which was modified to fit the local context. There were also some new features added by engineers on the procurer side. The implementation of the system began in April 2010. After tests conducted in autumn 2010, the system was fully operational by spring 2011. The system installed in the Jihlava Hospital was a pilot installation, to be followed by installations in the whole network of regional hospitals in Vysočina. The project utilized state-of-the-art non-European know-how from Taiwan in order to raise the level of healthcare services. Apart from improving the user experience and providing a more efficient patient handling system for health providers, the project also raised prestige. It would help to sustain the recognition of Vysočina as the leading 'e-health region' in the Czech Republic.

The case provides an interesting example of a public procurement project leading to a combination of diffusion and innovation. This was a diffusion project in the sense that the solution was based on an existing system that had been developed elsewhere. The system eventually installed however had undergone several modifications. Changes were made in the design of the user interface, taking into account differences between the graphic cultures of European and Taiwanese users. The patient registration procedure was simplified towards higher user-friendliness. Tasks that required the user to click three times in the original system required only one click in the new version. An automated report generating utility was added to the system at the request of doctors and management of the hospital as well as of the region. For doctors, a summary of patients' records was introduced, as well as a 'blacklist' function implemented to keep track of patient registering for doctors' appointments without showing up. After the third time of not showing up, users are removed from the system, with restrictions on future registration. This function would then release hospital resources for genuine patients. The Czech version also included a notification service for patients that would confirm and remind patients about booked appointments through e-mail and/or SMS.

The project evolved similarly to the phases specified in the pre-commercial procurement model. There was a feasibility study where different solutions were explored. This was followed by a prototype phase where the existing system was adjusted to the local context. Then followed a pilot test phase at the regional hospital in Jihlava. For the pilot project a multidisciplinary team was created of experts from Vysočina Regional Authority, Jihlava Hospital and a Taiwanese team. From the Czech side, the project manager was dedicated from the administrative staff of Vysočina Regional Authority. The team included experts from the regional IT department as well as from Jihlava Hospital IT department. The Taiwanese partner created a project team consisting of members with extensive e-hospital and e-healthcare experience from III, e-ToYou International Inc. (a subsidiary company of III) and Soloman Solution Services Corporation (a cooperative partner of III). The supplier team was managed by an account manager and the procurer side was managed by a project manager. After completion of the pilot phase, a commercial phase would conclude the project, leading to the system being installed for all Vysočina Region hospitals. As the overall costs for the implementation of the e-registration system were under the threshold values requiring a formal procurement procedure, no other procurement procedures were required.

One interesting feature of the project was the sharing of the costs. The procurer and the selected supplier agreed to share the costs of the prototype and pilot phases. This set-up also meant sharing the R&D risks, as both partners would be affected should the project fail. Thus this project started out as a project where the partners shared costs and risks, ending as a commercial public procurement project. The overall budget of the pilots was slightly over €120 000. Two-thirds of this funding came from Vysočina and, interestingly, the remaining one-third from Taiwanese national funds.

The Public Safety Radio Project

This case concerns the procurement of a new digital TETRA-based radio system for the emergency response authorities in Norway. The project meant a shift from analogue radio systems to a digital safety system, as well as a shift from separate systems to a system shared by the different authorities. Thus, apart from the rather radical technical features offered by the new technology, this organizational innovation was central to the project. The project also reflected an increased emphasis on the importance of communication between responding units from different branches of the emergency services, derived from conclusions drawn from emergency cases occurring in the recent past (DSB, 2000). This meant that the new system had to take into account user requirements for three public agencies, the National Police Directorate, the Directorate for Civil Protection and Emergency Planning (responsible for the fire and rescue service) and the Directorate for Health and Social Affairs. The new system would not only facilitate interdepartmental communication but also lead to cost savings for the community as a result of synergy effects (Norwegian Government, 2004, p. 2). One technical improvement in the system was the ability to prevent unauthorized monitoring of the radio traffic (ibid., p. 3).

The important dates for the project are shown in Table 7.2. The need for the renewal of a communication system was first reported to the Norwegian parliament in 1997. The Norwegian parliament gave the go-ahead to the project in the budget proposition for 2005. It was decided that procurement should be financed in its entirety by investments granted in the national budget, and that the state would be the owner of the technical components required for the realization of the procurement project. This, it was argued, would obviate costly funding solutions and provide better control of the safety network (ibid., p. 10). The proposition also emphasized that the tender specifications should be made technologically neutral, that is, in terms of functionality as perceived by the end user. Another requirement was robustness of the network and the technologies eventually chosen. The intention was to avoid the project becoming purely a development project (ibid., p. 10).

Table 7.2.   Important dates in the procurement project.

Autumn, 1995	Pre-study carried out
May, 1996	Pre-study published
Autumn, 1998	Initiation of feasibility study
Spring, 2000	Initiation of pilot study
5 March 2001	Publication of report from the feasibility study
24 March 2000	Tender call for pilot study
12 March 2001	Enquiry for consultancy services in preparing an invitation to tender
7 August 2004	Publication of TETRA pilot project final report
2 December 2004	Norwegian Parliament decision to procure a new digital radio communication system
15 December 2004	Tender Call Published: The delivery of Norwegian Public Safety Radio Network, Services and Control Rooms

The procurement consisted of the following elements: realization of the radio network with subsequent operation and maintenance; equipment in the control rooms of the services integrated in the network; and radio terminals for the users (hand-held and vehicle-mounted). This NOK 3.6 billion project included installation of new technology in 2000 existing telecommunication rooms, in aerial masts and in tunnels. New equipment needed to be installed in emergency control centres, emergency wards, centres for doctors on call, fire stations and police stations. Around 37 000 vehicle-mounted and hand-held radio terminals were to be procured (Norwegian Government, 2004). This was a rather big project that relied on several different contracts, for instance: framework agreements on consultancy services; a specific tender process for the installation of equipment used in a pilot study before the full-scale implementation; and the tender process for the full implementation of the system. In order to prepare for the specification of the main system, different positions were offered by the Department of Justice. In 2001, the department advertised to employ a head engineer, senior adviser, senior engineers, and a secretary to be located in Oslo (Department of Justice and the Police, 2001). This meant that traditional employment procedures were applied in order to attach competences to the project.

Three distinct learning activities are identifiable in the pre-procurement phase, which suggests that the procurers had to deal with uncertainty.

There was a pre-study, a feasibility study and a pilot study before the full commercial tender process was initiated. The pre-study gathered user requirements. The market was also surveyed for potential solutions. After the identification of several technological advantages as well as taking into consideration that TETRA was about to become an established standard in Europe, this option was chosen (Teleplan, 1999). The feasibility study concluded that existing radio technology was not meeting emerging demands. With the application of TETRA technology, the emergency agencies would be able to use one technical platform in a common network with a nationwide coverage. It would still be possible for users to have their 'own' communication network within the nationwide network. Through the possibility of sending text messages, images, geographical positions or parts of maps offered by the TETRA technology, the use of the resources would be more efficient. Other qualities associated with the TETRA-based system were the improved sound quality, the ability to protect communication from being monitored, and the possibility of retrieving database information via the network. Apart from these technical innovations, the TETRA-based system would also offer a reduction in cost through economies of scale, as compared to the case if the emergency agencies developed their own systems. A further point favouring the TETRA-based solution was found in relation to the Schengen Convention, article 44, where the importance of communication between countries, in particular in border areas, was stressed; as several other countries had chosen the TETRA standard, it suggested that Norway would do the same.

In 2000, a pilot project was initiated and a TETRA-based digital radio system was established in the Trondheim region. The pilot system was operational from autumn 2000 to June 2003. The purpose of the project was to evaluate technical, financial and organizational issues associated with the implementation of the safety network (Department of Justice and the Police, 2004). The final report from the pilot project concluded that the TETRA-based system satisfied the emergency services' most important requirements for radio communication, both within individual agencies and between different agencies, and also that the technology was mature enough for operational use. The tender call for the full-scale implementation of the system was published in 2004. The full contract was awarded to Nokia Siemens Networks two years later. The implementation of the system was to be done in two steps. The initial step included the Oslo area and 53 other municipalities in eastern Norway. The second step included implementation in the remaining parts of the country. Step 1 was delayed by two years. The initial budget for the first implementation step was NOK 900 million. The actual implementation cost increased by 18 per cent (DNK, 2011). The main reasons for these problems appear to be found in the coordination challenges associated with the project. One of the main experiences gained was that the project 'was complicated by the fact that the three departments for emergencies each had a long list of functionalities that they wanted the public safety network to fulfil, but few of them knew what was economically feasible. Moreover, it was difficult to get three autonomous departments to work together' (Sylvest, 2008, p. 51).

The Case of Passive Houses

In the mid-2000s the public housing company Hyresbostäder i Växjö, owned by Växjö Kommunföretag AB, a public company in turn owned by Växjö Municipality in Sweden, engaged in a project leading to the production of eight-storey homes built in wood utilizing passive energy solutions. It was the combination of both these features, multi-storey buildings in wood applying passive technologies, that was the central innovative component in the project. Historically, building wooden houses with that number of storeys was not allowed in Sweden. It became possible as a result of a change in the legislation. Although passive houses had been built in Germany since the early 1990s, these principles were not particularly common in Sweden at that point.

The new houses did not have any central heating systems. Instead they utilized passive technologies that captured heat energy from inhabitants and electrical equipment. Hot water was delivered to flats partly through distributed heating and partly by reusing heat energy in outgoing waste water. Heat in outgoing air was also recycled back to the house. It was claimed that using wood would reduce the energy consumption in the building process. Another claim was that using wood would increase sustainability, as it would produce less carbon dioxide than other building materials. Each flat was equipped with a device that measured consumption of cold and hot water and energy consumption. This device was associated with expectations of changing user behaviour. The idea was that giving tenants the opportunity to monitor energy consumption would reduce their level of consumption. Another factor, which came with the permission to build taller buildings in wood, was a concern for fire safety. The houses were equipped with fire extinguishers and fire alert systems that would shut down the electrical supply if smoke was detected. The users of the new homes, the inhabitants, had to adjust their behaviour somewhat in terms of ventilation habits as compared to living in conventional houses. Inhabitants would also undergo fire safety training.

Solar panels placed on the roofs of the houses were expected to produce 28 000 kWh per year.

The gains for the procurers were that the project communicated awareness of environmental issues. The project also attracted publicity and attention in the media. This harmonized well with the general policy development in Växjö Municipality, where environmental issues and energy efficiency had been emphasized for many years. There were some expectations that this project would help to change building practices towards green technologies and energy efficiency. Another expectation was that the project would help to stimulate the local wood industry. The project was also justified because it would create new homes for a community where there was a shortage of homes. Some key events of the project are summarized in Table 7.3.

Table 7.3.   Key events of the passive houses case

May 2006	Pre-study finished
2007	Tender call. Negotiated procedure with a tender's notice
25 April 2008	Project lounge
January – September 2008	Development meetings
March 2009	First house pressure tested

The houses were supplied by NCC, one of the leading Nordic construction and property development companies, employing approximately 20 000 employees, in collaboration with architects BSV Värnamo and Seth Bengtsson and a set of other sub-suppliers: Martinssons byggsystem, Gröna Rum, Service and Klimat AB, NVS Installation, ELUB and Siemens. Attached to the building project were different research projects funded by the Swedish Governmental Agency for Innovation Systems.

The idea to use wood was not in the project initially, but was introduced in the post-procurement development phase, essentially reflecting a policy decision made by municipality leaders to stimulate the local wood industry. The use of wood was initially not a fully understood process. For instance, there was a risk that the wood would crack and not be energy-efficient enough. Using wood required some extra considerations in order to comply with fire safety standards. In general there seems to have been a lot of interactive learning going on between the procurer, supplier and different experts attached to the project as new ideas and problems emerged. There were also organized training activities for the contracted staff working with the project. The project interacted with the local city planning council and the fire and rescue service. A series of assessments concerning energy consumption, humidity and temperatures was conducted.

For the procurer, Hyresbostäder i Växjö, emphasizing energy efficiency and sustainability was not really a new rationality. It had over the years conducted several projects generating experiences in energy-efficient housing. In that sense it was a 'competent procurer'. In addition, the supplier had long experience in construction. There were however some project-specific uncertainties that were managed in different ways. Concerning the uncertainties about the market for the new flats, the political leadership decided that it would accept that not all the flats would be occupied from the start. In principle the risk was also distributed in the owner structure. On a general level the procurers acted on municipality decisions. If any problems had occurred, the chances are that the political decision makers, rather than the procuring agency, would be the ones to take the blame. For the procurers, a more risky situation would have been if they had engaged in procurement activities where energy efficiency and sustainability were not promoted.

The supplier was responsible for coordinating the supply-side subcontractors and expertise necessary to deliver according to specification. In that sense the supplier carried the risk in the actual project. Fines (0.5 per cent of the total cost of the project) would be paid by the supplier for each new week a deliverable did not meet the contract specification. The supplier also conducted a risk and opportunity analysis before submitting the bid. In the budget money was allocated to cover unforeseeable cost related to the perceived risks. One keystone event of the project was to pressure-test the buildings before delivery. The supplier performed these tests ahead of the contract deadline to allow room for any improvements before the deadline.

Different research activities funded by Swedish national agencies were involved in the project. The project was also a part of the Sustainable Energy Systems in Advanced Cities (SESAC) project funded by the European Commission. In that sense, the project contributed to the development and diffusion of knowledge that might contribute to further development of the usage of green and energy-efficient technologies in housing production.

SUCCESS FACTORS FOR PUBLIC PROCUREMENT OF INNOVATION

'Failure' is in general understood as lack of its counterpart, 'success', and is often feared because with it come different kinds of damage, such as bad reputation, the risk of losing one's job or any other punishment. This is problematic, especially in innovation, when failure is a natural vehicle for learning towards subsequent success (Rolfstam, 2001). Successful projects might also incorporate 'failure-like' experiences, useful for doing things even better next time. For the purpose of the exercise conducted here, success is understood as public procurement of innovation projects that delivers the initially expected outcome. Taking what in this light becomes a snapshot view, four of the cases, the maritime radio case, the biofuel case, the e-ambulance case and the passive houses case, appear successful in the sense that the innovative item was delivered. This happened also for three of the other cases, the patient briefcase, the silver-coated catheter and the public safety radio. In these cases, however, the procurers encountered certain problems producing outcomes that did not fully live up to the initial expectations. Again, given success understood as something being eventually acquired, one of the cases falls outside that group. In the woodchip case, the procurers had to terminate the project without identifying a supplier. This variation opens up the possibility of comparing and identifying a pattern of common features in successful projects and also common features of not-so-successful projects. If the projects are compared, a number of success factors emerge. These are discussed in the following.

Expertise on Public Procurement Procedures and Relevant Law

What might appear a trivial remark is that public procurement of innovation requires access to knowledge of the underlying legal framework and the procurement process itself. However, for some of the cases this was a lack that affected the projects in a negative way.

One important feature of the maritime radio case and the biofuel case was that the public procurers made an effort to allocate expertise on procurement law to the project. In the maritime radio case, an engineer recruited in-house was assigned to the task to maintain legal compliance. This task was accentuated up to the point where the contract was awarded. The engineer participated for instance in the negotiation meetings to ensure that any information given from one supplier did not leak to any other supplier. In the biofuel case, the expertise task was fulfilled by an experienced consultant who worked in the initial stages of the project. In the case of the public safety radio net, legal expertise among other consultancy services was acquired through specific tender calls. In the passive houses case the procurers relied on both in-house competence and externalized knowledge in producing manuals to proceed with the project. In the e-ambulance case, a formal tender process was avoided, as the value of the procured system was below threshold values. In the case of the patient briefcase, the procurers had to seek and sometimes pay for external legal advice on the European level and from domestic lawyers before the commercial contract could be awarded. For the woodchip case, one might argue that lack of legal confidence on the procurer's side as well as lack of legal awareness among suppliers affected the outcome in a negative way. The procurer chose not to make any commitment as a future customer of the planned power plant, because it feared that such an act would be against the EC directives. These findings suggest that it is important to allocate *competence* on public procurement law to projects dealing with public procurement of innovation.

Technical Competence for the Specification

An often discussed element of public procurement of innovation is the specification. The application of a functional specification is often stressed, that is, the procedure where desired functions and outcomes rather than technical details of the item to be procured are given. One should note, however, that the application of functional specifications should not be regarded as a generic solution to any problem that may occur. The procurer must still have a clear understanding of the intended outcomes. This might be more critical than the application of functional specifications per se.

The maritime radio case to some extent, the biofuel case, the case with the patient briefcase and the passive houses case applied a functional specification. Interestingly these cases also included a high level of 'procurement competence' on the procurer side, that is, they knew what they wanted to achieve. In both the maritime radio case and the biofuel case, sufficient technical competence for the specification was available. In the maritime radio case, the project manager had made an effort to draw on existing knowledge and experiences to define the requirements of the radio system to be procured. In the biofuel case, an experienced consultant added the necessary competence. In the passive houses case, the procurer used a functional specification that was incomplete in the sense that the idea of using wood could be included in the project after the contract had been awarded. Although the development of the case of the patient briefcase was stalled at the upscaling stage of the project, the initial functional specifications given by the head physician worked very well to generate the prototype that provided the starting point for the project. Functional specifications were also applied in the case of the public safety radio net. This case also included an interesting tension between the initial pre-procurement learning activities and the specifications in the tender call. The conclusion arrived at through the pre-study, the feasibility study and the pilot test was that the system to be procured should be based on the TETRA standard, which would lead to exclusion of any other solutions. Even if one of the bids ultimately submitted was based on other standards, it could be argued that the quite specific recommendations arrived at in the pre-procurement phase undermined the potential benefits of applying functional specifications (Sylvest, 2008). Another specification challenge in the case of the public safety radio net was that three different emergency agencies were supposed to agree on one specification. The fact that this was not easily achieved constituted one reason why the project was delayed. In the woodchip case, the issue related to the specification can be seen in the restricting effect the tender call requiring green technologies had on suppliers. Had the requirements been formulated in a more open manner, solutions based on already existing technologies could have been submitted. The tender call also assumed the supplier to be a fairly big firm, which excluded any bids from smaller firms. In the case with the silver-coated catheter the innovation was identified after an open call to the market, where suppliers were asked to propose solutions that could help to solve the problems with healthcare-associated infections. One locus of competence was the Rapid Review Panel, which gathered some of the country's most competent physicians. Although the positive evaluation of the Rapid Review Panel could analytically be seen as some kind of approval of the specification, the approval per se was insufficient for successful diffusion of the silver-coated catheter into NHS hospitals. In the e-ambulance case, the situation was similar in the sense that the solution was built on an already existing system. The amendments made to fit the system into the local context imply at least some awareness of the expected outcome and absorptive capacity, as well as the ability to implement the system in the local context.

One should therefore not confuse the application of functional specification with 'unknowing procurement'. If functional application is applied, the procurer needs to have in its possession adequate procurement skills to know what to ask for. Specification might be problematic in cooperative public procurement of innovation, in particular in situations where there is no institutional match. Even if procurer competence is available, which was the situation in the cases of both the silver-coated catheter and the public safety radio net, in collaborative projects involving different rationalities with different user needs it may be problematic to apply such competence. This is also an important insight for any attempts to bundle demand. Even if purchasing power is attained, other problems might emerge owing to associated coordination challenges.

Coordinating Competence for Cooperative Demand

Public procurement of innovation may mean that a public agency attempts to satisfy an intrinsic need. In some cases public procurement of innovation takes place as a collaboration project between several stakeholders with slightly different requirements. The most critical role for procurers in such projects may not be to find the single best specification, but to arrive at a specification that would work for all stakeholders involved.

For the maritime radio case, the requirement for coordinating competence was less demanding, as the project essentially was a direct procurement satisfying intrinsic needs. To some extent this was true also in the e-ambulance case, which was essentially an intrinsic project. One should note, however, that both these projects had a project structure with clearly defined communication channels between the procurer and supplier that helped to keep the developments under control. For the biofuel case, interaction and coordination with an array of different stakeholders appear to have been central success factors for the project. The procurers and future operators not only coordinated demand but also made an effort to coordinate with other institutional stakeholders. In the case with the patient briefcase, which should have developed as an intrinsic project, the initial prototype stage developed quite smoothly. It was in the upscaling phase, when other units within the regional authority became important for progress, that problems emerged. Both the woodchip case and the case with the silver-coated catheter suffered from coordination problems that affected the outcome in a negative way. In the woodchip case certain factors were outside the procurer's control, for instance the fact that there were no tenants and future customers available at the pre-procurement phase. The set-up that meant that the operator would be identified through the tender call practically prevented any coordination attempts from the operator in the pre-procurement phase. There were also challenges because of institutional mismatch among the partners in the project. In the case of the silver-coated catheter, the decentralized structure of the NHS can in this perspective be seen as a coordination barrier. This suggests that coordinating competence is importance for public procurement of innovation in cases of collaborative procurement, something already suggested in the literature (Hommen and Rolfstam, 2009).

One point sometimes ignored in the debate is that public procurement of innovation should not merely refer to the tender process. For adoption and diffusion of the procured item it may be necessary to initiate other changes to make an innovation match the intended use context. Future users also need to be consulted in order to make sure that innovations match user requirements. Measures such as budget reorganization to avoid silo budget problems, evaluation studies to convince physicians of the innovation's usefulness, and development of business cases to establish the value of the innovation for an organization were institutional coordination activities discussed in the case of the silver-coated catheter. In the e-ambulance case, local engineers made certain adaptations to make the system fit to the local context. Institutional coordination concerns not only the procuring organization but also any institutional actor. Initiated by the public procurers in the biofuel case, an array of coordination activities took place over the years, including the opening up of new markets for biofuel and fertilizers, as well as changing waste sorting habits among households.

Managerial Control

Public procurement of innovation is not different from other innovation projects in the sense that the outcome may be determined by the quality of the project management. Project management concerns not so much creation as delivery of the intended outcome. A common feature of many successful projects involving public procurement of innovation is that they have been allocated an experienced manager either from within the organization or as an external consultant (Wade and Björkman, 2004). This means that successful public procurement of innovation requires allocation of management resources. It also requires a situation that it is possible to manage.

In the maritime radio case, all information exchange between the procurer and the supplier went through the project manager. In the e-ambulance case the project set-up had only one contact point linking the procurer side with the supplier side. In the maritime radio case emphasis was placed on meeting deadlines and sticking to decisions made, disallowing any alternative suggestions that emerged. One reason for the success in the biofuel case was the allocation of the experienced consultant who played an important role to design the project. The project organization was also formally defined in a project handbook. For the woodchip case the project management were restricted by the fact that the person who had championed the vision of a green power plant passed away halfway through the project. It seems as though the set-up in the woodchip case failed to identify a leading organization able to coordinate the stakeholders' different objectives. In the case with the patient briefcase the project lost time in the upscaling stage. If some kind of innovation management organization had been available on the regional level, the time loss and the funding problems encountered might have been avoided. In both the case of the public safety radio and the case of the silver-coated catheter, management had to struggle with negotiating mismatching rationalities to some extent outside their control. Managers in the public safety radio case had to negotiate the different user needs among the different emergency response agencies. In the case with the silver-coated catheter, managers had to find ways of stimulating adoption of the innovative catheter among sub-units in a decentralized organization.

One aspect of management concerns the risks associated with innovation. Conducting public procurement of innovation requires management of technological risks, organizational and societal risks, market risks, financial risks and turbulence risks (Tsipouri *et al.*, 2010). Even if the cases discussed here offer no clear demarcation line between risk management and managerial control in general, examples of actions that could be labelled as 'risk management' are as follows. The perhaps clearest example is the biofuel case, where the procurers made sure that all necessary commitments were established before they commenced with the tender call. This was also of central concern for the procurers in the maritime radio case. Many of the contracts used among the cases regulated exceptional situations, typically imposing fines for suppliers failing to meet deadlines. One exception on this account is the initial stages of the case with the patient briefcase, which was unregulated and entirely based on trust. If risk management is understood as preventing risks from materializing, the woodchip case and the public safety radio case appear to be the cases where risk identification failed in relation to the situations that actually occurred.

Allocation of Resources for Public Procurers

Public procurement of innovation requires resources that are typically not available within existing operative routines and budgets. Specifications of what to procure need to be developed; finding technologies and suppliers potentially able to deliver a solution requires time-consuming search; the appropriation and use of the procured item may require fundamental changes within the organization; and so on. Resources can thus be understood in terms of allocating resources, essentially in the form of money. Resources can also be understood in terms of the extent to which the procuring organization creates the conditions for the procurers to work with a project. This is especially important where innovation is a non-routine task.

The general pattern here is that the more successful cases included adequate resource allocation. In the maritime radio case, a group of people with assigned responsibilities worked full time on the project. The procurer had a clear understanding of the price it would be able to afford for the final system. For the actual procurement, the procurers in the biofuel case relied on funding from the national government, the EU and bank loans. The development project benefited from support through Agroptigas project funding, allocated through the 5th Framework Programme of the European Commission (Agroptigas, 2000). The e-ambulance case includes one interesting circumstance, namely that a third of the funding came from the Taiwanese authorities, that is, from the home country of the supplier.

In the case with the patient briefcase, the initial prototype stage was well provided in terms of resources. It was when funding was required to diffuse the innovation to other hospitals that problems occurred. The region did not have an organization ready to manage the allocation of funding and other resources required for the further diffusion of the product. The project relied to a large extent on funding from the supplier. In the woodchip case, the public procurers were supposed to run the power plant project at the same time as fulfilling their ordinary tasks, which was a working condition that reduced the chances of success. The fact that they did not themselves have the resources to buy the power plant also affected the procurement set-up. The resource lack in the case with the silver-coated catheter mainly concerned diffusion costs. In hospitals where the silver-coated catheter was introduced and diffused, this happened because local hospital management allocated additional funding to override the silo budget problem. Additional resource allocation for local studies might also have helped to ameliorate physicians' organized scepticism.

Political Support

Understood as an exceptional activity, public procurement of innovation requires political support and decisions in order to enable procurers on the operational level to carry out the work. Political support also increases the chances of sufficient resource allocation. This is however not always the case.

Most of the cases include some political support. Both in the maritime case and in the case with the public safety radio net, the procurement projects were direct responses to national government decisions including funding for the project. For the maritime case, the political support, as well as the associated funding, was sufficient for the success of the project. In the case of the public safety radio net, the procurers appreciated that financial resources were not unlimited. The project also became more expensive than initially envisaged. The passive houses case occurred essentially as an extension of local policy implementing energy efficiency and building materials that would promote the local forest industry. The case with the silver-coated catheter, the woodchip case and the biofuel case also included procurement projects that were in line with national or local policies. The political support was however not directly or not completely associated with funding. Although the case with the silver-coated catheter was intended to help solve problems related to hospital-acquired infections, which among policy makers was a highly prioritized problem, the project struggled with the institutional barriers inside the adopting organization. Additional funding could have helped to ameliorate this problem. Allocating money on the hospital level was one measure that helped diffusion of the catheter. The biofuel case constituted a project perfectly in harmony with national policies aimed at moving away from fossil-based fuels. However, even if the political support included part of the funding, the success of the project relied also on the procurers' success in allocating funding from complementary sources, such as support from the EU and bank loans. Although the woodchip case included political support, it did not include intrinsic resource allocation. The project lacked funding and other resources. The case with the patient briefcase is interesting, as this project attracted a lot of attention from the national level and the policy emphasis ameliorating the demographical challenges. This endogenous project however struggled when funding became an important issue for commencing, owing to lack of support on the regional level.

Commitment from Other Institutional Actors

Public procurement of innovation may involve the development of technology where success is determined not only by the supplier and the procurer that are part of the formal transaction. Success may sometimes be co-determined by other institutional actors. Examples of such institutional actors may be users and or consumers of future services or products delivered by the procurement project. Another category can be other organizations such as public agencies and/or NGOs with some kind of exogenous authority. To a third category belong people and organizations that neither are direct customers nor have any formal authority for the innovation. One example on the individual level would be the next of kin of someone who received a new innovative hearing aid procured by a public health agency. The biofuel case offers some examples of how the procurers worked to establish commitment from other institutional actors such as regulators and industry organizations. The procurers held meetings with households to establish commitment to new waste handling routines required to make the waste compatible with the new system. There were also public discussions about the new power plant regarding smell, risk and so on. The relocation of the powerplant that was necessary in the bio-fuel case also underscores the importance of taking into account that public procurement of innovation may also have certain effects on existing industries in the local context. Local commitment may be weakened if the procured technology is perceived as a threat to existing industries. In the catheter case, one of the problems was that there was a lack of commitment. Even if the new catheter got included in the hospital's supply chain, healthcare staff were less inclined to choose the innovation in preference to conventional catheters. In the case with the patient briefcase the success was co-determined by the existence of a fast routine for setting up the communication between the patient briefcase and the hospital. This was done by negotiating a contract with a telecommunication service provider. The developers of the patient briefcase also had to deal with a lack of institutional commitment from the regional authorities in the stage where they wanted to upscale. Securing stakeholder commitment before the start of a development project may be a very good way of avoiding problems that could potentially emerge once a new facility is built, as illustrated by the biofuel case.

Appreciation and Understanding of Public Procurement Procedures

It is important to distinguish between insufficient knowledge about how public procurement is carried out, and the perception that the procurement rules are insufficiently adopted for innovation. It appears at least, as if many problems initially claimed to belong to the latter, after some further scrutiny more adequately should be counted as examples of the former. A recent Swedish public inquiry concluded also that the negligence of using public procurement, an innovation policy tool, could partly be explained by the lack of available academic education on the topic (SOU, 2013). Although public procurement of innovation in principle is not very different from private procurement of innovation, there are some elements of public procurement of innovation practices that require some attention. Certain ways of conducting public business come from requirements in the EC directives on public procurement. Others come from endogenous traditions and policies developed over many years within a specific public agency. Firms' failed attempts to become suppliers to the public sector can at least sometimes be explained by lack of basic understanding of how public procurement works. Typically firms that fail do not fully appreciate or understand the legal framework regulating public procurement. This was a problem in the woodchip case, where some of the actors showed little interest in complying with public procurement law. In the case of the patient briefcase the supplier also felt frustration about what was perceived as a too slow public decision process. The pedagogic skills of the public procurer may help to remedy this problem, given that such skills are available. Clear information regarding, for example intentions, requirements and administrative procedures given throughout a procurement process may reduce the risk that suppliers become exposed to 'surprises' that may lead to complaints.

Institutional Match

Public procurement of innovation involves at least two organizations, the public procurer(s) and the supplier(s) and/or other organizations, all with different rationalities. A successful project occurs to the extent that there prevails an institutional match between the organizations involved. Many of the success factors discussed here, for example coordinating competence, managerial control and availability of technology champions, are vehicles for negotiating institutional mismatch. Sometimes such management and coordination factors are insufficient, in relation to associated transaction costs which become too high, for an institutional match to be achieved. This assertion has some implications, for example, for the selection of partners in public procurement of innovation.

Different accounts of institutional mismatch prevailed in the case with the silver-coated catheter, the woodchip case, the case with the patient briefcase and the case with the public safety radio. In the case with the silver-coated catheter institutional mismatch prevailed between efficiency rationalities manifested as digital supply systems, framework agreements and also paradigmatic rationalities such as organized scepticism among physicians. In the other case evolving in a hospital environment, the case with the patient briefcase, the mismatch occurred between the endogenous innovation endeavours at the healthcare unit and the regional administration working mainly by operation or efficiency rationalities. The region did not initially see its role as a facilitator of innovation. Neither did there exist initially adequate knowledge to do so. Both the woodchip case and the public safety radio case involved institutional mismatch among participating partners. In the woodchip case, the organizations involved each emphasized different rationalities, such as green technology, commercial viability and legal compliance, a mix that in the end did not match. A side story in the biofuel case was the initial attempt to build a biofuel plant to run on ley crops delivered by farmers in a region relying heavily on the forest industry. For one of the municipalities involved, Ljungby, the intended facility would also have reduced commercial viability in existing waste handling systems. In the public safety radio project the institutional challenge occurred when different public agencies were supposed to agree on one design for the shared radio system.

It appears then as if the power of the coordination might sometimes be insufficient in relation to the transaction costs that have to be carried somehow by someone. For all economic organizations there is a limit to what different coordination actions, user involvement and other forms of interaction realistically can achieve or how much effort can be spent on such measures. Although presumably difficult as an *ex ante* analysis, public procurers may still consider to what extent foreseen institutional mismatches are too great to be carried. The generic assertion is that institutional mismatch sometimes occurs, and other ways forward than the initially intended one should be considered. This happened in the biofuel case, where the public procurers found another location for the power plant. It happened also in the case with the patient briefcase, where the first commercial customer was found abroad.

Technology Champions

Technology champions are in general considered 'key to the implementation of technologies, and their actions appear directly related to the success or failure of many innovations' (Lawless and Price, 1992, p. 342). The importance of technology champions appears to be increasing with increasing institutional mismatch and in situations of endogenous innovation, that is, where the initial idea is not initiated by an exogenous decision made by for example a government.

The general pattern for all the cases is that for each successful case it is typically also possible to identify individuals or a group that act as technology champions. In the maritime radio case, both the project manager and the legal expert functioned as technology champions. In the biofuel case an experienced engineer contributed with dedication to the idea as well as procurement competence. In the case of the patient briefcase the head physician, together with his team of medical staff, was instrumental in initiating the project. The supplier was an important driver of the project, especially in the situation when the regional level hesitated. Correspondingly, many of the less successful cases lacked a clear technology champion. The woodchip case was negatively affected by the death of the technology champion and the problem of finding a replacement. In the case of the silver-coated catheter, the diffusion of the catheter suffered from the fact that its use fell outside the core interest of any of the medical disciplines and therefore lacked a natural technology champion in the hospital organization that could have helped to negotiate prevailing institutional barriers.

Choosing the Universally Best Solution

The general principle to apply for public procurement of innovation is that the 'best' solution should be awarded a contract, regardless of its origin. This principle contrasts with local political rationalities that sometimes strive to promote local (national, regional) champions. Going against local pressure for policies promoting endogenous firms and local trajectories in general may be challenging for any political leadership. Considering this issue strictly as an innovation problem, however, the long-term costs for persisting in support of underachieving endogenous technology are probably higher.

One proxy for determining if a public procurement of innovation project has delivered the universally best offer is the origin of the supplier, that is, whether the supplier is a domestic company or not. Among the seven cases that delivered a finalized item, six had a foreign or international supplier. This suggests at least that the solutions eventually chosen were superior to any solution that could be offered by domestic firms. In some cases this was also a clear ambition. In the maritime radio case the procurers made an effort to scan markets globally in order to find the best supplier. Another example is the initiative by the Department of Health to set up the Rapid Review Panel to enable innovation, as happened in the case with the silver-coated catheter, leading to the attempt to diffuse a product that had previously been successful on the US market. In the biofuel case both the upgrading plant and the storage silos were supplied by foreign firms. In the e-ambulance case the Czech public procurers were able to utilize the spillover effects through localization of (global) state-of-the-art knowledge from Taiwan. The in-house technological experts managed to identify a global leader in the technological field of their interest and were also able to collaborate and contribute in the innovation work themselves by adding 'local' features to the system. The e-ambulance case is thus an 'ideal case' in the sense that it allowed for the sourcing of state-of-the art technology while at the same time enabling local learning.

CONCLUDING REMARKS

One immediate danger associated with assembling lists of the kind presented here is that it might imply a too functionalistic interpretation of how the world works. This might lead to less constructive discussions on the extent to which a specific element qualifies as a success factor or not. Such discussions should ideally be avoided. Instead, the intention here is to show that public procurement of innovation is determined by many factors, among which most prevail on other institutional levels than that of the EC directives. It is in that sense also noteworthy that none of the success factors discussed here are directly connected to the EC directives. Even if allocating competence of the directives is important, this does not mean that the directives themselves hinder innovation, as was proposed in earlier literature. A revision of the EC directives in itself may therefore be relatively unimportant as a means to stimulate public procurement of innovation, at least as far as the success factors discussed here are concerned. Having said this, it should still be noted that, even if the success factors pinpointed in this chapter are substantiated empirically, there remain some methodological and analytical challenges deriving from the characteristics of the phenomenon under study. Some of the success factors are nested and to some extent affected by each other. For instance, institutional coordination may be less important if there is already an institutional match between actors in a project. Another example concerns risk management. If a high-risk project is supported politically and publicly, the risks perceived by the public procurers might not be as high as would otherwise be the case. There are also elements that appear in some of the cases that still were not regarded as success factors in this display. One example is the observation that some of the cases included a supplier that provided parts of the funding. This happened for instance in the case with the patient briefcase, where the supplier actually contributed most of the funding for the development of the system. In the e-ambulance case the supplier benefited from support from the Taiwanese government. Although supplier co-funding was not treated as a success factor here, its role in certain situations should still be acknowledged. Finally, it is important to acknowledge again the need for critical realistic precautions. The occurrence per se of a certain success factor does not allow for the generic conclusion that its re-creation in another context will determine success. What could be claimed however is that the *likelihood* of success will increase for each realized success factor discussed here.

There are two reasons for claiming that the success factor exercise endeavoured in this chapter might steer clear of some of the problems described above. First, most of the success factors discussed here are 'subsidiarity friendly' in the sense that they are discernible without being definite, and their realization might be attained by those who are trying to copy them, in many different ways. They are in that sense outcomes that in turn may depend on many other specific events. Second, and connected to the first reason, their identification relies on cross-case analysis of cases that have evolved in different countries, in different sectors, involving the procurement of different kinds of technology. Applying such a set-up would help to minimize the risks of identifying success factors that would be relevant only in special cases. The limitation of this holistic approach is its tendency to ignore sector-specific particularities. Public procurement of innovation in for example med-tech or construction comes with sector-specific challenges and rules of the game that are not captured in the exercise undertaken here.

NOTE

1. This case study was conducted by Irina Zálišová and her EPMA colleagues in the context of the PreCo project (Turkama *et al.*, 2012).

8. Concluding remarks

Appreciating that research on public procurement of innovation has gained new momentum in the last decade this chapter contains a few reflections on what appear to be two emerging sub-fields within the general endeavour to gain new knowledge on public procurement of innovation. The assertion made is that this book positions itself in one of these streams. This is followed by a brief summary of, and subsequently some elaborations on the findings of this book. Even if these findings align well on a general level with earlier work in innovation studies drawing on institutional frameworks, they nevertheless challenge some of the existing literature devoted to public procurement as an innovation instrument. This 'anomaly' is explained. A discussion on innovation policy concludes the chapter.

RESEARCH ON PUBLIC PROCUREMENT OF INNOVATION

There are two discernible approaches to research on public procurement of innovation. The one that has attracted most attention deals profoundly with the policy level and in particular the development of the demand-side argument, and is closely associated with the arguments related to the promotion of lead markets. One important recent example of this approach is Edler and Georghiou's research policy article from 2007. There is also other work that resides on the same conceptual level (Cave and Frinking, 2003; Rolfstam, 2005; Hommen and Rolfstam, 2009; Lember *et al.*, 2010; Myoken, 2010). The de facto starting point for this literature is the understanding of demand-based innovation policy defined as a 'set of public measures to increase the demand for innovations, to improve the conditions for the uptake of innovations or to improve the articulation of demand in order to spur innovations and the diffusion of innovations' (Edler, 2007, p. 1). This book belongs to a complementary and more endogenous approach often taking as a starting point individual or several real cases seeking understanding on 'purchasing activities carried out by a public agency that lead to innovation'. Both approaches share the same ultimate goals, to inform policy development ultimately to sustain competitive advantage in a global economy. The former is more conceptual and in a way normative, as it strives to identify and attract attention to the potential that lies in public procurement of innovation. The latter approach is more inductive and draws on public procurement practice, in ways which sometimes come close to mode 2 knowledge production (Gibbons *et al.*, 1994). The latter is also less restricted by dogmas sometimes prevailing in innovation studies, seen for instance in its attempt to draw on other related disciplines, such as law, and its ambition to take into account how public procurement of innovation is carried out in real life. In other words, the focus here lies in engaging with a multifaceted practice.

This approach has also proven its value. Quite early it helped to demonstrate that the challenges lying ahead for implementing public procurement of innovation policies concerned not so much the EC procurement directives but other institutional levels (Edler *et al.*, 2005; Rolfstam, 2007, 2009a; Rolfstam *et al.*, 2011), an insight that went against what was then established knowledge (Edquist et al., 2000). It was also this direction that EU policy development took initially. Rather than chasing for any innovation-inhibiting properties within the directives, an array of activities have been initiated ultimately to demonstrate how public procurement of innovation could be achieved within the existing legal framework. This perspective has also produced some inspiration within the academic community. Soini and Keinonen (2011) for example discuss the role of stakeholder commitment in precommercial procurement. Morrar (2011) discusses how public and private collaboration emerge in public–private innovation networks. Others have studied cases of public procurement of innovation drawing on institutional theory (Abonce Perez, 2011; Hjaltadóttir, 2011; Veizaj Greisen, 2012). Especially now that the directives are under revision the role for this perspective is clear: to remind policy makers that most of the determining factors for successful implementation of public procurement of innovation policies reside on other institutional levels than the level of the EC directives. This generic claim is discussed below.

SUMMARY OF FINDINGS

The theoretical framework outlined in this book holds public procurement to be a versatile tool that can work to stimulate innovation as summarized in the Hommen matrix. Public procurement of innovation can lead to the initiation of new technology, and also to the removing of depreciated technology from the market. It can take place as intrinsic procurement projects where one public agency acts to satisfy intrinsic needs, or in more distributed forms where the public actor facilitates the process to satisfy needs identified elsewhere. It may vary in scale from aiming at procuring a multimillion-euro facility for synchrotron radiation-based research to locally produced food for homes for the elderly. These are however probabilistic claims substantiated through *ex post* analysis of selected public procurement of innovation cases. A holistic analysis may give reason for moderation if these claims are extrapolated too far. This point, which is discussed further below, is related to the other important contribution of this book, the understanding of public procurement of innovation as governed not only by regulation on the EU level. Other institutions also need to be taken into account. The three institutional modes elaborated here underscore the importance of conducting a multilevel institutional analysis, consider that institutions are endogenous and exogenous, and take into account that endogenous institutions may work as rationalities determining outcomes.

All of the cases discussed in this book have elements that could be included in such analysis. The case of the maritime radio, for example, relied on support from the national level and was successful because of an endogenous institutional set-up 'regulating' public procurement law as something you have to master, and public procurement of innovation as something you need to manage, for instance by establishing clear goals of what should come out of the process. In the case with the silver-coated catheter, an attempt on the national level to diffuse an innovative catheter faced problems on lower institutional levels. Different rationalities among health staff and organizational design mainly following operational or efficiency rationalities became institutional barriers to introducing the innovation. In the woodchip case an array of different stakeholders on different institutional levels acted according to their own rationalities, leading to a situation where the procurer had to cancel the tender process without identifying a supplier. The biofuel case relied on support and interest from European, national, regional and local institutional levels. This case also included an array of organizations among which there prevailed an endogenous institutional match. An array of success factors were also found in the comparison of eight cases of public procurement of innovation. Some of these success factors prevailed on agency or practice levels, and others on regional, national or international levels. Problems encountered manifested themselves for example as institutional mismatches between collaborating partners, or between different levels within an organization.

What should be noted is the generic conclusion that emerges from an institutional analysis of the cases discussed in this book. The empirical studies demonstrate that institutions matter, that is, that the behaviour and outcome of public procurement of innovations are affected by institutions. However, the studies fail to support the proposition that the EC procurement directives in general inhibit public procurement of innovation. Instead, the results indicate that, to fully understand the institutional effects on public procurement of innovation, other institutions on other institutional levels than the EU directives also need to be taken into account. A pragmatic account of justification for the claims made here is the activities seen recently on national levels. The fact that public agencies do engage and succeed in procuring innovations also overthrows the general claim that the EC directives inhibit innovation. Apparently some public agencies are able to find their way through, in spite of the alleged problems. Blaming the EC directives for incorporating a 'tension' that prevents innovation thus becomes problematic in the light of available practical experience. In a way, these are not particularly novel assertions. W. Scott (2003, p. 886), for example, emphasizes the importance of taking interpretative aspects of formal laws into account, thus at least implying that institutions other than formal ones may determine behaviour. The multilevel approach to institutions is emphasized even further by Hollingsworth (2000, p. 600), who is explicit about the point that 'we must be sensitive to multiple levels of reality'. This is also a generic point that aligns with an array of sources cited in this book. The results however contrast with claims made on public procurement of innovation specifically (Edquist and Hommen, 2000; Nyholm *et al.*, 2001; Edquist and Zabala-Iturriagagoitia, 2012) and therefore deserve some explanation.

AN ONTOLOGICAL EXPLICATION

The argument brought forward in this book has essentially a critical-realistic relationship to the Edquistian claim. The difference between intransitive knowledge and transitive knowledge is useful in explaining this point (Bhaskar 1975, cited in Sayer, 2000). These two knowledge dimensions distinguish analytically between the object under study, the intransitive dimension, and the way it is studied, the intransitive dimension. There might be certain properties of particles that interest the physicist, or a social phenomenon that interests the social scientist. How certain objects are studied is governed by theories and paradigms to which the researcher subscribes. These might change as the result of scientific revolutions, while the objects in the real world, the particles or the social phenomena, will remain the same (Sayer, 2000, pp. 10–11). Furthermore, critical realists distinguish between the real, the actual and the empirical. The real is what exists regardless of whether it is perceived as an empirical object. Specimens of animals may exist in the deep oceans although they have never been observed by humans. Structures and powers or capacities that the object might exercise are also part of the real. A creature living in the deep oceans might be able to swim or feed in a particular way. It is also possible that, although this creature has these powers, it might not employ them all the time. The actual, which is the second component in this critical-realist ontology, refers to what happens when these potential structures are employed. In the case of the deep-sea fish, the actual can be the fish eating, or any activations of its motoric system. The empirical, then, is the domain of experience. The empirical is either the real or the actual. What a scientist sees in the deep sea may be what exists, that is, something real and/or something actual. The experience may also depend on structures which are not observable to the scientist. A challenge emerges regarding how the observations should be understood. Observability may create confidence, but is not a guarantee of fully complete claims about reality in relation to what is real. Even if what you see is adequate, what you see might not be what you think you see. Assume for instance that a new fish specimen that lives in the deep sea is discovered and that the particular feature of this fish is that it shines. This would be an observation producing bold headlines and celebration among the researchers responsible for the discovery. After further research it is found that it is only the female fish that shines, that is, a finding that limits the original claim. Yet further research reveals that this shining among female fish of this specimen occurs only in the mating season, which occurs for a few weeks in the spring every year. Even if the phenomenon observed all through this progression remains the same, the understanding has evolved from the discovery of a shining fish to a fish which is like any other fish, albeit with a particular feature occurring among females related to the specimen's reproduction in a scarcely lit environment. The critical-realist explanation is, thus, that, unlike most other scholars and policy makers who have worked in this field in recent years, Edquist persists in claiming he has discovered a fish that shines.

Critical-realist philosophy is applicable to institutional theory for understanding innovation in the following sense. Formal laws are perfectly observable and thus potentially run the risk of creating false confidence. Applying a critical-realist ontology to the study of institutions such as the EC procurement directives would prompt the researcher to go out to study the actual effects of the directives when they are employed, rather than attempting an analysis of the literal law, understood as something real, as was done in Edquist *et al.* (2000). The work by Edquist and Zabala-Iturriagagoitia (2012) is interesting, as it confirms the claims made in this book without the authors being aware of it. In what is actually a literature review of some cases of public procurement of innovation (including one case study this author conducted together with Leif Hommen some years ago, Gavras *et al.*, 2006), the problems they describe, that is, insufficient level of competence, inability to choose the universally best offer, lack of commitment, poor specification or the importance of adequate organization for successful outcomes, are all items that would fit in the analysis presented in this book as occurring on endogenous levels. The EC procurement directives have relatively low explanation value in regard to these phenomena. Still the authors maintain that the 'EU regulation of public procurement has been an important obstacle to [public procurement of innovation]' (Edquist and Zabala-Iturriagagoitia, 2012, p. 25). They also claim that it is *'evident* that the EU procurement rules have inhibited collaboration and interaction for innovation in [public procurement of innovation] processes for a long time (ibid., italics added). There are two main weaknesses in those statements. Making such claims without providing supporting observable facts violates the most basic requirements for a scientific claim (Chalmers, 1999). Second, the claims are problematic in the light of a transitive knowledge dimension as outlined in this book.

If the directives are treated not as something real but as something empirical or actual, the analysis is prompted to take into account that the significance of the law 'is often negotiated by various actors in the field – ranging from legislators and judges to policy administrators and managers' (W. Scott, 2003, p. 886). This is indeed a central observation for anyone appreciating an understanding of the world as multi-institutional. Anyone who has met experts in public procurement from different countries might also have experienced that they are all quite certain of what is allowed and what is not allowed. The problem is that this certainty varies between countries and contexts. A more rigorous look at agency and practice levels would probably also reveal differences in understandings of the interpretations of the directives. This follows at least from an evolutionary line of thinking where the endogenous institutional set-up is organization-specific. A public agency should from that perspective be understood as a locus for development of organization-specific norms and routines regarding its procurement behaviour. This is in itself an interesting reflection. In Sweden, for example, estimations suggest there exist about 4000 entities ranging from local municipality levels to national agencies that carry out their procurement activities according to the EC procurement directives, while the corresponding number for all EU member states is around 100 000 (European Commission, 2012). The latter would also be the number of distinct agency-specific variations of interpretations out there.

Initially appearing mostly as anecdotal evidence, but also confirmed by others (Carlsson and Waara, 2006, p. 30), variation is also distinguishable on the individual level. It appears possible to distinguish between one category of public procurers, who find the law to be problematic, bureaucratic and not particularly well suited for public procurement of innovation, and another category, which consists of 'entrepreneurial' public procurers who appreciate the possibilities within the restrictions of the law that enable successful public procurement of innovation. One could suspect that organizations dominated by the second category of entrepreneurial procurers are most likely to engage in public procurement of innovation and, vice versa, organizations nurturing a negative attitude towards the EC directives would probably be less inclined to explore the possibilities as given by the rules. In this variation there probably lies a clue as to why public procurement would fail, or be perceived as problematic, and consequently underutilized; the institutional set-up of some organizations may be less encouraging to public procurement of innovation than that of others. Similarly, success is not determined by chance, but is associated with institutions safeguarding adequate development of certain success factors, as was discussed in Chapter 7. Viewed in this light, the question whether the EC directives per se inhibit or stimulate innovation becomes inadequate. To pursue the answer to such a question would require isolation of the effects that come from endogenous institutions. This would be impossible in practice.

IN SEARCH OF THE POSSIBILITIES

If one instead commits to an analysis of the EC procurement directives that assumes them to support innovation, some noteworthy points emerge. For example, the requirement to choose the most economically advantageous offer may prompt the procurer to search with an open mind for suppliers able to deliver the most economically advantageous solutions. This happened for example in the maritime radio case, where the procurers conducted a global search for suppliers before issuing the formal tender call. One could also argue that the problems encountered in the procurement of the X2000 high-speed train (Edquist *et al.*, 2000), as discussed in Edquist and Zabala-Iturriagagoitia (2012), happened because of lack of attention to the development going on elsewhere, which led to a solution that never reached an international market. Had the principles in the current directives been applied at the time, the chances are that the solution eventually selected would have been more attractive to an international market. The benefit of the 'restriction' that favours the most economically advantageous bid obviously requires an appreciation of the difference between national industrial policy aiming at supporting domestic firms and innovation policy understood as achieving solutions based on the most advantageous technologies available globally. The restriction is only a restriction for those who believe in supporting domestic champions rather than engaging in activities aiming at acquiring state-of-the-art technology.

Another point concerns the requirement of specification, which is sometimes treated as a problem. The typical question raised is how public procurement of innovation, understood as procuring something which does not exist and is therefore at least partly unknown, can take place if the specifications must be included in the tender call. The pragmatic answer to this question is to look at how public procurers typically deal with such situations. One common technique is to split up a project into different phases, where each step increases clarity. The first tender call might deliver a pre-study or feasibility study where the problem is analysed and maybe different solutions are explored. This might be followed by a pilot study or some kind of test-batch being tested. Eventually the procurer gains sufficient knowledge to enable a tender call aiming at procuring a full realization of the final solution. This way of managing uncertainty is implemented in the pre-commercial procurement model (European Commission, 2007a), and was also a central feature in the technology procurement model applied in Sweden in the 1970s (SOU, 1976; Rolfstam and Ågren, forthcoming). One example of such splitting-up in this book was seen in the public safety radio case. Another way of dealing with this problem is to apply functional specification or performance-based procurement (e.g. Wade and Björkman, 2004). It is in that sense important to make the distinction between knowing what is the intended outcome and being able to specify in detail how this should be achieved. The former is crucial for the procurer, but the latter may be left to the supplier. Yet another approach acknowledges that contracts may be incomplete and therefore require measures that regulate actors' behaviour although certain things are unknown at the time the contract is signed (Ågren and Landin, 2012). One case where this approach was applied was the case of the passive houses. The benefit of that requirement emerges if specification is looked upon as an instance of knowledge conversion (Nonaka, 1994), that is, the process where tacit knowledge is externalized as explicit written knowledge. In that light specification becomes a learning process prompting the procurer to establish what is to be achieved before commencing with the formal tender call. The directives work in that sense as a support mechanism for the execution of well-prepared projects.

The critics' allegations concerning a lack of innovation-friendliness in the directives connects to a critique of the ideologies on which the directives were originally developed that is less convincing. It is true that the underlying rationalities shaping the EC directives from the beginning rested on neoclassical economics and neoliberal policies (e.g. Cox and Furlong, 1996) that included very little consideration for innovation. On the other hand, preventing fraud and maintaining competition and transparency are not in themselves innovation inhibiting. Some restrictions do emerge in the directives, for instance that the procurer cannot change the specifications or the evaluation criteria once the procurement process is initiated. These are however restrictions that impose fewer problems in well-prepared projects. In the more successful cases discussed in this book, the public procurers made an effort to establish the intended outcome before publishing the tender calls. This was clearly seen in both the maritime radio case and the biofuel case. The EC directives have also been criticized for inhibiting interactive learning. Again, it is clear that certain things are not allowed. If, for instance, the open procedure is applied, interaction is not allowed. Other procedures such as the negotiated procedure and the competitive dialogue do allow interaction. One should note, however that these are procedural restrictions with an institutional range limited to the life-time of the tender procedure which may, again, cause little problems for well-prepared projects. If one looks at the cases discussed here, interaction was never raised as an issue. Also, it appears the reason why public procurement projects produce complaints have very little to do with lack of possibilities for interaction. A Swedish study on court cases from the construction industry found that most of the reasons for complaining concerned flaws in the tender documents, such as lack of clarity, lack of objectivity, and inconsistency between the tender document and evaluation criteria (Carlsson and Astrom, 2008). The general amelioration for such problems, it could be argued, is improved procurement competence and maybe sometimes improved supplier competence, which are both problem areas that belong to the endogenous levels.

Here a challenge emerges for the innovation research community. It could be argued that the integrity and credibility of innovation research are at stake. Informing the implementation of public procurement of innovation policies based on reading legal texts only signals a simplistic understanding of how public procurement of innovation actually occurs in real life that should not be considered a part of sound institution-based innovation research. The challenge for the innovation research community is to make that clear for policy makers and other stakeholders. In other words, the innovation research community needs to acknowledge past mistakes and set things straight again. The subsequent parts of the chapter attempt to draw attention to some issues it is relevant to consider in that pursuit.

DRIVERS OF INNOVATION

A central idea in the policy debate on public procurement of innovation concerns its potential to create demand for innovation. This is in turn built on the assumption of an 'innovation gap', that is, the existence of currently commercially unexploited scientific or other forms of knowledge. By applying public demand this potential could be transformed into commercially viable innovations that would eventually help to sustain growth. Although there certainly exist cases where public procurement has delivered innovation, the question is whether these occurrences warrant an exclusive understanding of public procurement of innovation as a demand-side tool. At least in the light of the literature reviewed below, the questioning of such a claim appears to have some justification.

Different views on what is driving innovation have each had their period of dominance. The prevailing view of the 1950s regarded innovation as a process that began with research, which led to development, followed by production, and was concluded by marketing. In the mid-1960s, perspectives developed in which market pull was seen as the engine for innovation. Instead of stimulating developments and advances within universities and government laboratories in expectation that this would eventually lead to the emergence of new products on the market, R&D was perceived as being directed by demand (Rothwell, 1994). The demand-pull preference eventually diminished in importance for reasons that appear to have been broadly accepted by the innovation research community. Mowery and Rosenberg, for instance, argued that 'the uncritical appeal to market demand as the governing influence in the innovation process simply does not yield useful insights into the complexities of that process' (Mowery and Rosenberg, 1979, p. 139). In a similar way, Malerba argued:

> In reality, this relationship is more complex than the mere pulls of the various demand segments of innovation. In a more articulated way, this relationship is a dynamic and a two-way one. On one hand, there are the effects of demand structure on technical change. ... On the other hand, technological change may create new structures of demand by opening up completely new types of demand. (Malerba, 1985, p. 293)

Kline and Rosenberg (1986) proposed an innovation model that emphasized the chain-linked relationships between research, invention, innovation and production. Instead of viewing the innovation process as a linear flow from research to market, the model took into account that, for instance, a 'perceived market need will be filled only if the technical problems can be solved, and a perceived performance gain will be put into use only if there is a realizable market use' (ibid., p. 289). Dosi and Orsenigo made the point that innovation 'involves specific, often idiosyncratic, partly appropriable knowledge which is accumulated over time through equally specific learning processes, whose directions partly depend on firm-specific knowledge and on the technologies in use' (Dosi and Orsenigo, 1988, p. 16). Dosi emphasized also that 'technological change cannot be described as simple and flexible reactions to changes in market conditions'; instead, 'it is the nature of technologies themselves that determines the range within which products and processes can adjust to changing economic conditions' (Dosi, 1988, p. 233). For the systemic approaches that emerged, an interactive understanding of innovation was a central theme. For instance, Lundvall (1992, p. 2) states that a 'system of innovation is constituted by elements and relationships which interact in the production, diffusion and use of new, and economically useful, knowledge'. Recent open models of innovation make innovation explained by demand appear even more of an abstraction (Pénin et al., 2011).

If one looks at understanding of the demand notion itself, it is noteworthy that demand has also been understood as an *ex post* innovation selection mechanism which is different from the demand-pull understanding of the notion. One starting point for this view is that 'the basic function of demand is to select between the varieties that are made available by innovation' (Andersen, 2003, p. 3). This understanding regards demand as routine behaviour that takes place with limited foresight and is only changed by (Schumpeterian) entrepreneurs (Andersen, 2003, p. 1). Furthermore, it essentially incorporates demand for already existing, regular products. This perspective aligns with a mainstream application of the demand–supply dichotomy, that is, demand understood as one element of the price determining mechanism, in the sense that it does not take into account any influence from demand on supply. In the view of Edquist and Hommen (1999) the point of departure is the existence of a certain set-up of technology. In the system, there are mechanisms that create diversity, that is, novel developments from the initial technological set-up. Then there is a selection mechanism that reduces the diversity, that is, some of the novel developments become more emphasized while others diminish in importance.

This brief historical summary puts current emphasis on the demand side into perspective. One cannot help but note that accepting the notion of an innovation-driven economy does not necessarily mean that innovation is demand driven. Anyone who would argue that demand in general stimulates innovation would run into problems in relation to prevailing knowledge that suggests a more interactive relationship between demand and supply. The current emphasis on the demand side must therefore be understood more as a policy discourse than as an argument stemming from any theoretically justified preference for the demand side as a driver for innovation. As far as the review above goes, public procurement of innovation could also be understood as selection, that is, a destructive activity. Understanding public procurement of innovation as something that 'occurs when a public agency places an order for a product or system which does not exist' (Edquist and Hommen, 1999, p. 65) clearly connects to a demand-pull understanding; the public agency 'commands' on the demand side to achieve supplier-side innovation. In the same way as demand policies were criticized in the past, the relevance of this exclusive understanding fades away when compared with the variety of how public procurement of innovation projects may evolve.

The empirical material discussed in this book is a case in point. In the maritime radio case, the procurers awaited the maturity of digital technology before they eventually proceeded with what was their second attempt to procure a new maritime radio system. Even if they achieved innovation, they made an effort to procure a technology that had already proven its functionality elsewhere. A central concern was to find a supplier that could demonstrate the capability to deliver the envisaged solution. The case with the silver-coated catheter concerned a supply-side innovation coming from elsewhere. The eventual tender process in the biofuel case was a formal manifestation of ideas emerging among farmers some 15 years before the facility was built. The case with the patient briefcase, which concerned a universal innovation, evolved mainly driven by the head physician and an entrepreneurial firm where the formal procurer on the regional level played almost an averse role. There are also examples in the literature where a literal understanding of public procurement of innovation as a demand-side instrument lose relevance. One case concerns the procurement of digital hearing aid technology where the National Health Service in England essentially acted in response to a need formulated by the patient association (Phillips *et al.*, 2007). Procurement projects have also been conducted where suppliers were involved early in the process, not only through suggesting solutions but also by defining the problems (van Valkenburg and Nagel-kerke, 2006). A study of the effects of public procurement of innovation in Germany appears to confirm this general pattern. The firms found to be involved as suppliers were already innovative and arguably in posses-sion of sufficient levels of absorptive capacity (Aschhoff and Sofka, 2009). In other words, the successes of these firms were determined by capacities commonly associated with the supply side.

The literature reviewed above points to the risk with a too explicit focus on public procurement of innovation as a demand-side tool. It might even be tempting to infer that the current policy discourse on public procurement of innovation should be disqualified because of lack of theoretical foundation, as the role of demand appears to be far from settled. A more sound position to take is probably reached, for instance, by considering the empirical material discussed in this book. The cases discussed here give reason to underscore the variations in which public procurement of innovation manifest, which somewhat reduces the rel-evance for the concern to what extent it occurs on the demand-side or not. What appears to be more important is policy stimulating innovation-enabling procurement activities of all its forms, rather than a specific focus on 'demand'. Sound policy development should take into account that public procurement of innovation may certainly occur also as responses to supply-side innovation. As was discussed in Chapter 4 regarding the case with the silver-coated catheter, the effects from public procurement of supplier-side innovation will also contribute to increased competitive advantage although the exchange mechanism is different. Instead of getting a price for committing to innovation, supplying firms attain return on investment from already performed innovative activities that can be re-spent in further innovative efforts. One practical issue in this context is the ability to deal with unsolicited bids for innovations. This was essentially the situation in the case with the patient briefcase, which was also a situation that the regional level was not fully prepared to deal with.

QUALIFYING THE UNDERSTANDING OF PUBLIC PROCUREMENT OF INNOVATION

Obviously all public procurement projects manifest themselves as some kind of written specification in a tender call. An exclusive emphasis on this formal aspect of public procurement may however take focus away from the real game that is played to reach that point. This might also produce misplaced conclusions on how to change the rules of the game to make them more innovation-friendly. The perspective developed in this book attempts to carry out 'a careful analysis of preconditions and limits', appreciating even that public procurement may not necessarily have as 'an intentional or explicit objective the promotion of innovation' (Uyarra and Flanagan, 2010, p. 127). To what extent innovation, intended as well as unintended, is generated in public procurement projects can typically be established only as *ex post* phenomena. The final result is often also determined by factors that have very little to do with the formal aspects. The connection to growth, which is the starting point for this whole policy discourse, is far from clear cut. This is discussed further below.

Like any institution, any individual public procurement of innovation project has a specific range. It may invoke and affect local suppliers, local markets, local users and other local institutional actors. One example would be a municipality setting up contracts for innovative ways of supplying locally produced traditional food. A preliminary assumption would be that such procurement projects would be determined by local supply and demand. The other extreme are cross-national procurement projects affecting developments internationally that could potentially establish standards like the NMT or TETRA standards, which will affect endogenous levels. Common to both these extremes however is that it is hard to predict their actual range, especially over time. Sometimes an idea emerging in a local context can evolve to become an internationally sold innovation. This is what happened in the case of the patient briefcase. Sometimes what to adopters is an exogenous innovation faces diffusion problems that if ignored slow down or even inhibit commercial success on local markets. This was essentially the struggle in the case with the silver-coated catheter. It is also conceivable that public procurement of innovation activities performed in one institutional context produce effects or are affected by other exogenous effects. One Swedish example that evolved some years ago was a public dentist clinic that procured what in Sweden was a state-of-the art system for patient administration. Although the actual system had superior features, it eventually had to be abandoned as a result of a standard war. This first-mover initiative was built on the IBM OS/2 technology, which was later outcompeted by solutions built on Microsoft technologies. A similar story evolved in the 1980s, where a national project aiming at developing a computer to be used in Swedish schools was abandoned owing to the emergence of the PC/DOS standard (Kaiserfeld, 2000). Although both these cases were successful on the endogenous level, they both failed because of exogenous effects.

Thinking of institutional range for public procurement of innovation also highlights the importance of taking into account adoption and diffusion. The formal understanding of public procurement of innovation tends to neglect that success should be understood as *appropriation* of the procured innovation as codetermined also by events and activities residing outside the scope of formal bidding and contract awards. The existence of a contract is in that sense only a necessary but not sufficient condition for success. One example is centrally negotiated framework agreements which might not be used by their intended clients. This was at least the problem identified in a Danish review of the matter. Although centrally negotiated framework agreements were found to offer cost savings and reduce the administrative burden for the individual public agency, they have not been utilized to the extent envisaged by policy makers (Larsen *et al.*, 2006). Diffusion is also important in public procurement of innovation. Several of the cases discussed in this book included diffusion problems as well as measures to negotiate them. The problems encountered in the case of the silver-coated catheter were essentially all about institutional barriers that prevented diffusion. The problems encountered in the case with the patient briefcase essentially emerged at the diffusion stage. In the maritime radio case, the procurers interacted with the users of the system to be replaced in order to learn and facilitate the shift to the new system. In the biofuel case, the procurers interacted with an array of stakeholders to secure future operations. One of the reasons for the termination of the woodchip case was that such interaction could not take place. In the e-ambulance case the procurers took different steps to adopt the procured system to fit the local context.

A Schumpeterian understanding of innovation underscores the role of destruction (as was incorporated in the extended Hommen matrix) as both an enabling condition and an effect. The success of a particular innovation is determined by its ability to make existing knowledge obsolete. As with any innovation, this means that successful public procurement of innovation may affect prevailing technologies and those firms engaged therein in destructive ways. This might in turn render secondary effects, for instance on the job market. It appears that public procurement of innovation projects initially may help to create jobs, as they tend to increase demand for skilled labour during the development phase. When the solution is delivered and in operation, the efficiency gains might however lead to job cuts in the context in which the innovation is introduced (Sylvest, 2008). Public procurement of innovation may in the same way affect (negatively) any other stakeholders involved in the replaced technology. One example is when Danish fire brigades recently shifted to TETRA-based communication systems. Almost overnight, the old equipment transferred from being a critical technology for the provision of rescue services to something that was collected and shipped to the scrapyard. These mechanisms have implications in turn for public procurement of innovation understood as a tool supposed ultimately to generate growth. Even if successful public procurement of innovation projects might increase competitive advantages among the suppliers involved and generate efficiency gains for the procurer, secondary effects such as job cuts and depreciation of technology might reduce the total benefits. This in turn calls for a holistic approach to understanding public procurement of innovation – an understanding that also takes into account these secondary effects. Even if public procurement of innovation may be a powerful vehicle for change, the full benefits might not be secured unless applied together with other policy measures also addressing these negative effects.

IMPLICATIONS FOR INNOVATION POLICY

After this broadened discussion in the preceding paragraphs, the remaining parts of this chapter address some implications for public procurement of innovation policy that emerge in light of the findings of this book. The starting point is the unfortunate tendency to perceive the EC directives as the exclusive determining variable. What from an innovation policy perspective has been problematic is that the alleged innovation-unfriendliness in the EC directives has worked to remove any incentives to develop the conditions necessary for success in public procurement of innovation. What sane actor in a public agency would initiate projects attempting to learn more about or even go about procuring innovations when 'science' says it cannot be done anyway? Another problem with the single-minded focus on the directives is the implication for the directives themselves. As the natural remedy for perceived legal inadequacies is legal revision, any solutions required that go beyond legal revision might be overlooked. There is therefore a risk that phenomena occurring on other institutional levels that actually are causing the problems might be unaffected. Huge amounts of resources might be spent on legal revision and transposition of the new directives into national legislation without solving the problems that are important. In addition, any revision carried out in the name of increasing interaction may run the risk of bringing back the situation that prompted the development of the EC directives in the first place, which would mean a reduction in the efficiency gained, that is, increases in prices, and potentially pave the way for fraud.

The results reported give reason to be less concerned with the directives but instead search for success factors prevailing on lower institutional levels. The generic argument would be that innovation policies should be developed that help to negotiate the institutional barriers seen on lower institutional levels. What are essentially exogenous funding schemes as seen both on the EU level and on national levels need to be complemented with initiatives that address the problems on endogenous levels. To some extent activities such as training programmes and establishment of learning networks may be helpful. However, a fundamental paradigmatic change of the perception of what a public agency is supposed to do might also be required. The established primary activity of any public agency is typically to deliver public services. Innovation is generally treated as an exceptional activity that often clashes with the prevailing institutional set-up. In order to fully utilize public procurement of innovation, innovation should be integrated as a complementary continuous activity alongside daily operations. This in turn calls for a revised understanding of what public procurement of innovation policy is. The necessity to understand public procurement of innovation policy making as a multilevel activity is also stressed.

The theoretical framework developed in this book acknowledges the importance of being sensitive to institutional variety and the existence of functional equivalents (Amable, 2000, p. 647), for our purposes here the insight that the role of public procurement of innovation might not be implemented in the same way everywhere. Other tools might have evolved that in some sense replace the role public procurement of innovation is intended to have. One example is in Denmark, where the policy focus has been on more blended forms of public–private innovation partnerships where the relationship between the public partner and private supplier is of a more collaborative nature than envisaged in the command paradigm (Weihe *et al.*, 2011; Albers, 2012; Rolfstam and Pedersen, forthcoming), which in turn reflects the negotiated economy that is characteristic for Denmark (Maskell, 1996). In Denmark, the most accepted form of collaboration between a public agency and private firms is the public–private innovation project (in Danish 'offentlig privat innovation', OPI). An interesting peculiarity with this form is the Danish legal perception of a public partner. Any possibility for interactive learning given by a public agency is considered as a value that may constitute state aid, unless the beneficiaries, the participating firms, are crediting the public partner. If for example a supplier is given access to a hospital ward to try out a new product the supplier must pay the public partner. Another feature of this model is that it typically does not involve a tender call aiming at procuring the actual outcome of the learning activities. This understanding contrasts with the way public procurement of innovation is understood here, where the expected outcome would be a procured innovation. The interactive learning involved is understood as a natural and essential element suppliers in public procurement of innovation projects need to be a part of, not something they should pay for. These are examples of context-specific differences that may cause confusion in policy discussions, and it may also be crucial to take them into account to work out the best way to diffuse and implement public procurement of innovation policy. Another endogenous Danish feature concerns the role of private firms. In Southern Jutland, the most southern area in Denmark, for example, there is a tradition for corporate responsibility towards the local community. Successful firms tend to engage in activities driven by a combination of philanthropic and commercial rationalities such as funding of research conducted in the local university or initiating and co-funding of local road construction projects. Exogenous attempts to introduce public procurement of innovation where the role of public agencies is moved towards the demand and command side may clash with the established perception of the relation between public agencies and firms. In such contexts policy makers might instead have to consider how to further stimulate and facilitate *private* procurement of innovation. An exclusive emphasis on the public agent as the commander might fit less well in such contexts. There are at least reasons to expect that the implementation of such policies would face endogenous challenges that, if not handled well, would reduce the chances of success.

Accepting institutional variety and the existence of functional equivalents justifies a subsidiarian approach to innovation policy where policy implementation takes into account the endogenous institutional set-up. As with any organization, public agencies evolve in and develop unique institutional set-ups and are therefore to be considered as distinct unique entities. Context-specific advice therefore requires context-specific knowledge, where applying a probabilistic checklist of success factors might be insufficient in a context requiring determining actions. This positioning should be seen in the light of what is commonly the case in practice. Policy makers may attempt to copy success stories seen elsewhere into their own domains. This 'naïve borrowing of "best-practices"' has been questioned in the context of policy making for Asian economies in transition (Lundvall *et al.*, 2006, p. 16). Similarly, authors writing about regional policies maintain that 'successful borrowing or copying of a single institutional idea is quite difficult to achieve, since it is often the case that the imitated institution will not function in the same way in the context of another institutional set-up or configuration' (Eriksson, 2005, p. 53). In a similar manner, Tödtling and Trippl (2005, p. 1204) argue that '[i]t would be misleading ... to conclude that innovation activities required to secure competitiveness are the same in all kinds of areas'.

POLICY AS INSTITUTIONAL INTERACTION

The approach applied in this book concurs with the view that 'the institutional set-up of an economy consists of many different kinds of institutions which more or less hang together and are related to one another. They form a complex system, which taken as a whole fulfils some functions in relation to both the cohesion and change of the economy' (Johnson, 1997, pp. 55–6). If organizations are shaped by the wider institutional environment (DiMaggio and Powell, 1983), a change in the wider institutional environment would somehow prompt change in an organization prevailing on a lower institutional level. Such a view provides a basic foundation for innovation policy understood essentially as an act of diffusion. The complexities that emerge with a multi-institutional understanding may on the other hand reduce the expectations of what policy can achieve (Uyarra and Flanagan, 2012). Scholars have also played with the idea of non-intervention and instead underscored the importance of enabling learning, as a generic approach to handling uncertainty (Dalum *et al.*, 2010), which in comparison is a more distributed understanding of innovation policy. Questions may therefore arise as to where in this dichotomy lies the optimal path to follow. Essentially three questions emerge. What kind of change is required, who should change and how is the change achieved?

   To pursue an answer to the first question requires a qualifying discussion. Would it suggest a striving towards an increase in the number of public procurement of innovation projects carried out? Or would it be achieved by launching a few multinational mega-projects set up to address some grand challenge? Would it be measured in terms of the quantitative ambitions formulated over the years, such as the Lisbon 3 per cent target, or an increase of the share of innovation in the 16 per cent of EU GDP that today stems from (all kinds of) public procurement?

Who would then carry out these additional projects: those that are already familiar with using public procurement as a means to generate innovation or maybe those that have not yet developed the necessary innovation-friendly institutional set-up? The answer given here is partly a non-answer. Although these numbers may have worked well to place the role of public procurement as an innovation policy instrument on the agenda, their usefulness as goals per se might be limited. The same goes for any attempts to use such quantitative effects as measures in policy evaluation. The empirical material in this book provides some further clues for such a discussion, which essentially is a discussion about additionality. One could argue that there is a tension between what perhaps could be labelled genuine public procurement of innovation and policy-induced public procurement of innovation. The former notion would refer to public procurement of innovation projects driven by intrinsic or endogenous actual needs. To the latter notion would belong any cases that are largely responses to different kinds of exogenous policy pressure and/or funding programmes, for example, as has been seen recently, obligations to direct parts of procurement budgets to 'innovation'. The question is similar to the discussions that have emerged on gender quotas as a means to attain gender equality or the extent to which entrepreneurs can be created. Most of the cases discussed in this book would belong to the former category. Even if they sometimes depended on exogenous funding and were executed in line with exogenous policies, most of them rested on endogenous endeavours evolving within either the procuring agency or the endogenous context. Any expectation of success with public procurement of innovation projects without similar endogenous anchorage appears less realistic.

Accepting the requirement of endogenous anchorage has implications for what could be expected from public agencies that are involved in public procurement of innovation as the quality and intensity of public procurement of innovation activities may also reflect the life cycles of prevailing technology. A public agency that has just procured an innovative solution, for example a power plant or a completely sustainable bus fleet, will probably not initiate a similar project aiming at satisfying the same need in the near future. Instead, for each such 'radical' project there would probably follow a lull, where public procurement of innovation is directed towards smaller amendments and incremental improvements. Implementation of exogenous innovation policy failing to take into account these internal dynamics would probably run the risk of creating tensions between the requirement to harvest the potential gains in already procured innovations, and innovation because of exogenous pressure. Successful policy implementation would probably therefore require some kind of monitoring where focus is set on technology at the end of its life cycle and public agencies that have traditionally not given much attention to public procurement of innovation.

To address the 'who question' requires some reflections on innovation policy itself. Markets have been liberalized and globalized, meaning that procurement projects seen in the past that rested on monopolistic situations will probably not emerge today. The transformation from being stand-alone countries in Europe to becoming member states in the EU has not only imposed additional institutional layers such as the EC procurement directives but also provided new possibilities for initiatives on regional levels. This can be seen for instance in Denmark, where the regional level appears to have run ahead of the national level when it comes to concrete measures to explore and utilize public procurement of innovation. A multilevel institutional view of the world as outlined in this book acknowledges the existence of local and context-specific traject-ories in innovation, but also in innovation policy (Uyarra and Flanagan, 2012). This situation affects the condition for 'governance'. 'The impli-cation is that national governments no longer have the ability to direct society toward specific goals. Instead, they must play a part within de-centered and shifting assemblages of power' (Irwin, 2008, p. 584). 'This in turn suggests that we should shift our attention away from heroic attempts at mechanistic evaluation and towards a better understanding of learning processes in relation to public policy interventions over time (including learning from failures), experimentation and trial and error' (Uyarra and Flanagan, 2012, p. 157). This in turn brings us back to an emphasis on Lundvallian learning (Lundvall, 1992).

PUBLIC PROCUREMENT OF INNOVATION LEARNING NETWORKS

One general implication derived from institutional analysis conducted concerns 'governance'. Although there thus exists some knowledge on how public procurement can be used to stimulate innovation it is noteworthy that most of the recent literature discusses or specifies certain conditions that need to be set, or *preferred states* for successful public procurement of innovation. Although adaptation to change has been studied in the context of for example climate change (e.g. Keskitalo and Kulyasova, 2009), one relatively neglected issue concerns *how* the processes would look that lead to these preferred states, that is, processes that enable the implementation of the new innovation policies for public procurement. The institutional framework developed here provides some implications useful for further scrutinizing of that issue. For instance, the analysis conducted here advances an emphasis on heterarchical governance modes rather than hierarchical ones (Borrás and Edler, 2012). The Royal Swedish Academy of Engineering Sciences (IVA) points to the need for building new networks and the fact that networking per se is a crucial success factor for different players (government, industry, academia and so on). If it is not clear whether players in the system have found their roles yet, then networking is certainly a prerequisite for the flexibility that will apparently be necessary in the future. The question is essentially: what sort of cooperation can we expect to see (IVA, 2003, p. 8)?

The relation between institutional levels becomes in this analysis reciprocal, where one institutional level exercises influence over and is influenced by other institutional levels. Understanding an organization as driven by rationalities reinforces further the limitations of a command-and-control way of thinking. A change in the EC directives will obviously change the exogenous institutional set-up for any lower institutional level. The impact on rationalities and long-term endogenous institutions' set-ups on lower institutional levels might however be substantially less certain. A procurement division with rationalities that have not earlier promoted the development of ingenious public procurement of innovation practices will not suddenly do so because of changes made in the EC directives. The extent to which any organization will harmonize with innovation policies prompting for change is determined by the organization's adaptive capacity, in turn determined by the organization's rationalities and institutional set-up as well as institutions out of range of the organization. Even the most eager procurement division would end up in difficulties when engaging in public procurement of innovation if for example national policies and/or the institutional set-up within the public agency did not also harmonize with the innovation policies. 'Adaptive capacity is thus fundamentally differentiated depending on the capacity of the actors to work within or influence the relevant systems' (Keskitalo and Kulyasova, 2009, p. 61). Realizing such change requires that considerations not only of 'hard' institutions such as law but also of 'softer' institutions such as norm and culture are taken into account. Here the notion of metagovernance is useful, which:

> refers to higher-order governance transcending the concrete forms of governance through which social and economic life is shaped, regulated and transformed. If governance is defined as a both formal and informal process through which a plurality of actors regulates a multiplicity of social, political

and economic practices in accordance with some predefined goals, metagovernance can be defined broadly as 'the governance of governance'. (Sørensen and Torfing, 2009, p. 245)

A central feature of such metagovernance understood in this context is to find an institutional match between the relevant institutions on all relevant levels.

This all implies that, if public procurement as a means to stimulate innovation is to be increasingly applied, it should not remain an issue only for public procurers or for innovation policy makers on the EU level. Networks gathering managers in public agencies, policy makers on different levels, suppliers and other not-for-profit organizations that may play a part in public procurement projects should be exposed to the potential of public procurement as a means to stimulate innovation. This is a development seen in the last few years, stimulated for instance by coordination actions and other forms of funding schemes set up on the EU level. If information is more generally diffused, this might create possibilities for the institutional redesign that may sometimes be necessary in order to use public procurement as a means to stimulate innovation. Caution should, however, be exercised in order not to lose sensitivity to context and also, to avoid cognitive lock-in. One example is the perception of public procurement as a demand-side policy tool which becomes pointless at best, if not potentially misleading. Instead, much more emphasis should be placed on the interactive characteristics of public procurement of innovation where a multi-institutional analysis is a central feature, and what implications this might have for public procurement organizations. In this way, chances are that public procurement of innovation will become diffused as a versatile innovation policy instrument for the future.

The final reference in this book will be made to a reflection concerning control versus reality, which essentially concerns the evolution of exogenous institutions:

Certain forms of knowledge and control require a narrowing of vision. The great advantage of such tunnel vision is that it brings into sharp focus certain limited aspects of an otherwise far more complex and unwieldy reality. This very simplification, in turn, makes the phenomenon at the centre of the field of vision more legible and hence more susceptible to careful measurement and calculation. Combined with similar observations, an overall, aggregate, synoptic view of a selective reality is achieved, making possible a high degree of schematic knowledge, control and manipulation. (J. Scott, 1998)

The question any researcher needs to ask is where to position oneself in this control/schematic-versus-reality spectrum. This is at least true for anyone interested in understanding public procurement of innovation.

References

Abonce Perez, E.G. (2011), 'Exogenous institutional redesign for successful procurement of innovation: the case of the public health sector in Southern Denmark', Participatory Innovation Conference, 13–15 January 2011, Sønderborg, Denmark.

Ågren, R. and A. Landin (2012), 'Contract design for procuring complex projects', in G. Piga and S. Treumer (eds), *The Applied Law and Economics of Public Procurement*, London: Routledge.

Agroptigas (2000), *Project Handbook*, NNE/2000/484, http://www.vafabmiljo.se/filarkiv/agroptigas/pdf/deliverable%20nr%201.pdf (accessed 6 January 2013).

Agroptigas (2005), 'WP 4: Communication and information forum for rural–urban co-operation', Deliverable D10, Agroptigas Project.

Aho, E., J. Cornu, L. Georghiou and A. Subira (2006), *Creating an Innovative Europe: Report of the Independent Expert Group on R&D and Innovation Appointed Following the Hampton Court Summit* (Luke Georghiou, Rapporteur), EUR 22005, Luxembourg: Office for Official Publications of the European Communities.

Albers, B. (2012), 'Farvel til leverandøren – goddag til implementeringsteamet! Offentlig-privat samarbejde om udsatte børn, unge og familjer', OPP-Nyt. 2. halvår 2012, pp. 9–12.

Amable, B. (2000), 'Institutional complementarity and diversity of social systems of innovation and production', *Review of International Political Economy*, **7** (4), 645–87.

Amit, R. and M. Belcourt (1999), 'Human resources management processes: a value-creating source of competitive advantage', *European Management Journal*, **17** (2), 174–81.

Andersen, E.S. (2003), 'Innovation and demand', in H. Hanusch and A. Pyka (eds), *Elgar Companion to Neo-Schumpeterian Economics*, Cheltenham, UK and Northampton, MA, USA: Edward Elgar Publishing.

Argyris, C. (1994), *On Organizational Learning*, Oxford: Blackwell Publishers.

Arnheim, R. (1962), *Picasso's Guernica: The Genesis of a Painting*, Berkeley CA: University of California Press.

Arrowsmith, S. (2004a), 'Public procurement: an appraisal of the UNCITRAL model law', *International and Comparative Law Quarterly*, **53**, January, 17–46.
Arrowsmith, S. (2004b), 'An assessment of the new legislative package on public procurement', *Common Market Review*, October, 1277–1325.
Arrowsmith, S. (2005), *The Law of Public and Utilities Procurement*, London: Sweet & Maxwell.
Aschhoff, B. and W. Sofka (2009), 'Innovation on demand: can public procurement drive market success of innovations?', *Research Policy*, **38**, 1235–47.
Baky, A. (2006), *Socio-Economic Analysis of the AGROPTI-Gas System*, final report WP5 Socioeconomic, Uppsala: Institutet för jordbruks- och miljöteknik.
Baxter, P. and S. Jack (2008), 'Qualitative case study methodology: study design and implementation for novice researchers', *Qualitative Report*, **13** (4), December, 544–59.
Beckert, J. (1999), 'Agency, entrepreneurs, and institutional change: the role of strategic choice and institutionalized practices in organizations', *Organization Studies*, **20**, 777.
Bengtsson, S., D. Berggren, M. Falås, M. Lindmark, C. Palomeque, C. Thengqvist and K. Karlsson (2006), 'Agroptigas: ett projekt, två utfall', unpublished project report, Teknik- och vetenskapshistoria, Uppsala Universitet.
Berggren, C. and S. Laestadius (2003), 'Co-development and composite clusters: the secular strength of Nordic telecommunications', *Industrial and Corporate Change*, **12** (1), 91–114.
Bettison, P. and A. McCormack (2002), 'Foreword', in *Bracknell Forest Town Centre Masterplan: Final Report*, http://www.bracknell-forest.gov.uk/bracknell-town-centre-master-plan.pdf (accessed 4 December 2006).
Bodewes, H., S-E. Hargeskog, L. Müller, M. Ottolander, P. Thevissen, C. Veys, N. Widmark and M. Rolfstam (2009), 'Exploring public procurement as a strategic innovation policy mix instrument', OMC–PTP Project funded within the 6th Framework Programme of the European Commission.
Borrás, S. (2004), 'System of innovation theory and the European Union', *Science and Public Policy*, **31** (6), 425–33.
Borrás, S. and J. Edler (2012), 'The governance of change in socio-technical and innovation systems: some pillars for theory-building', paper presented at the Governance of Innovation and Socio-Technical Systems in Europe: New Trends, New Challenges conference, 1–2 March, Copenhagen Business School, Denmark.

Boyle, R. (1994), 'E.C. public procurement rules: a purchaser reflects on the need for simplification', *Public Procurement Law Review*, **3**, 101–13.

Bracknell Forest Borough Council (2007), 'A history of regeneration', http://www.bracknell-forest.gov.uk/environment/env-planning-and-development/env-regeneration/env-history-of-regeneration.htm (accessed 17 July 2007).

Bracknell Town Centre Masterplan: Final report (2002), http://www.bracknell-forest.gov.uk/bracknell-town-centre-master-plan.pdf (accessed 4 December 2006).

Braun, E. (1981), 'Government policies for the stimulation of industrial innovation, Technology Policy Unit, University of Aston in Birmingham', in R. Rothwell, 'Pointers to government policies for technical innovation', *Futures*, June.

Braun, P. (2003), 'Strict compliance versus commercial reality: the practical application of EC public procurement law to the UK's private finance initiative', *European Law Journal*, **9** (5), December, 575–98.

Brenner, P. (2009), 'Tesla against Marconi: the dispute for the radio patent paternity', in *EUROCON 2009: IEEE Conference Proceedings*, New York: IEEE, pp. 1035–42.

BRP (Bracknell Regeneration Partnership) (2006a), 'Things you didn't know about Bracknell Forest', http://www.changebracknell.com/_downloads/dont_know.pdf (accessed 11 December 2006).

BRP (Bracknell Regeneration Partnership) (2006b), 'What will people get?', http://www.changebracknell.com/features_list.htm (accessed 11 December 2006).

Bryn, K. (2010), 'Foreword', in Tore Grønningsæter (ed.), 'This is EFTA 2010', European Free Trade Association, http://www.efta.int/publications/this-is-efta.aspx (accessed 10 February 2011).

Buchanan, J.M. and W.C. Stubblebine (1962), 'Externality', *Economica*, **29** (116), November, 371–84.

Cabral, L., G. Cozzi, V. Denicoló, G. Spagnolo and M. Zanza (2006), 'Procuring innovations', in N. Dimitri, G. Piga and G. Spagnolo (eds), *Handbook of Public Procurement*, Cambridge: Cambridge University Press.

Callender, G. and D. Mathews (2002), 'The economic context of government procurement: new challenges and new opportunities', *Journal of Public Procurement*, **2** (2), 216–36.

Carlsson, L. and K. Astrom (2008), 'Court decision in public procurement: delineating the grey zone', in *3rd International Public Procurement Conference Proceedings*, IPPC, pp. 191–204.

Cave, J. and E. Frinking (2003), 'Public procurement and R&D: short analysis of the potential and practices', in J.P. Gavigan (ed.), *Public*

Procurement and R&D: A JRC/IPTS-ESTO Fast Track Working Paper, Brussels: European Commission Joint Research Centre, Institute for Prospective Technological Studies, European Science and Technology Observatory, pp. 11–44.

Central Procurement Directorate, Department of Finance and Personnel, UK (1994), 'Integrating environmental considerations into public procurement', Procurement Guidance Note 04/04 (revised 27 April 2010), http://www.dfpni.gov.uk/index/procurement-2/cpd/cpd_publications/content_-_cpd_-_policy_-_procurement_guidance_notes/content_-_cpd_procurement_guidance_notes_pgn_04_-_04.htm.

Chalmers, A.F. (1999), *What Is This Thing Called Science?*, 3rd edn, Buckingham: Open University Press.

Coase, R. (1937), 'The nature of the firm', *Economica*, **4** (16), November, 386–405.

CONCERTO (2006a), 'CONCERTO', http://www.CONCERTOplus.eu/index.php (accessed 3 January 2007).

CONCERTO (2006b), 'What is CONCERTO?', http://www.CONCERTOplus.eu/what_is_CONCERTO.php (accessed 3 January 2007).

Coombs, R., P. Saviotti and V. Walsh (1987), *Economics and Technological Change*, New York: Macmillan.

Coriat, B. and O. Weinstein (2002), 'Organizations, firms and institutions in the generation of innovation', *Research Policy*, **312**, 273–90.

Cox, A. and P. Furlong (1996), 'The jury is still out for utilities procurement: the impact of the EU procurement directives on the location of utility contract awards in the "twelve" member states', *Public Procurement Law Review*, **5**, 57.

Cross, N. (1992), 'On design ability', in *Proceedings of International Conference on Theories and Methods of Design, Gothenburg*, p. 49.

CSES and OR (2011), *Final Evaluation of the Lead Market Initiative: Final Report*, July, Sevenoaks: Centre for Strategy and Evaluation Services and Oxford Research.

Currie, I. (2005), 'Using Canadian government procurement to improve technology diffusion, adoption and adaptation: maximising benefits and managing risks', discussion paper prepared for the Prime Minister's Advisory Council on Science and Technology (PMACST), 12 June.

Dahlman, C.J. (1979), 'The problem of externality', *Journal of Law and Economics*, **22** (1), 141–62.

Dalpé, R., C. DeBresson and H. Xiaoping (1992), 'The public sector as first user of innovations', *Research Policy*, **21**, 251–63.

Dalum, B., B. Johnson and B-Å. Lundvall (1992) 'Public policy in the learning society', in B-Å. Lundvall (ed.), *National Systems of Innovation: Towards a Theory of Innovation and Interactive Learning*, London: Anthem Press.

Daniel, D.R. (1961), 'Management information crisis', *Harvard Business Review*, **39** (5), September/October, 111–21.

Department of Health (2002), 'Getting ahead of the curve: a strategy for combating infectious diseases', http://image.guardian.co.uk/sys-files/Society/documents/2003/12/05/idstrategy2002.pdf (accessed 13 February 2007).

Department of Health (2003), 'Winning ways: working together to reduce healthcare associated infection in England', http://www.dh.gov.uk/assetRoot/04/06/46/89/04064689.pdf (accessed 13 February 2007).

Department of Justice and the Police (2001), 'Diverser stillinger til TETRA-prosjektet', job advertisement, http://odin.dep.no/odinarkiv/norsk/dep/jd/2001/annet/012101-180008/dok-bn.html (accessed 19 January 2005).

Department of Justice and the Police (2004), *TETRA Pilot Project Final Report*, Version 1.0, 7 August.

DiMaggio, P.J. and W.W. Powell (1983), 'The iron cage revisited: institutional isomorphism and collective rationality in organizational fields', *American Sociological Review*, **48**, April, 147–60.

DNK (2011), 'Evalueringsrapport Nødnett trinn 1', Direktoratet for nødkommunikation, http://www.dinkom.no/Global/Dokumenter/rapporter/evalueringsrapport_trinn_1_ver1_1.pdf (accessed 6 January 2013).

Donk, W.B.H.J. van de and I.T.M. Snellen (1989), 'Knowledge-based systems in public administration: evolving practices and norms', in I.T.M. Snellen (ed.), *Expert Systems in Public Administration: Evolving Practices and Norms*, Amsterdam: Elsevier.

Dosi, G. (1982), 'Technological paradigms and technological trajectories', *Research Policy*, **11**, 147–63.

Dosi, G. (1988), 'The nature of the innovation process', in G. Dosi, C. Freeman, R. Nelson, G. Silverberg and L. Soete (eds), *Technical Change and Economic Theory*, London: Pinter.

Dosi, G., C. Freeman, R. Nelson, G. Silverberg and L. Soete (1988), *Technical Change and Economic Theory*, London: Pinter.

Dosi, G. and L. Orsenigo (1988), 'Coordination and transformation: an overview of structures, behaviours and change in evolutionary environments', in G. Dosi, C. Freeman, R. Nelson, G. Silverberg and L. Soete (eds), *Technical Change and Economic Theory*, London: Pinter.

DSB (2000), 'Nytt felles radiosamband for nöd- og beredskapsetatene: TETRA pilotprosjekt i Trondheimsområdet', DBE-448, http://www.dsb.no:81/File.asp?File=PDF/bestillingslista/tetra.pdf (accessed 22 January 2005).

Dunleavy, P. (1981), *The Politics of Mass Housing in Britain 1945–1975: A Study of Power and Professional Influence in the Welfare State*, Oxford: Oxford University Press.

Edler, J. (2007), 'Demand-based innovation policy', Manchester Business School Working Paper no. 529, http://www.mbs.ac.uk/research/workingpapers/.

Edler, J. and L. Georghiou (2007), 'Public procurement and innovation: resurrecting the demand side', *Research Policy*, **36** (9), 949–63.

Edler, J., S. Ruhland, S. Hafner, J. Rigby, L. Georghiou, L. Hommen, M. Rolfstam, C. Edquist, L. Tsipouri and M. Papadakou (2005), *Innovation and Public Procurement: Review of Issues at Stake*, study for the European Commission, Karlsruhe: Fraunhofer ISI.

Edmondson, A.C., R.M. Bohmer and G.P. Pisano (2001), 'Disrupted routines: team learning and new technology implementation in hospitals', *Administrative Science Quarterly*, **46** (4), 685–716.

Edquist, C. (ed.) (1997), *Systems of Innovation: Technologies, Institutions and Organizations*, London: Pinter.

Edquist, C., P. Hammarqvist and L. Hommen (2000), 'Public technology procurement in Sweden: the X2000 high speed train', in C. Edquist, L. Hommen and L. Tsipouri (eds), *Public Technology Procurement and Innovation*, Boston, MA: Kluwer Academic Publishers.

Edquist, C. and L. Hommen (1999), 'Systems of innovation: theory and policy for the demand side', *Technology in Society*, **21**, 63–79.

Edquist, C. and L. Hommen (2000), 'Public technology procurement and innovation theory', in C. Edquist, L. Hommen and L. Tsipouri (eds), *Public Technology Procurement and Innovation*, Boston, MA: Kluwer Academic Publishers.

Edquist, C., L. Hommen and L. Tsipouri (eds) (2000), *Public Technology Procurement and Innovation*, Boston, MA: Kluwer Academic Publishers.

Edquist, C. and B. Johnson (1997), 'Institutions and organizations in systems of innovation', in Charles Edquist (ed.), *Systems of Innovation: Technologies, Institutions and Organizations*, London: Pinter.

Edquist, C. and J.M. Zabala-Iturriagagoitia (2012), 'Public procurement for innovation as mission-oriented policy', *Research Policy*, **41** (10), 1757–69.

EFTA (2006), 'Overview of the Vaduz Convention', http://secretariat.efta.int/Web/EFTAConvention/AboutTheConvention/OverviewOfThe VaduzConvention/view.

Eisenhardt, K.M. (1989), 'Building theories from case study research', *Academy of Management Review*, **14** (4), October, 532–50.

Eliasson, G. (2010), *Advanced Public Procurement as Industrial Policy: The Aircraft Industry as a Technical University*, New York: Springer Science, Business Media.

Emmerson, A.M., J.E. Enstone, M. Griffin, M.C. Kelsey and E.T.M. Smyth (1996), 'The second national prevalence survey of infection in hospitals: overview of the results', *Journal of Hospital Infection*, **32**, 175–90.

Environmental Industries Unit (2006), *Bridging the Gap between Environmental Necessity and Economic Opportunity: First Report of the Environmental Innovations Advisory Group*, London: Department for Environment, Food and Rural Affairs/Department of Trade and Industry, UK.

Erdmenger, C. (ed.) (2003), *Buying into the Environmental Experiences, Opportunities and Potential for Eco-Procurement*, Sheffield: Greenleaf Publishing.

Eriksson, M-L. (2005), 'Organising regional innovation to support Sweden's industrial development centres as regional development coalitions', Ph.D. thesis, Department of Technology and Social Change, Linköping University.

Europe Innova (2008), 'STEPPIN', http://standards.eu-innova.org/Pages/Steppin/default.aspx (accessed 12 July 2008).

European Commission (1998), *Public Procurement in the European Union*, Communication from the Commission, COM(1998) 143 final, Brussels: European Commission.

European Commission (2002a), *The Lisbon Strategy: Making Things Happen*, COM(2002) 14, Brussels: European Commission.

European Commission (2002b), *More Research for Europe towards 3% of GDP*, COM(2002) 499, Brussels: European Commission.

European Commission (2003a), *Raising the EU R&D Intensity: Improving the Effectiveness of the Mix of Public Support Mechanisms for Private Sector Research and Development*, Brussels: European Commission.

European Commission (2003b), *Investing in Research: An Action Plan for Europe*, COM(2003) 226, Brussels: European Commission.

European Commission (2004a), *A Report on the Functioning of Public Procurement Markets in the EU: Benefits from the Application of EU Directives and Challenges for the Future*, Brussels: European Commission.

European Commission (2004b), *Buying Green! A Handbook of Green Procurement*, SEC(2004) 1050, Brussels: European Commission.

European Commission (2005), *Implementing the Community Lisbon Programme: More Research and Innovation – Investing for Growth and Employment: A Common Approach*, COM(2005) 488, Brussels: European Commission.

European Commission (2006), *Creating an Innovative Europe: Report of the Independent Expert Group on R&D and Innovation Appointed Following the Hampton Court Summit*, EUR 22005, Brussels: European Commission.

European Commission (2007a), *Pre-Commercial Procurement: Driving Innovation to Ensure Sustainable High Quality Public Services in Europe*, COM(2007) 799 final, Brussels: European Commission.

European Commission (2007b), *Guide on Dealing with Innovative Solutions in Public Procurement: 10 Elements of Good Practice*, Commission Staff Working Document SEC(2007) 280, Brussels: European Commission.

European Commission (2010), *Europe 2020 Flagship Initiative: Innovation Union*, Communication from the Commission to the European Parliament, the Council, the European Economic and Social Committee and the Committee of the Regions, COM(2010) 546 final, Brussels: European Commission.

European Commission (2011), *Green Paper on the Modernisation of EU Public Procurement Policy: Towards a More Efficient European Procurement Market*, COM(2011) 15 final, Brussels: European Commission.

European Commission (2012), *Annual Public Procurement Implementation Review 2012*, SWD(2012) 342 final, Brussels: European Commission.

European Council (2000), *Lisbon European Council 23 and 24 March 2000: Presidency Conclusions*, Brussels: European Council.

European Council (2005), *Council Recommendation of 12 July 2005 on the Broad Guidelines for the Economic Policies of the Member States and the Community (2005 to 2008)*, 2005/601/EC, Brussels: European Council.

European Parliament and Council (2004a), 'Coordinating the procurement procedures of entities operating in the water, energy, transport and postal services sectors', EC Directive 2004/17/EC, *Official Journal of the European Union*, 30 April.

European Parliament and Council (2004b), 'On the coordination of procedures for the award of public works contracts, public supply contracts and public service contracts', EC Directive 2004/18/EC, *Official Journal of the European Union*, 30 April.

Fagerberg, J. (2005), 'Innovation: a guide to the literature', in J. Fagerberg, D. Mowery and R. Nelson (eds), *The Oxford Handbook of Innovation*, Oxford: Oxford University Press.

Fagerberg, J., D. Mowery and R. Nelson (eds) (2005), *The Oxford Handbook of Innovation*, Oxford: Oxford University Press.

Freeman, C. (1982), *The Economics of Industrial Innovation*, Cambridge, MA: MIT Press.

Fridlund, M. (1999), 'Den gemensamma utvecklingen: staten, storföretaget och samarbetet kring den svenska elkrafttekniken', symposium, Stockholm.

Gavras, A., L. Hommen, M. Rolfstam, N. Vasileiadis, M. Mavis, L. Sousa Cardoso and D. Tsigos (2006), *Procurement as an Innovation Instrument*, Heidelberg: Inno-Utilities/EC 5th Framework Programme for Research and Technological Development.

Gelderman, C.J., P.W.T. Ghijsen and M.J. Brugman (2006), 'Public procurement and EU tendering directives: explaining non-compliance', *International Journal of Public Sector Management*, **19** (7), 702–14.

Georghiou, L. (2007), *Demanding Innovation: Lead Markets, Public Procurement and Innovation*, Provocation 02: February, London: National Endowment for Science, Technology and the Arts (NESTA).

Geroski, P.A. (1990), 'Procurement policy as a tool of industrial policy', *International Review of Applied Economics*, **4** (2), 182–98.

Gibbons, M., C. Limoges, H. Nowotny, S. Schwartzman, P. Scott and M. Trow (1994), *The New Production of Knowledge: The Dynamics of Science and Research in Contemporary Societies*, Thousand Oaks, CA: Sage.

Gjerløv-Juel, P. (2012), 'Who loses a leader without losing ground? Unexpected death in top management teams and firm performance', Working Paper, 26 June, DRUID, Aalborg University.

Granstrand, O. (1984), 'Technology procurement as a special form of buyer–seller interaction in industrial marketing', CIM Report no. 84:06, Department of Industrial Management, Chalmers University of Technology, Gothenburg.

Granstrand, O. and J. Sigurdsson (eds) (1985), *Technological Innovation and Industrial Development in Telecommunications: The Role of Public Buying in the Telecommunications Sector in the Nordic Countries*, Oslo: Nordic Cooperative Organization for Applied Research/ Research Policy Institute.

Green, P. (1994), 'The Utilities Directive 93/38: the extent to which it applies to contracting entities', *Public Procurement Law Review*, **3**, 173–86.

Gregersen, B. (1992), 'The public sector as a pacer in national systems of innovation', in B-Å. Lundvall (ed.), *National Systems of Innovation: Towards a Theory of Innovation and Interactive Learning*, London: Pinter.

Grønningsæter, T. (ed.) (2010), 'This is EFTA 2010', European Free Trade Association, http://www.efta.int/publications/this-is-efta.aspx (accessed 10 February 2011).

Guy, K. *et al.* (2003), *Raising EU R&D Intensity: Improving the Effectiveness of the Mix of Public Support Mechanisms for Private Sector Research and Development*, Report to the European Commission by an Independent Study Group, Brussels: European Commission.

Hall, B. (2005), 'Innovation and diffusion', in J. Fagerberg, D. Mowery and R. Nelson (eds), *The Oxford Handbook of Innovation*, Oxford: Oxford University Press.

Health Protection Agency (2006), 'Rapid Review Panel', http://www. hpa. org.uk/infections/topics_az/rapid_review/default.htm (accessed 17 October 2006).

Heller, J. (1994), *Catch-22*, New York: Simon & Schuster.

Henderson, R.M. and K.B. Clark (1990), 'Architectural innovation: the reconfiguration of existing product technologies and the failure of established firms', *Administrative Science Quarterly*, **35** (1), 9–30.

Hippel, E. von (1976), 'The dominant role of users in the scientific instrument innovation process', *Research Policy*, **5**, 212–39.

Hippel, E. von (1988), *The Sources of Innovation*, Oxford: Oxford University Press.

Hjaltadóttir, R.E. (2011), 'Endogenous institutions for user–producer interaction in public procurement of innovation', Participatory Innovation Conference, 13–15 January, Sønderborg, Denmark.

Hodgson, G.M. (2006), 'What are institutions?', *Journal of Economic Issues*, **XL** (1), March, 1–25.

Hollingsworth, J.R. (2000), 'Doing institutional analysis: implications for the study of innovations', *Review of International Political Economy*, **7** (4), 595–644.

Hommen, L. and M. Rolfstam (2005), 'Public technology procurement in relation to markets and social need: a strive towards a typology', seminar, 8 November, Department of Design Sciences, Lund University.

Hommen, L. and M. Rolfstam (2009), 'Public procurement and innovation: towards a taxonomy', *Journal of Public Procurement*, **9** (1), 17–56.

IEA (International Energy Agency) (2000), 'Annex III: Co-operative procurement of innovative technologies for demand-side management', in *Implementing Agreement on Demand-Side Management Technologies and Programmes: Final Management Report*, Stockholm, IEA.

Irwin, A. (2008), 'STS perspectives on scientific governance', in E. Hackett, O. Amsterdamska, M. Lynch and J. Wajcman (eds), *The Handbook of Science and Technology Studies*, Cambridge, MA: MIT Press, pp. 583–607.

Isaksen, S. (2003), 'Maritime radio – from Marconi to GMDSS', http://www.maritimradio.no/english/engelsk3.htm (accessed 29 March 2005).

IVA (2003), *Technical Development in Deregulated Markets: What We Can Learn from the Telecom, Energy, Railway and Defence Sectors – Executive Summary*, Stockholm: Royal Swedish Academy of Engineering Sciences.

Jacoby, S.M. (1990), 'The new institutionalism: what can it learn from the old?', *Industrial Relations*, **29** (2), 316–40.

Jegrelius (2010), *The Art of Buying What Is Not Available on the Market: Blood Bags – A Pilot Case to Stimulate Eco-Innovation within the Healthcare Sector*, Final Report, Vinnova Project reg. no. 2008-0381, October, Östersund: Jegrelius Institute for Applied Green Chemistry.

Jepperson, R.J. (1991), 'Institutions, institutional effects, and institutionalism', in Walter W. Powell and Paul J. DiMaggio (eds), *The New Institutionalism in Organizational Analysis*, Chicago: University of Chicago Press, pp. 1–38.

Johnson, B. (1992), 'Institutional learning', in Bengt-Åke Lundvall (ed.), *National Systems of Innovation: Towards a Theory of Innovation and Interactive Learning*, London: Pinter, pp. 23–44.

Jones, C., W.S. Hesterly and S.P. Borgatti (1997), 'A general theory of network governance: exchange conditions and social mechanism', *Academy of Management Review*, **22** (4), 911–45.

Kaiserfeld, T. (2000), 'A case study of the Swedish public technology procurement project "The Computer in the School" (COMPIS), 1981–1988', in C. Edquist, L. Hommen and L. Tsipouri (eds), *Public Technology Procurement and Innovation*, Boston, MA: Kluwer Academic Publishers.

Keskitalo, E.C.H. and A.A. Kulyasova (2009), 'The role of governance in community adaptation to climate change', *Polar Research*, **28**, 60–70.

Kline, S.J. and N. Rosenberg (1986), 'An overview of innovation', in R. Landau and N. Rosenberg (eds), *The Positive Sum Game*, Washington, DC: National Academy Press.

Kuhn, T.S. (1996), *The Structure of Scientific Revolutions*, 3rd edn, Chicago, IL: University of Chicago Press.

Larsen, P., H. Mortensen, H. Thorup, H.A. Møller, J. Lebech and E. Larsen (2006), *Beretning om staten som indkøber*, Copenhagen: Statsrevisoratet.

Lawless, M.W. and L.L. Price (1992), 'An agency perspective on new technology champions', *Organization Science*, **3** (3), August (Focused Issue: Management of Technology), 342–55.

Lember, V., T. Kalvet and R. Kattel (2010), 'Urban competitiveness and public procurement for innovation', *Urban Studies*, **48** (7), 1373–95.

Levinson, O. (2006), 'The Whiz Clean Catch: the rocky road to marketing an innovative product into the NHS – procuring for healthcare 2006: investing in innovation', *HES Magazine*, June.

Li, Y. (2011), 'Public procurement as a demand-side innovation policy tool in China: a national level case study', DRUID Society Conference on Innovation, Strategy, and Structure, 15–17 June, Copenhagen Business School, Denmark.

Lissoni, F. and S. Metcalfe (1996), 'Diffusion of innovation ancient and modern: a review of the main themes', in M. Dodgson and R. Rothwell (eds), *The Handbook of Industrial Innovation*, Cheltenham, UK and Brookfield, VT, USA: Edward Elgar Publishing.

Lister, S. (2004), 'NHS is world's biggest employer after Indian rail and Chinese Army', *Times Online*, 20 March, http://www.timesonline.co.uk/tol/news/uk/health/article1050197.ece (accessed 25 February 2008).

Lundvall, B-Å. (1988), 'Innovation as an interactive process: from user–producer interaction to the national system of innovation', in G. Dosi, C. Freeman, R. Nelson, G. Silverberg and L. Soete (eds), *Technical Change and Economic Theory*, London: Pinter.

Lundvall, B-Å. (ed.) (1992), *National Systems of Innovation: Towards a Theory of Innovation and Interactive Learning*, London: Pinter.

Lundvall, B-Å. and S. Borrás (1997), 'The globalising learning economy: implications for innovation policy', report based on contributions from seven projects under the TSER programme, DG XII, Commission of the European Union, ftp://ftp.cordis.lu/pub/tser/docs/globeco.doc (accessed 10 March 2013).

Lundvall, B-Å. and S. Borrás (2005), 'Science, technology and innovation policy', in J. Fagerberg, D. Mowery and R. Nelson (eds), *The Oxford Handbook of Innovation*, Oxford: Oxford University Press.

Lundvall, B-Å., P. Intarakumnerd and J. Vang (2006), 'Asia's innovation systems in transition: an introduction', in B-Å. Lundvall, P. Intarakumnerd and J. Vang (eds), *Asia's Innovation Systems in Transition*, Cheltenham, UK and Northampton, MA, USA: Edward Elgar Publishing.

Maidique, M.A. (1980), 'Entrepreneurs, champions and technological innovation', *Sloan Management Review*, **21** (2), Winter, 59–76.

Malerba, F. (1985), 'Demand structure and technological change', *Research Policy*, **14**, 283–97.

Mani, S. (2003), *Deregulation, Entry of MNCs, Public Technology Procurement and Innovation Capability in India's Telecommunications Equipment Industry*, April, Tokyo: United Nations University, INTECH, Institute for New Technologies.

Maritim Radio (2005a), 'Generelle tjenester Kystradio', http://www.maritimradio.no/generelt/1g-kystradio.htm (accessed 29 March 2005).

Maritim Radio (2005b), 'Telenor Networks Maritime Radio', http://www.maritimradio.no/english/engelsk1.htm (accessed 30 March 2005).

Martin, J.F. (1996), *The EC Public Procurement Rules: A Critical Analysis*, Oxford: Clarendon Press.

Martin, S., K. Hartley and A. Cox (1997), 'Public purchasing in the European Union: some evidence from contract awards', *International Journal of Public Sector Management*, **10** (4), 279–93.

Maskell, P. (2006), 'Learning in the village economy of Denmark: the role of institutions and policy in sustaining competitiveness', Working Paper no. 96-6, Danish Research Unit for Industrial Dynamics (DRUID).

McCrudden, C. (2004), 'Using public procurement to achieve social outcomes', *Natural Resources Forum*, **28**, 257–67.

McDonough, W. and M. Braungart (2002), *Cradle to Cradle: Remaking the Way We Make Things*, New York: North Point Press.

Medisat (2011), Press release, http://www.medisat.dk/en/Start.aspx (accessed 12 October 2011).

Ministry of Economic Development (2005), *New Zealand Government Procurement Policy Review, Part Two: Realising the Potential for Innovation*, October, Wellington: Regulatory and Competition Policy Branch, New Zealand Ministry of Economic Development.

Morrar, R. (2011), 'Conceptual framework for public private innovation networks (PPIN): a technological perspective', Participatory Innovation Conference, 13–15 January, Sønderborg, Denmark.

Mowery, D. and N. Rosenberg (1979), 'The influence of market demand upon innovation: a critical review of some recent empirical studies', *Research Policy*, **8**, 102–53.

Murray, J.G. (2009), 'Towards a common understanding of the differences between purchasing, procurement and commissioning in the UK public sector', *Journal of Purchasing and Supply Management*, **15** (3), 198–202.

Myoken, Y. (2010), 'Demand-orientated policy on leading-edge industry and technology: public procurement for innovation', *International Journal of Technology Management*, **49** (1/2/3), 196–219.

Nassimbeni, G. (1998), 'Network structures and co-ordination mechanisms: a taxonomy', *International Journal of Operations and Product Management*, **18** (6), 538–54.

National IST Research Directors Forum Working Group (2006), 'Pre-commercial procurement of innovation', http://europa.eu.int/rapid/pressReleasesAction.do?reference=IP/06/373&format=DOC&aged=0&language=EN&guiLanguage=en (accessed 13 April 2006).

Neij, L. (2001), 'Methods of evaluating market transformation programmes: experience in Sweden', *Energy Policy*, **29**, 67–79.

Nelson, R.R. (ed.) (1993), *National Innovation Systems: A Comparative Analysis*, Oxford: Oxford University Press.

Nelson, R.R. (2008), 'What enables rapid economic progress: what are the needed institutions?', *Research Policy*, **37**, 1–11.

Nelson, R.R. and K. Nelson (2002), 'Technology, institutions, and innovation systems', *Research Policy*, **31**, 265–72.

Nelson, R.R. and N. Rosenberg (1993), 'Technical innovation and national systems', in R.R. Nelson (ed.), *National Innovation Systems: A Comparative Analysis*, Oxford: Oxford University Press.

Nelson, R.R. and B.N. Sampat (2001), 'Making sense of institutions as a factor shaping economic performance', *Journal of Economic Behaviour and Organization*, **44**, 31–54.

Nelson, R.R. and S.G. Winter (1982), *An Evolutionary Theory of Economic Change*, Cambridge, MA: Belknap Press of Harvard University Press.

NHS PASA (2008), 'NHS procurement', http://www.pasa.nhs.uk/PASAWeb/NHSprocurement/AboutNHSPASA/LandingPage.htm (accessed 25 February 2008).

Nonaka, I. (1994), 'A dynamic theory of organizational knowledge creation', *Organization Science*, **5** (1), February, 14–37.

North, D.C. (1990), *Institutions, Institutional Change, and Economic Performance*, Cambridge: Cambridge University Press.

Norwegian Government (2004), 'Future radio communication for the emergency and preparedness services', Proposition no. 1 to the Storting, Supplement no. 2 (English translation), http://www.nodnett.dep.no/stortingsdok/Proposition%20v1.0%20-%20Norwegian%20Public%20Safety%20Radio%20Network.PDF (accessed 24 January 2005).

Nyholm, J., L. Normann, C. Frelle-Petersen, M. Riis and P. Torstensen (2001), 'Innovation policy in the knowledge-based economy: can theory guide policy making?', in D. Archibugi and B-Å. Lundvall (eds), *The Globalizing Learning Economy*, Oxford: Oxford University Press.

OECD (2011), *Demand-Side Innovation Policies*, Paris: OECD Publishing, http://dx.doi.org/10.1787/9789264098886-en (accessed 8 December 2011).

OPI-Lab (2011), 'OPI-Lab: laboratorium for offentlig-privat innovation og vælfærdsteknologi', http://www.opi-lab.dk/ (accessed 17 August 2011).

Orlikowski, W.J. (1992), 'The duality of technology: rethinking the technology in organizations', *Organization Science*, **3** (3), 398–427.

Ostrom, E. (2005), *Understanding Institutional Diversity*, Princeton, NJ: Princeton University Press.

Palmberg, C. (2002), 'Technical systems and competent procurers: the transformation of Nokia and the Finnish telecom industry revisited?', *Telecommunications Policy*, **26**, 129–48.

Pénin, J., C. Hussler and T. Burger-Helmchen (2011), 'New shapes and new stakes: a portrait of open innovation as a promising phenomenon', *Journal of Innovation Economics*, **1** (7), 11–29.

Persson, A. (2004), *Teknikupphandling som styrmedel: metodik och exempel*, 30 March, Stockholm: Statens Energimyndighet.

Persson, B. (2008), 'The development of a new Swedish innovation policy: a historical institutional approach', CIRCLE Electronic Working Paper Series Paper no. 2008/2.

Petersen, O.H. (2011), 'Public–private partnerships: policy and regulation – with comparative and multi-level case studies from Denmark and Ireland', Ph.D. thesis, Ph.D. series 8.2011, Copenhagen Business School.

Phillips, W.E., L.A. Knight, N.D. Caldwell and J. Warrington (2007), 'Policy through procurement: the introduction of digital signal process (DSP) hearing aids into the English NHS, *Health Policy*, **80** (1), 77–85.

Plowman, R., N. Graves, M.A.S. Griffin, J.A. Roberts, A.V. Swan, B. Cookson and L. Taylor (2001), 'The rate and cost of hospital-acquired infections occurring in patients admitted to selected specialities of a district general hospital in England and the national burden imposed', *Journal of Hospital Infection*, **47**, 198–209.

Pratt, R.J. and B.O. O'Malley (2007), 'Supporting evidence-based infection prevention and control practice in the National Health Service in England: the NHS/TVU/Intuition Approach', *Journal of Hospital Infection*, **65** (52), 142–7.

Pratt, R.J., C.M. Pellowe, J.A. Wilson, H.P. Loveday, P.J. Harper, S.R.L.J. Jones, C. McDougall and M.H. Wilcox (2007), 'epic2: National

Evidence-Based Guidelines for Preventing Healthcare-Associated Infections in NHS Hospitals in England', *Journal of Hospital Infection*, **65** (52), S1–S64.

Ragin, C.C. (1987), *The Comparative Method: Moving beyond Qualitative and Quantitative Strategies*, Berkeley, CA: University of California Press.

Renaissance (2006), 'Renaissance', http://www.CONCERTOplus.eu/projects/RENAISSANCE.php (accessed 3 January 2007).

Rhodes, R.A.W. (2007), 'Understanding governance: ten years on', *Organization Studies*, **28** (8), 1243–64.

Robinson, P.J., C.W. Faris and Y. Wind (1967), *Industrial Buying and Creative Marketing*, Boston, MA: Allyn & Bacon.

Rogers, E.M. (1995), *Diffusion of Innovations*, 4th edn, New York: Free Press.

Rolfstam, M. (2001), 'Design as handling and reflecting of errors', Master's thesis, Department of Informatics, Lund University.

Rolfstam, M. (2005), 'Public technology as a demand-side innovation policy instrument: an overview of recent literature and events', DRUID Winter Conference, 27–29 January, Skoerping, Aalborg, Denmark.

Rolfstam, M. (2007a), 'Organisations and institutions in public procurement of innovations: the case of the energy centre in Bracknell Forest, UK', DRUID Winter Conference, 27–29 January, Skoerping, Aalborg, Denmark.

Rolfstam, M. (2007b), 'The Utilities Directive and how it might affect innovation: the case of innovative procurement of maritime radio technology', *Public Procurement Law Review*, **16** (6), 435–60.

Rolfstam, M. (2008), 'Public procurement of innovation', Ph.D. thesis, Centre for Innovation, Research and Competence in the Learning Economy (CIRCLE) and Department of Design Sciences, Lund University.

Rolfstam, M. (2009a), 'Public procurement as an innovation policy tool: the role of institutions', *Science and Public Policy*, **36** (5), June, 349–60.

Rolfstam, M. (2009b), 'Public procurement of innovation as network governance', International Conference on Governance Networks: Democracy, Policy Innovation and Global Regulation, 2–4 December, Sørup Mansion, Denmark.

Rolfstam, M. (2010), 'A tentative model of a demand system for public procurement of innovation', *Proceedings of the International Public Procurement Conference*, 26–28 August, Seoul, South Korea.

Rolfstam, M. (2012a), 'An institutional approach to research on public procurement of innovation', *Innovation: European Journal of Social Science Research*, **25** (3), 303–21.

Rolfstam, M. (2012b), 'Understanding public procurement of innovation: definitions, innovation types and interaction modes', working paper, 26 February, http://ssrn.com/abstract=2011488 or http://dx.doi.org/10. 2139/ssrn.2011488.

Rolfstam, M. (2012c), 'Good rules or bad rules in public procurement of innovation: but is it really the (right) question?', *Halduskultuur: Administrative Culture*, **13** (2), 109–29.

Rolfstam, M. and R. Ågren (forthcoming), 'Public procurement of innovation in Sweden', submitted book chapter.

Rolfstam, M. and O.H. Pedersen (forthcoming), 'Public procurement for innovation policy: the case of Denmark', submitted book chapter.

Rolfstam, M., W. Phillips and E. Bakker (2011), 'Public procurement of innovations, diffusion and endogenous institutions', *International Journal of Public Sector Management*, **24** (5), 452–68.

Rothwell, R. (1981), 'Pointers to government policies for technical innovation', *Futures*, **13** (3, June), 171–83.

Rothwell, R. (1984), 'Creating a regional innovation-oriented infrastructure: the role of public procurement', *Annals of Public and Cooperative Economics*, **55** (2), 159–72.

Rothwell, R. (1994), 'Issues in user–producer relations in the innovation process: the role of government', *International Journal of Technology Management*, **9** (5/6/7), 629–49.

Rupp, M.E., T. Fitzgerald, N. Marion, V. Helget, S. Puumala, J.R. Anderson and P.D. Fey (2004), 'Effect of silver-coated urinary catheters: efficiency, cost-effectiveness, and antimicrobial resistance', *American Journal of Infection Control*, **32** (8), 445–50.

Schön, D.A. (1983), *The Reflective Practitioner: How Professionals Think in Action*, New York: Basic Books.

Schumpeter, J. (1934 [1969]), *The Theory of Economic Development*, New York: Oxford University Press.

Schumpeter, J. (1976), *Capitalism, Socialism and Democracy*, London: Routledge.

Scott, J.C. (1998), *Seeing like a State: How Certain Schemes to Improve the Human Condition Have Failed*, New Haven, CT: Yale University Press.

Scott, W.R. (2003), 'Institutional carriers: reviewing modes of transporting ideas over time and space and considering their consequences', *Industrial and Corporate Change*, **12** (4), 879–94.

Searle, J.R. (2005), 'What is an institution?', *Journal of Institutional Economics*, **1** (1), 1–22.

SFS 1992:1528, Lagen om offentlig upphandling, http://www.notisum.se/ rnp/SLS/LAG/19921528.HTM (accessed 5 May 2004).

SFS 2007:1091, Lag om offentlig upphandling, http://www.notisum.se/ rnp/sls/lag/20071091.htm (accessed 10 March 2013).
Soete, L. (2010), 'The costs of a non-innovative Europe: the challenges ahead', http://eur-lex.europa.eu/LexUriServ/LexUriServ.do?uri=COM: 2005:0474:FIN:en:PDF (accessed 3 July 2011).
Soini, K. and T. Keinonen (2011), 'Building up commitment at the Finnish renovation industry', Participatory Innovation Conference, 13–15 January, Sønderborg, Denmark.
Sørensen, E. and J. Torfing (2009), 'Making governance networks effective and democratic through metagovernance', *Public Administration*, **87** (2), 234–58.
SOU (1976), 'Teknikupphandling: betänkande av Teknikupphandskommittén', SOU 1976:69.
SOU (2013), 'Goda affärer – en strategi för hållbar offentlig upphandling', SOU 2013:12.
Stolterman, E. (1991), 'Designarbetes dolda rationalitet: en studie om metodik och praktik inom systemutveckling', doctoral dissertation, Department of Information Processing, Umeå University.
Suvilehto, H-M. and E. Öfverholm (1998), 'Swedish procurement and market activities: different design solutions and different markets', *Proceedings of the ACEEE 1998 Summer Study on Energy Efficiency in Buildings*, Washington, DC: ACEEE.
Sylvest, J. (2008), *Opportunities for Public Technology Procurement in the ICT-Related Sectors in Europe: Final Report*, commissioned by the European Commission, Directorate-General for Information Society and Media, Copenhagen: Rambøll Management.
TED (2005), 'UK – Bracknell Forest: wood-fired power station', Contract Notice 2005/ S 6-005350, *Tenders Electronic Daily*, http:// ted.europa.eu (accessed 11 December 2006).
TED (2006), 'UK – Bracknell Forest: wood-fired power station, additional information', 2006/ S 70-072649, *Tenders Electronic Daily*, http://ted.europa.eu (accessed 11 December 2006).
Teleplan (1999), 'Felles radionett for nödetatene: sammendrag av forstudie', www.nodnett.dep.no/arkiv/Forprosjekt_kortversion.doc (accessed 22 January 2005).
Thai, K.V. and R. Grimm (2000), 'Government procurement: past and current developments', *Journal of Public Budgeting, Accounting and Financial Management*, **12** (2), 231–47.
Tödtling, F. and M. Trippl (2005), 'One size fits all? Towards a differentiated regional innovation policy approach', *Research Policy*, **34**, 1203–19.
Tsipouri, L. *et al.* (2010), *Risk Management in the Procurement of Innovation: Concepts and Empirical Evidence in the European Union*,

EC Expert Group of Public Procurement and Risk Management, Brussels: European Commission.

Turkama, P., I. Zálišová, M. Rolfstam, S. Ikävalko, Á. de Oliveira and M. Nina (2012), 'Policy recommendations for advancing pre-commercial procurement in Europe', project report, PreCo (Enhancing Innovation in Pre-Commercial Purchasing Processes), funded by the European Commission, Directorate-General for Information Society and Media.

TV Energy (2005), 'TV Energy company profile', http://www.tvenergy.org/pdfs/tve-company-profile-25-02-2005.pdf (accessed 2 January 2007).

Tvarnø, C.D., with H. Andersen, F. Cao and P. Wang (2010), *Public–Private Partnerships: An International Analysis – From a Legal and Economic Perspective*, Nottingham: EU Asia Inter University Network for Teaching and Research in Public Procurement Regulation.

University of Reading (2004), 'Bracknell Forest to become a European beacon for green energy', press release, 20 May, http://www.extra.rdg.ac.uk/news/details.asp?ID=368 (accessed 3 January 2007).

US–China Business Council (2010), 'Issue brief: new developments in China's domestic innovation and procurement policies', http://www.dudebin.com/library/Chinadomesticinnovation.pdf (accessed 6 January 2013).

Utterback, J.M. (1994), *Mastering the Dynamics of Innovation: How Companies Can Seize Opportunities in the Face of Technological Change*, Cambridge, MA: MIT Press.

Uttley, M.R.H. and K. Hartley (1994), 'Public procurement in the Single European Market: policy and prospects', *European Business Review*, **94** (2), 3–7.

Uyarra, E. and K. Flanagan (2010), 'Understanding the innovation impacts of public procurement', *European Planning Studies*, **18** (1), 123–43.

Uyarra, E. and K. Flanagan (2012), 'Reframing regional innovation systems: evolution, complexity and public policy', in P. Cooke (ed.), *Reframing Regional Development: Evolution, Innovation and Transition*, London: Routledge.

Valkenburg, M. van and M.C.J. Nagelkerke (2006), 'Interweaving planning procedures for environmental impact assessment for high level infrastructure with public procurement procedures', *Journal of Public Procurement*, **6** (3), 250–73.

Vanberg, V.J. (1997), 'Institutional evolution through purposeful selection: the constitutional economics of John R. Commons', *Constitutional Political Economy*, **8**, 105–22.

Veizaj Greisen, A. (2012), 'Public procurement of innovations: promoting awareness on the factors enhancing and hindering the practice of public procurement of innovations', Master's thesis, University of Flensburg and University of Southern Denmark.

Wade, C. and L. Björkman (2004), 'Study on performance-based procurement of IFI and donor-funded large, complex projects: final report', procurement study for IFI, World Bank Contract 7122679/ 7126720, WB Appointment UPI 248035.

Weele, A.J. van (2002), *Purchasing and Supply Chain Management: Analysis, Planning and Practice*, London: Thomson Learning.

Weihe, G., S. Højlund, E.T. Bouwhof Holljen, O. Helby Petersen, K. Vrangbaek and J. Ladenburg (2011), *Strategic Use of Public– Private Cooperation in the Nordic Region*, TemaNord 2011: 510, Copenhagen: Nordic Council of Ministers.

Weltzien, K. (2005), 'Avoiding the procurement rules by awarding contracts to an in-house entity: the scope of the procurement directives in the classical sector', *Public Procurement Law Review*, **14** (5), 237–55.

Westling, H. (1991), *Technology Procurement for Innovation in Swedish Construction*, D17: 1991, Stockholm: Swedish Council for Building Research.

Williams, I.P. and S. Bryan (2007), 'Cost-effectiveness analysis and formulary decision making in England: findings from research', *Social Science and Medicine*, **65**, 2116–29.

Williams, R. (2004), 'The new procurement directives of the European Union', *Public Procurement Law Review*, **13** (4), 153–9.

Yin, R.K. (1994), *Case Study Research: Design and Methods*, 2nd edn, Thousand Oaks, CA: Sage.

Zsidisin, G.A. and M.E. Smith (2005), 'Managing risk with early supplier involvement: a case study and research propositions', *Journal of Supply Chain Management*, **41** (4), 44–57.

Index